STRATAGEMS AN

PAVILION SERIES

General Editor: F. G. Bailey

STRATAGEMS AND SPOILS

A Social Anthropology of Politics

F. G. BAILEY

PAVILION SERIES

SOCIAL ANTHROPOLOGY

OXFORD
BASIL BLACKWELL
1980

ⓒ Basil Blackwell 1969
Fourth impression 1980

ISBN 0 631 11760 1

Library of Congress Catalog Card No:
69-14381

Reproduced from copy supplied
printed and bound in Great Britain
by Billing and Sons Limited
Guildford, London, Oxford, Worcester

Contents

Is it possible to be a pragmatic idealist?

Introduction

In 1963 I watched on television in America an enquiry by a committee of their Senate into a criminal organization called *cosa nostra* ('our thing' or 'our affair'). A man named Valachi, once a member of the organization, had been persuaded to 'sing', and for several days a large television audience watched and listened while he spoke in an unassuming, undramatic, friendly, indeed almost homely fashion, about the techniques of crime, about the contests for gang leadership, about violence and about murder.

The 'Valachi hearings', as they were called, aroused a great deal of local interest. Much of the cross-examination was reported verbatim in the newspapers, especially those parts which enlivened local history by revealing that it was in the nearby town that X had arranged for the murder of Y or that one of the leaders of *cosa nostra* (which the newspapers also called the 'Mafia') had been a locally resident and apparently respectable businessman. The television performances gripped their audience because they showed a contest between Valachi and his cross-examiners, because they were about life-and-death struggles for power in the criminal world, and because they revealed a degree of organization in that criminal world, which, although revealed many times before, continued both to frighten and to fascinate. The casting too, if one may put it like that, was good: particularly striking were Valachi's patient and good-humoured explanations to one of his senatorial inquisitors who appeared to be slow-witted. Finally there was always the chance that the *cosa nostra* might silence Valachi by murdering him: it might even be seen on the television.

At first sight it is the history (and possibility) of violence which fascinates in an affair like this. But interest was in fact sustained not by the stories of murders and massacres but by the revealed orderliness of the criminal world. Of course one quickly understands that large scale rackets have to be run on business-like principles. But beyond this, even when *cosa nostra* leaders fought and murdered one another to gain supremacy, they seemed to do so in predictable ways, even, one might say, according to the rules of their game. Certainly, leaving aside the question of how consciously the gangsters themselves thought in terms of right and wrong conduct within their own world, the manoeuvres in which they engaged were capable of being analysed. Indeed, for a tantalizingly brief moment, there appeared on the television screen charts which showed the process by which one leader replaced another.

Those charts, of which I had no more than a glimpse and have never seen again, started this book. After looking at them for a few seconds, and taking in the pattern of competitive interaction which they pictured, I had the strongest of feelings that I had seen them before. At first I thought they might have been in a newspaper report of an earlier day's hearings: but this was not so. Then I realized that while I had not seen those particular charts before, I was familiar with the pattern of interaction which they described. Not long before I had been arguing about it with some of my colleagues and with students: it was a pattern of contests for leadership described by a Norwegian anthropologist, Fredrik Barth, writing about the Swat Pathans, who live near the north-western frontier of Pakistan. The people of Swat and the criminals of the American *cosa nostra* arranged their violent successions in broadly the same fashion.

So what? What does it matter to any civilized person if they do? What conceivable benefit, intellectual or otherwise, can be got out of knowing a fact like that? The behaviour of murderous ruffians, whether they belong in the backward mountain vast-nesses of Asia or in the barbarous enclaves that remain in our civilized societies of the west, may be of use to the world of entertainment, but it has nothing to do with the world of science and learning. Social anthropology, it seems, picks on the exotic and the eccentric and the deviant and the aberrant: it cannot deal with the normal and the usual. The subject is, as one par-ticularly obtuse critic said, merely barbarology: and my implied excitement at discovering the Pathans behaved like the *cosa nostra* gangsters would have confirmed him in this view.

But that view is wrong. It is wrong in point of fact because we anthropologists are interested also—indeed, many of us primarily—in our own 'civilized' society. The reader will find that the train of thought started by the Valachi hearing and the Swat Pathans led me also to thinking of villages where I had lived in India, to my colleagues' descriptions of life in rural Britain and rural America, to Harold Nicolson fighting an election in pre-war Britain, to the manoeuvrings of Asquith and Lloyd George in the autumn of 1916, to General de Gaulle and the *colons* of Algeria, and—constantly—to what goes on around me in the university. It is true that I am deeply interested in the behaviour of 'exotic' peoples like the Indian villagers among whom I lived (in fact they live hard-headed and relatively humdrum lives): but this is because by understanding what they do and what they think and why they think that way, I can better understand what goes on in all societies, our own included. In this book the ideas tend to arise out of 'anthropologists' societies' (Indian villagers or the wild Pathans), because it is on those societies that I have cut my analytic teeth: but I will have failed if the reader remains unconvinced that just the same patterns of political competition can be perceived alike in the behaviour of Valachi's associates, Indian villagers, university committee-men, General de Gaulle, and that most civilized of men Herbert Henry, Lord Oxford and Asquith. Beneath the contextual variations and cultural differences, political behaviour reveals structural regularities.

The view that exotic societies are somehow unfitted for serious study is not only disproved by the fact that anthropologists do study them and with profit: it is also a distasteful view—even an evil view. To believe this is to believe that your own culture and your own society—people like you—are certainly superior to other kinds of people if not unique. Unhappily every society makes these kinds of discriminations, ranging from full members allowed to bear responsibility and to command the corresponding privileges down to categories of people who are defined as scarcely human at all. It is not easy to extricate oneself from this assumption. It comes so readily to judge as good and bad, sensible and ridiculous, admirable and contemptible the customs and values of our society as against the customs of another society. But the truth is that one must *first* perceive and understand differences as just differences and nothing more: the judgement of good and bad is a luxury which comes later.

A more restrained and more thoughtful comment could come from those who acknowledge the significance and legitimacy of the study of peasant or primitive societies, who agree that comparisons between such societies and the modern state are profitable, but who would deny my assertion that in certain fundamental ways political activity is the same at both ends of the spectrum. The immense and sophisticated bureaucracies which manage a modern state, the complex and subtle methods of rational competition followed by its politicians and the highly-organized and highly-codified legal systems deny affinity with the Swat tribesmen or the unlettered peasants of India, who are governed by tradition (not to say superstition), acting not after rational calculation and foresight like the politicians and bureaucrats of the modern state but merely out of habit. Of course such critics are right to the extent that a society managed on bureaucratic legal-rational principles is different from a 'traditional' society. But these terms stand for concepts, for 'ideal types'. When we come down to the real world we experience not these pure types but mixtures. In fact there is a high element of rationality in the management of public affairs in Swat or in rural Indian communities, a rationality which is denied in our stereotype of those kinds of society. Furthermore, we close our eyes too easily and too frequently in face of the blind emotions which shape political action in our own modern states. America, apparently so rational and so calculating in its internal political affairs, happy in the myth of an ordered rational political marketplace, throws up the witch-hunting Joseph McCarthy. The rational, logical, eminently self-interested Frenchmen succumb to the emotional appeal of what they call a 'rally' and accept the imperative of national glory and strong leadership. That 'anthropological' societies and modern states are alike enough to be comparable is a point argued through the book: these examples are enough to show that the argument is worth opening.

There may also be critics who, thinking with their hearts and not their heads, simply reject without argument or with only the slenderest rationalization, the implied similarities between, say, a British Prime Minister struggling to lead his nation through the most exacting war of its history and an anonymous Pathan chieftain squabbling with another anonymous Pathan over a field boundary mark. To some the comparison will seem to be absurdly over-stretched: it may seem even to be in bad taste. I know of no *a priori* way of convincing such critics that they are wrong: my arguments are presented later in the course of the book and in the demonstration of similarities. But those who filter these arguments through a conviction that the peoples of the world are ordered into a hierarchy of importance, or significance, or simple merit will probably not be convinced. I regret this, because the book is written—to some extent—for the benefit of just such people: or perhaps I should say for that part of such people which exists in us all and which unthinkingly and automatically classifies those who are different as morally inferior. Writing in Britain in the spring of 1968, in the midst of an apparently spontaneous outburst of racial antagonisms (still happily largely confined to print and shouting), it seems unlikely that social anthropology will ever be a subject of wide appeal, for its central tenet goes hard against popular assumptions: beneath the differences (of race, of colour, of customs) human behaviour is ordered in fundamentally similar and comprehensible ways—that is what makes us human. To fasten upon the differences and use them to scale people into superior and inferior is scientifically unprofitable (because it blocks systematic enquiry) and it is also immoral.

That argument places me alongside what one set of newspaper writers have been calling the 'wishy-washy liberals'. However, the field of activity in which I have chosen to argue the main point and the way in which I define this activity—political competition—will provoke (and has elsewhere provoked) the opposite criticism: that my approach is unduly hard-headed, not to say cynical. The politicians (of whatever culture) who appear in this book are all caught in the act of outmanoeuvring one another, of knifing one another in the back, of tripping one another up and they all appear to be engrossed in winning a victory over someone. This approach, the critics might say, totally ignores the well-known fact that by and large the nation's rulers are statesmen acting in the interest of what they conceive to be the general good.

But this criticism misses the point. Indeed everyone claims to be acting for the general good, and I suppose many would not be able to act with such passionate intensity if they did not also sincerely believe that they were fuelled on altruism. But the fact remains that even such people will encounter others whom they perceive as motivated by self-interest, who advocate opposing policies, and who therefore must be tripped up, knifed in the back, or in some other way disposed of so that the general good may be served. No statesman is effective unless he knows the rules of attack and defence in the political ring. Our interest is in finding out what these rules are, both in particular cultures and cross-culturally; the moral evaluation of the participants' motives is beside the point. Our business is not to sort out the good men from the bad men but to distinguish between effective and ineffective tactics and to say why they are so. Only after we understand the rules can we start evaluating the behaviour and so in the end come to a judgement on the men, if we wish to do so.

There is one other matter in the book which has moral resonances. It arises because I sympathize with the attitude stated in two lines of Yeats:

'The best lack all conviction, while the worst
Are full of passionate intensity.'

This is a personal view and I am not speaking for social anthropologists: they say only that you should suspend convictions, while still trying to find out the truth. The view is also a temperamental one and difficult to defend in a logical fashion. I know very well that my present life would probably be less pleasant than it is now, if a certain amount of passionate intensity had not been whipped up in Britain in the early 1940s. On the other hand, the difficulty might not have arisen if it had not been for the supercharged intensity of Nazi Germany: and so on. The argument runs into the sand. For in the end this is not a matter of logic at all: it is a matter of faith, as indeed is the conviction that it is wrong to assume and never question the innate superiority of one's own culture. I know only that at least in the little affairs of university life I am alarmed by those who jet themselves through issues and arguments with a burning moral conviction. The result is nearly always bad: if there is someone else burning with an opposed flame, then nothing gets done; alternatively decisions are taken in the white heat of moral virtue, and no-one has thought out how the work is to be done or what will be the consequences. It is better to follow out the cumbersome, tedious and sometimes devious rituals of compromise. At least then it seems less likely that 'mere anarchy' will be 'loosed upon the world'.

I have picked out in this introduction certain moral themes which ride between the lines of the book. Behind these themes—and behind the whole endeavour—is a repugnance for disorder, for the mere jumble of facts in which no pattern can be perceived, for 'mere anarchy'. My central situation is not the game (which connotes only orderliness) nor the fight (where no holds are barred) but competition which, unlike the game, lies close to the edge of anarchy because the contestants do not 'lack all conviction', because, in other words, they think that what is at stake is important. This edge of anarchy is fenced off by rules: and this book is about the rules which regulate political combats, and about the regular patterns which exist within them. We shall be making propositions about how a politician's support is eroded; how, in a particular culture, challenges are issued; how the protagonists come to know that one of them has won and the other has lost; and so forth.

This says no more than that in any culture there are regular and accepted ways of getting things done and of prevailing over others; that actions have a determinate range of consequences; and that the actors in any particular culture believe they know what these consequences are. In other words, they know the rules; they know—or sometimes only think they know—how to act effectively. Some have written down this wisdom in the form of handbooks for politicians: a range which runs from Kautilya and Machiavelli to Cornford and Plunkitt.

This book is not a handbook for politicians in particular cultures. Behind the cultural diversity there lies a common structure. We attempt to discover some of the general principles in political manoeuvre which transcend cultures and which provide questions which could be the tools of research in a variety of different cultures. This is not a systematized repository of the accepted wisdom of any part of anthropology or political science: it is not, in other words, a textbook. Its purpose is to stimulate ideas and provoke questions and, perhaps, to foster certain attitudes. But in the end, it is a bag of tools; not an artifact.

Parts of a draft were used for teaching and I have been aided and chastened by student reactions. My greatest debt is to Bruce Graham, a constant source of ideas and information. He and Bernard Schaffer instructed me in the politics of societies not 'anthropological'. I also thank Jeremy Boissevain, Richard Brown, Ken Burridge, Colin Leys, Anthony Low and Adrian Mayer. I should acknowledge, finally, the different committees on which I have sat beside infinitely eloquent and subtly resourceful colleagues, whose actions set me to wondering: Why?

1

A Political System

GAMES, FIGHTS AND POLITICS

To make a beginning, think of politics as a competitive game.[1] Games are orderly. Although the competitors are matched against one another, and may even dislike one another, the fact that they are playing a game means that they agree about how to play and what to play for. They agree that the prize is worth having and they accept some basic rules of conduct. A game is not a game if the outcome of the contest is certain: consequently the players must, within limits, be evenly matched. The weaker player should have, as we say, at least a sporting chance of winning. Furthermore, conduct which would make it impossible to play the game again is forbidden. Although particular opponents may be eliminated (and elimination is, of course, defined by the rules of the game), the total elimination of all opponents would mean that the game could never again be played. In short, rules are an essential part of games: indeed, in a sense a game *is* a set of rules, for it can only be defined by a statement of these rules.

Up to a point, this is true of a political structure: this, too, is a set of rules for regulating competition: beyond that point politics ceases to be a competition and becomes a fight, in which the objective (we cannot call it a prize, as we can in a game) is not to defeat the opposition in an orderly 'sporting' contest, but to destroy one 'game' and establish a different set of rules

But, it may be objected, the comparison between a game and politics is inept because politics is a serious business, while games are, by definition, trivial. Dejected losers are comforted, and puffed-up victors deflated by being told 'It's only a game'; meaning that games are a side-affair which are not to be compared with, nor allowed to interfere with, the serious side of life, with education, with making a living, and so forth. Sometimes people say of politics that it too is only a game: but this is only said in moments of anger or cynicism and the claim has an air of paradox not present when applied to actual games.

On the other hand there is a sense in which politics *are* secondary. When politics interfere with raising families or producing enough to eat, then people say that something has gone wrong with that political structure. This can happen when politics has ceased to be an orderly competition and become a fight: when conflict takes place without the control of an agreed set of rules; when, it seems, few holds are barred because the fight is to decide which set of rules will in future regulate political competition.

Some of my readers may already be thinking that 'real politics'—the politics which matter—are what I have just been calling fights. The day-to-day routine of Westminster, the complex but almost wholly predictable manoeuvres of American pressure politics[2] certainly have an intellectual fascination. Yet, somehow, they seem less important than those occasions when history leaps suddenly in a new direction—the coup of 1967 in Greece, the Congo disorders or the less violent emergence of other new nations, the Russian Revolution and so forth.

But what is the meaning of 'important'? Coups and revolutions are certainly more violent and more dramatic than the Westminster routine. But surely it is impossible to assert, in any absolute sense, that they are more important. Importance is relative to the values of whoever is making the judgement: it is not an attribute of events themselves.

Furthermore, understanding and analysing routine and relatively orderly politics is not an entirely different business from making sense of revolutions. In both, one has to ask questions about leaders and how they attract and hold and reward followers, how they take decisions and how they settle disputes among their followers. In both kinds of conflict there is an idiom of confrontation and encounter. Moreover, even in revolutions, some holds are in fact barred because, for one reason or another, they damage the attacker as well as his victim.

Even in 'real politics'—the politics of coups and revolutions—there are rules of how to get things done. These are not rules in

the sense of moral directives mutually agreed between the contestants, but rules which recommend courses of action as being
effective. These same 'pragmatic rules' (to be described shortly)
exist also in orderly politics, and their analysis is one of the
main objects of this book.

Let us begin by looking at an example.

HOW TO PLAY AND HOW TO WIN

In the autumn of 1935, when Harold Nicolson was about to
become a candidate for Parliament, he went to see his cousin.[3]

> Having dressed soberly but not unimpressively, I went to see Buck
> De LaWarr in the Ministry of Agriculture. He was very pleasant
> and cousinly. I told him I was in a difficulty. I knew nothing what-
> soever about the rules of the game. In fact my ignorance of even
> the elements was as if a man sitting down to play bridge with Mrs
> Keppel were to exclaim brightly, 'Tell me, Alice, are those clover-
> shaped cards spades or diamonds?'

In saying this, Nicolson was not undervaluing himself as a
politician or as a potential Member of Parliament: he was merely
disclaiming any expertise in electioneering. An electoral contest
was a kind of game, with rules of fair play, and other kinds of
rules about how to win, and of these—he said—he knew nothing.
So they began to teach him.

> [Jarvis] began by saying that it was most important that I should
> stand as 'The National Government Candidate' and not as
> 'National Labour'. I let Buck answer that point as I am all at sea
> about these labels. Buck said he agreed. I said, 'But supposing
> people ask me what party I belong to, what am I to say?' Buck
> said that I must say that I was a follower of Ramsay MacDonald.
> The conversation went on in this way with me sitting all good and
> quiet on the sofa. Then I realised that something must be done. I
> said it was no use asking me about these things, but that what was
> important was that I should not get a single vote under false pre-
> tences. I would be anything they liked except all things to all men.
> I would not pretend to be a Tory to catch the Tory vote and so on.
> I would get muddled if my own position was not quite clear and
> straight from the start. 'I am very bad,' I said, 'at *prolonged*
> deception.' Anyhow they agreed and told me not to fuss about
> MY HONOUR.

Almost the same thing happened when the lesson was continued at Leicester, where he was standing.

> I sat there twiddling my hat while I was discussed as if I were not present. They decided that I should stand as British Government candidate. Then I intervened. I said that was all very well. But that in fact I was standing as National Labour. I was quite prepared to call myself a 'National Candidate', but if asked, I should reply that I was a supporter of Ramsay MacDonald. They said that this would lose me votes. I said that if I suppressed the fact, I should be getting votes under false pretences. I would never agree to that. They looked down their noses. Mr. Flaxman said angrily, 'But surely, Mr. Nicolson, you do not suppose that a General Election is a vestry meeting?' I said that I would not stand as a candidate unless I started on an open and honest basis. Mr. Flaxman cast up his hands in horror. Jarvis said, 'Yes, you're right. Quite right.'

The two latter passages describe part of the lesson which Harold Nicolson received in how to win an election. He was being taught the rules of how to win the game, in particular a rule which says, very simply 'Don't link yourself with parties or people whom the electors don't like': or, more specifically in this case, 'Don't call yourself Labour if you hope to get Liberal and Tory votes.' Rules like this are not what we usually mean by 'rules of the game': they are practical instructions about how to win. 'Dress soberly but not unimpressively [to impress your sponsors].' These are *pragmatic* rules.

It seems, however, that for Harold Nicolson certain other rules were sacred and could not be sacrificed even to win an election. He wanted to be honest: and said so. His advisers at Leicester clearly thought this sentiment inappropriate: something, no doubt, which would sound well from the platform but did not belong in the Committee Rooms. But, after all, he was a beginner and so they humoured him by saying that he was quite right, but telling him that he should not fuss about HIS HONOUR (his capitals). Rules which express such ultimate and publicly acceptable values are called *normative* rules. Besides, he was learning the language of practical politics quickly enough to add that he was no good at *prolonged* (his italics) deception and would surely trip himself up. In this way he reinforced a rule which he saw as an ultimate value to be publicly pronounced 'One must be honest' with a pragmatic rule: 'It pays to be honest'. 'Austen always played the game,' said Lord Birkenhead of Austen Chamberlain, 'and always lost it.'

In this way politics has its public face (normative rules) and its private wisdom (pragmatic rules). My interest is largely in the latter kind of rule: that is, not so much in the ideals and ends and standards which people set themselves in public affairs, but rather how they set about winning. *This does not mean that I will be talking only about how individuals advance themselves: it is the tactics which are of interest, and the same tactics, by and large, apply whether it is a principle or an individual which is being advanced.*

The distinction between the two kinds of rule is important and requires elaboration.

Normative rules do not prescribe a particular kind of action, but rather set broad limits to possible actions. They leave some choice about what exactly the player will do. Some normative rules, like those implied in the concept of 'honesty' or 'sportsmanship', are extremely vague, and the most disparate kind of conduct can be condemned or defended in their name. Other rules, like the rule requiring that the referee shall be obeyed, are more precise: but even here there is a leeway for interpretation both because the word 'obedience' is itself vague, and through the notion that referees can exceed their powers and so forfeit the right to obedience.

Normative rules are very general guides to conduct; they are used to judge particular actions ethically right or wrong; and within a particular political structure they can be used to justify *publicly* a course of conduct. Use in this way is probably the readiest test of whether or not a particular rule is to be given normative status. For example, I can think of no part of our own society where a leader can say 'I did this because I enjoy ordering people about and I like to be famous': but he can say 'I did this for the common good.'

The further directives which come into existence to fill the empty spaces left by norms, are the pragmatic rules. These recommend tactics and manoeuvres as likely to be the most efficient: whether the scrum shall pack 3-2-3 or 3-4-1, in what conditions to bring on the slow bowlers, whether to box defensively or aggressively, how to dress when being interviewed by one's sponsor, and so forth. Pragmatic rules are statements not about whether a particular line of conduct is just or unjust, but about whether or not it will be effective. They are normatively neutral. They may operate within the limits set by the rules of the game: or they may not. They range from rules of 'gamesmanship' (how to win without actually cheating) to rules which advise on how to win by cheating without being disqualified (what may be done, for example, on the 'blind' side of the referee in the boxing ring).

Such devices are known to those who sit on committees, and some have been recorded in *Microcosmographia Academica*. When bankrupt of good arguments to defeat a motion, openly accept the principle of the motion but suggest that the wording could be improved. Cornford calls it 'starting a comma', picturing the pack of committeemen in full cry after the hare of punctuation. This at least delays acceptance of the motion if it does not wreck it altogether.[4]

Frankenberg, writing about a village in North Wales, tells of an acrimonious committee meeting, in which one side alleged that a certain matter had been agreed at their previous meeting, while the other claimed that it had not. They called for the minute book, but the secretary said that she had left it at home. When they offered to fetch it, she said that she had not written up the minutes. The secretary was on the side of those who had opposed the motion.[5]

There are hundreds of other examples of how people try to win their way in political competition, displaying a private wisdom which lies behind the public face of politics. Each culture— English politicians, academics, villagers in Wales, villagers in India, villagers anywhere, a Vatican Council, the racketeers of the American cities as revealed in Whyte's book[6] or in the 1963 Senate hearings, when Valachi took the lid off the *cosa nostra*— each culture has its own set of rules for political manipulation, its own language of political wisdom and political action. Like Harold Nicolson, you have to learn the appropriate language and the rules of the game before you can play effectively. Those stately manoeuvres which C. P. Snow[7] lovingly describes would not be effective among the *cosa nostra*, because the racketeers would literally not understand the signals which were being transmitted.

Nevertheless, one may look for similarities behind the wide variation. Just as different languages may have similar structures, so there may be a common structure behind the different kinds of 'private wisdom'. C. P. Snow's language of manoeuvre and the language of the *cosa nostra* may be structurally similar. Each culture—parliamentary elections, Welsh villages, American racketeers and the rest—has its own idiomatic set of rules which summarize its own political wisdom. Nevertheless, they have something in common, which makes it possible for us to look for the essentials of political manoeuvre, whatever be the culture.

We now ask what is meant by the word 'essentials'.

HOW TO FORECAST

Harold Nicolson was not, apparently, optimistic about his chances. Reports from his canvassers were not encouraging. When the Liberals put up a candidate, making it a three-cornered fight, he became even less sanguine because he had counted on getting both Liberal and Tory votes in a straight fight with the Labour candidate. In other words, his cognitive map of the situation contained elements which were neither normative nor pragmatic rules about how to behave, but were forecasts of how other people would behave. On such forecasts and assumptions, he and his helpers based their pragmatic rules for conducting their campaign.

If that campaign had been conducted thirty years later, not in 1935 but in 1965, the forecasting would have been considerably more sophisticated, for the techniques of sampling public opinion have developed considerably since that time. How even the most sophisticated methods would have fared with a majority which turned out eventually to be 87 in a poll of around 35,000, is open to question. Nevertheless, it is probable that modern techniques of analysis would have provided forecasts and insights into the state of the campaign which were not available to the competitors in 1935. It follows that there can be a level of understanding of how a game or a competition works, which may not be known to the players themselves.

These forecasts are not directives: not rules. They are hypotheses or statements: laws in the scientific and not the legal sense. To know that no football team has ever won the cup for more than two seasons in succession, or that no head of state has ever been re-elected more than a certain number of times sets a problem about the game or the political structure concerned. It may turn out that such events can be explained as consequences of the normative or pragmatic rules of the structure involved. Close analysis of any set of rules, whether normative or pragmatic, may reveal consequences unknown to those who play the game. Of course, if the unintended consequences become known to the players and they can make use of this knowledge to win, then what was an hypothesis becomes also a pragmatic rule. Harold Nicolson's advisers had such hypotheses about the popularity of Ramsay MacDonald among Liberal and Tory voters in Leicester. The politicians whom I knew in Orissa in India were continually trying to take practical advantage of what they hoped were analytic insights into voting behaviour.

The purpose of any scientific endeavour is to suggest verifiable propositions about relations between variables. Here is a facetious example, again from Harold Nicolson's diaries. He was being interviewed by the Executive Committee of the local Conservatives, before his selection as candidate.

> Luckily nearly all the first questions were about Abyssinia which I could answer off my hat. Then a man asked whether I had studied the mining question. I said that my ignorance of the question was as wide as it was deep. They looked startled at that and then the central lady said, 'Well, I am sure, Mr. Nicolson, that if you smile like that, it doesn't matter what you know or don't know.'

Perhaps she was right, for he was elected: and in a situation so confused as that election seems to have been, by Nicolson's own account, his smile might have tipped the balance: the brighter the smile the more the votes. It is a proposition about the relation between variables: but, I suppose it must be ruled out as scientific, since in practice verification is impossible.

A less frivolous example is the following statement.

> In village India the greater the number of tenants or landless labourers in proportion to resident landlords, the higher will be the

proportion of disputes taken to the village council as against those taken to the government courts.

The statement[8] suggests a connection between the pattern of land distribution and the pattern of judicial activity. These are variables in that there may be a range from a single land-holding family in one village to another village where every family owns land: equally the judicial pattern may vary from the village council settling every dispute to every dispute going before the government courts. Also the proposition could be proved false: by finding villages where there is a single landlord and every dispute goes to government courts: or watching one particular village where land is increasingly concentrated into the hands of fewer and fewer people, and yet the pattern of judicial action remains unchanged: and so forth.

Propositions which connect variables are not in the strict sense forecasts. Statements connecting a landholding pattern with judicial behaviour do not forecast what in fact will happen in particular villages: they predict only that *if* the landholding pattern changes, *then* the pattern of judicial behaviour will also change: and vice-versa. They do not say that Harold Nicolson will smile: only that *if* he smiles, he will be elected.

In short, we are seeking a level of understanding of how the game works which may not be known to those who play it. This is the level which the anthropologist or political scientist intends to reach, for until he does come to that stage he has merely *described* what the players themselves know, and has not begun to make his own *analysis*.

THE ENVIRONMENT

Between the years of 1946 and 1958, the French Fourth Republic[9] endured a far from tranquil life. The governments, each resting on compromises and usually uneasy parliamentary alliances, and succeeding one another with accelerating instability, were unable to act decisively to meet their many difficulties. On the economic front at the end of the war there was inflation, industrial discontent awaiting exploitation by the parties of the left, and agrarian discontent among the small farmers of the south and central regions. There was a widespread anti-Republican sentiment, later to be marshalled behind de

Gaulle. The period was not without its successes. Some governments were more stable than others. Economic and social difficulties were reduced and the stresses brought under control. A
ruinous war was begun in Indo-China in 1946 but it was also
ended by a Fourth Republican government, that of Mendès-
France. Nevertheless difficulties in the end became too much for
the regime and governments found themselves unable to control
even their major instruments of policy, in particular (in 1958)
the armed forces and the civilian government in Algeria. Unable
to find adjustment with such an environment, the Fourth
Republic came to an end. Particular political structures live or
die according to whether they can remain compatible with their
cultural and natural environment, either by making themselves
suitable to it or by modifying it to suit them. A political structure and its environment together constitute a political *system*,
and such systems are understood when the continuous process
of adaptation and adjustment between structure and environment is understood.[10]

It is easy to see how political structures are connected with
an environment, if the structures are stated in terms of *roles*.
A structure is a set of rules about behaviour: these rules list
the rights and duties of particular roles; they say what a king, a
subject, a judge, a voter, a party leader, a village headman and
so forth is expected to do in that particular capacity and what
he may expect others to do for him. But an individual is likely
to have many roles: the village headman may also be a father,
a brother, a farmer, a priest in the temple, and a part-time
trader; a voter may be a family man, a devout Roman Catholic
and a shop assistant. At the very least all these different roles
compete for a man's time and energy; they may also directly
influence his political behaviour, as when the headman uses his
official position to further his trading, or the voter accepts his
priest's directive on how to vote, or a candidate for office
mobilizes his kinsmen to campaign for him in the election, or
Harold Nicolson is aided by his influential cousin to become a
candidate. The environment both provides resources for political
use and puts constraints upon political behaviour.

If a particular political structure were intimately connected
with every other structure of social action, so that everything
which went on in economics or religion or on the domestic scene

vitally affected it, the task of analysis could never be finished. Happily this is not the case, for only some parts of an environment hinge onto a political structure. Furthermore all political structures contain rules, both normative and pragmatic, which attempt to shield them from an excess of demands from the environment. Sometimes they rule particular issues out of the political field, especially if these issues are explosive: Britain recently failed to do this with racial questions. There are other devices for compounding, ordering and so reducing demands.[11] There are also political structures which protect themselves by disqualifying whole classes of people from competing in politics. Conversely, other structures in the environment may attempt to protect themselves by disqualifying or discouraging politically active persons from taking on roles in that structure.[12]

The political structure *interacts* with its environment: the arrows of causation point in both directions. Nevertheless, since this interaction is in a series of discrete events, we can at our convenience analytically separate out the arrows which point in one direction only. Indeed, sometimes we can start with events which are not themselves reactions. Importing a new food staple, the drying up of a river and the decay of empires from failing irrigation, or the onset of new epidemic diseases are 'acts of God' which start a chain of causation: they are independent variables, and the political structure, which is adjusted, is the dependent variable. But, in turn, the political structure (that is to say, the people who compete in this structure) may change the rules or devise new ones to control the disease or to modify whatever else it is in their environment that is threatening the continuation of their regime. The modified environment in its turn will react upon the political structure: and so on until some kind of stability is reached or until that structure like the Fourth Republic is abandoned as beyond repair, and a new structure takes its place. For, to continue this profligate use of metaphor, lurking in the environment of some political structures are rival political structures, waiting to take the job over and show that they can do it better and more than willing to go in for sabotage. This brings up the question of a society having more than one political structure, to be discussed in the following two sections.

ENCAPSULATED POLITICAL STRUCTURES

The political philosophers who taught me a generation ago were quite clear that whatever was to be called 'political' must have something to do with the State: if phrases like 'University politics' or 'Church politics' were used, then they meant that these institutions were playing a part in State politics: otherwise the phrases were simply metaphors.

 But political structures can be recognized at all levels and in all kinds of activities and can, when appropriate, be compared with one another. The anthropologist must do this. Research has uncovered and made sense of societies which have no authorities and are not states and yet enable their people to live orderly lives.[13] Furthermore, given the anthropologist's strong interest in small communities encapsulated within larger societies—in villages, tribes within nations or colonial dependencies, sections of urban populations, and so forth—who seem to operate political structures in spite of the fact that the State authorities are only occasionally involved, he has no choice but to consider these as political structures, which are partly independent of, and partly regulated by, larger encapsulating political structures.

The procedure is not difficult, being, in fact, exactly the same as that outlined for relating a political structure to its environment. If, for example, the politics of a University are to be analysed, then the political structure of the local education authority, of the nation, and of various groups interested in higher education, are all to be treated as part of the environment. It is even sensible to follow this procedure when the external institution is formally sovereign. Dependency, as the word does not imply, is always in fact a two-way interaction. Exactly the same kinds of question about adjustment or failure to make adjustment between the encapsulated structure and its environment can be asked, even when some parts of the environment are themselves political structures.

CHANGE

The process by which a structure adjusts itself to changes in the environment, or modifies the environment to suit itself, is called *maintenance.* In anthropological books the idea of maintenance is conveyed through the term 'equilibrium', the metaphor being that of a disturbance throwing the structure off balance, redressive devices being brought into play, and the structure being balanced again at a point of equilibrium. Such an analysis does not ignore preventive action (structural modifications) to close off the source of disturbance, and, as in the analysis of a structure and its environment, equilibrium analysis allows the arrows of causation to run both ways: up to a point.

To make this clear consider an example, taking changes in the size of the population as the independent variable (cause) and rules defining membership of a particular kind of political team (the Kond clan) as the dependent variable (effect). The Konds are a tribal people living in the hills of Western Orissa, in India. The example is somewhat hypothetical in that it is a conjecture about the state of affairs which existed before either Hindu chieftains or the British Administration arrived in the Kond Hills.[14]

The environmental variable is the ratio of population to land. We assume that techniques of production remain constant. There are two critical values for this variable: one where numbers grow beyond the point where they can be supported on a given piece of land, and the other where the people grow too few to cultivate the land or to protect it from outsiders. Land is owned by clans: that is, a man has a right to land only in the territory of his own clan. A clan is a descent group so that membership is ascribed: you are born into it. But this rule can work only so long as the number of people born into the clan does not exceed or fall below the critical range suggested above. Too few members means that the role of defender of the clan land cannot be performed effectively: too many members means that competition for scarce land cannot any longer be controlled by allocating land according to descent. In other words, an independent variable in the environment (the rate of reproduction) can put a strain upon the Kond political structure.

A critical variation in one direction (excess population) can be controlled by acting directly upon the environment and deliberately restricting the number of people born into the clan. The Konds did in fact once practice female infanticide. But this kind of control obviously cannot be used when the critical variation is downward (inadequate population). One solution is to relax the rule of ascribed membership and permit achieved membership of clans: to allow excess population to leave one clan and join an underpopulated clan. Kond clans were in fact composite, being put together from lineages acknowledged to be not of the same descent. All that remains now is to express this relaxation in recruitment rules as a variable, suggesting that it is linked with the land-population ratio. The hypothesis then reads: productive technology remaining constant, variations beyond a critical range in the land-population ratio (the independent variable) will cause an increase in numbers recruited into clans by achieved criteria (adoption or alliance) as against those recruited by ascribed (birth) criteria (achieved–ascribed recruitment being the dependent variable). For the Konds this hypothesis has not been tested, since the information required to verify it is lost in the mists of unrecorded history: but it is in a form which could be tested.

Crises of this kind are perennial and ubiquitous: in all structures such adjustment is going on all the time, and the procedures for resolving strain become familiar and well-tried. Indeed, one recognizes this kind of 'routine' strain by seeing whether the structure already has a set of rules for dealing with it effectively. Such rules can be either normative or pragmatic. In the case of Kond recruitment they are normative (although they may have begun as pragmatic devices) because clan brotherhood achieved through alliance or adoption can be used to justify conduct no less than brotherhood by descent. The test, then, for distinguishing 'equilibrium' or 'maintenance' from more radical kinds of change is done by asking whether the structure contains effective rules for coping with this kind of crisis.

But what happens if the land-population ratio is varied even beyond those critical limits at which achieved recruitment rules can cope with strain? Suppose population increased sharply *everywhere*. A rule of achieved recruitment will be effective only when some clans grow in population while others decline. Other things being equal, an overall increase in population must result in a breakdown, if the rule of achieved recruitment remains the only device for coping with the crisis.

But equilibrium analysis, in its simpler form, does not allow for the possibility that a structure may be radically changed

Social chg accounted for in/by "tools" ① equilib/maintenance ② normative, prag. rules etc. ③ rival polit struct

or quite destroyed. The structure may remove sources of disturbance in its environment: but the possibility of the environment, so to speak, winning the battle is not allowed for, and the structure is always in effect treated as a constant.

A model of this kind runs manifestly contrary to experience, for revolutions do occur and political structures do go out of business.[15] Even without revolutions political structures are sometimes quietly transformed, and after a time the observer and the players come to realize that quite a different game is being played.

Therefore, although equilibrium analysis and the idea of maintenance are useful analytic tools up to a point, additional tools are needed to understand social change.

One such device is the distinction between normative and pragmatic rules. It provides a variable in propositions about change. For example: the more Untouchables in an Indian village become rich, the more often will village leaders of the dominant caste be compelled to find pragmatic loop-holes in the normative rule that only clean caste members have a say in the running of the village.[16] The ratio of normative to pragmatic rules can then reach a critical point at which the normative rules can no longer be sustained. To speak metaphorically, if a rule is bent often enough, it will break. The more often rich Untouchables are consulted about running the village, the more likely it is that their right to be consulted will become a normative rule, and so the political structure of that village will have changed.

Another tool is the idea that an environment may contain rival political structures. It is important to understand what this means. An opposition party, hoping to take control after the next election, is not a rival political structure: one would-be dictator, waiting his chance to murder the incumbent dictator, is not a revolutionary but a contestant operating with the rules of that particular structure (within the same arena). But an army leader who replaces a parliamentary democracy with his own brand of guided democracy does change the rules of the game, and while he was waiting and planning his coup and organizing support for it, he did constitute a rival political structure within the environment of the parliamentary democracy.

In what sense can political structures be rivals of one another? Teams within a structure are rivals because they compete for the same scarce prizes. Political structures are rivals insofar as they seek to use the same environmental resources of personnel, or available political energy, or funds. In this sense the traditional caste oligarchies of rural India are rivalled by the secular egalitarianism of modern democracy. The cumulated demands of the two political structures cannot be sustained by the environment: life is hard, so to speak, when both Government forces and rebel forces collect taxes from the peasants.

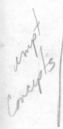

Changes from one political structure to another can be gradual and virtually unnoticed by the players. They can also be sudden, dramatic and take place overnight. There is, of course, a third possibility: that of anarchy and complete breakdown. When the same society contains two or more rival political structures, this constitutes a *political field*: the criterion being the absence of an agreed set of rules which could regulate their conflict. The distinction is similar to that drawn earlier between a game and a fight. The second concept we need is *stability*, which means that one political structure is replaced by another but the change takes place without a total breakdown; that is to say, without bringing complete disorder to the non-political structures of the social environment.

CONCLUSION

I have been putting on display a very abstract set of conceptual tools which can be used to dissect political systems. Here and there I have suggested hypotheses or in other ways shown the tools in use, partly to make the meaning clearer and partly to break the tedium of continued abstract statement. Such abstract exposition is not to be avoided—and indeed will continue into the next chapter—for in the social sciences the tools must go on exhibition along with and as part of the finished artifact.

In the centre of the complex of interconnected parts is a structure of rules about how people should interact with one another as political men. Some of these (the normative) say what is the right and proper thing to do: other rules (the pragmatic) tell you what is the effective thing to do, right or wrong. These rules are directives for the actors in a particular society: they are models of behaviour for particular contexts; they are institutions; they are part of the culture.

Any one item in this culture—any particular rule in the structure of political rules—is to be explained by showing that it is part of a structure. Explanation, in this sense, is putting things into context, showing that they are part of a pattern.

In the present chapter, in a broad and programmatic fashion, we have gone beyond that point to another level of explanation. Taking the political structure as a whole we have been asking how this whole fits into a larger context. We began with the idea that political structures must achieve some kind of balance with other social structures and must not get in the way of, for example, making a living or must not in other ways jeopardize human survival. Political actors have other roles—religious, economic, familial and so forth—and a set of political rules which too much inhibits the performance of these duties is probably self-liquidating.

All these other roles—these other structures—form the environment of a political structure. They are at once a constraint upon and a resource for the political actor. Beyond them are other structures which are not part of the culture and the society but of the natural world: demography, the physical environment, and so forth. These too are constraints upon and resources for the politician. Both kinds of environment, the social and the non-social, have a two-way causal relationship with the political structure. When they change they can change it: and the political structure can modify its environment. To understand a political system is to construct verifiable hypotheses about the mutual dependence of a political structure and its environment.

well put

NOTES   *wonderful man*

1. I am mathematically illiterate and this book, in consequence, makes no attempt to use the theory of games developed by Von Neuman and Morgenstern and their successors. In any case the highly limiting abstractions required by that theory are too far from the reality with which I hope to deal. Here I am making use only of an analogy and saying that the way people behave in

competitive games is similar to the way they behave when competing for power. For the applications of such theories to politics see *Boulding, Schelling, Rapoport,* and *Mackenzie,* pp. 119–37.

2. See *Bailey, S. K.*

3. These extracts are taken from *Nicolson.* The quotations are on pages 216, 217 and 219 respectively.

4. See *Cornford,* p. 21.

5 See *Frankenberg,* p. 140.

6. See *Whyte,* Part II.

7. See, for example, *The Masters* or *The Corridors of Power.*

8. This proposition clearly needs further refinement before it is ready for testing. The word 'dispute' would need to be more closely defined; one might like to limit the proposition initially to one region in India; and those who know India also know that the word 'tenant', standing undefined, could lead to inextricable confusion.

9. I owe this example to Bruce Graham. Sources used are *Graham* (1) and (2), *Werth,* and *Williams.*

10 The ideas developed in this section and in the final chapter derive partly from Easton's writings and partly from the stock-in-trade equilibrium analysis of post-war British social anthropology. My approach is, I hope, somewhat less mechanistic and less rigid than either of these. I feel uneasy when faced with any analysis which does not allow man a central role as an entrepreneur. In Britain Raymond Firth has been the proponent of this view and I acknowledge the influence of his writings and those of Fredrik Barth.

11. These are systematically discussed in *Easton,* (1), Chapters 6–9.

12. A sophisticated group of villagers in Orissa took great pains to keep State politics and the party political machines out of certain cherished village institutions. See *Bailey, F. G.* (4), Chapter 2.

13. See *Fortes and Evans-Pritchard,* and *Middleton and Tait,* for examples.

14. For a more detailed account see *Bailey, F. G.,* (2).

15. For another attack on equilibrium analysis see *Leach,* Introduction.

16. For an example see Chapter 9.

2

A Political Structure

In 1916, during the First World War, a Coalition Government in Britain which included Liberals, Unionists (under the leadership of Bonar Law) and a token Labour representation and was headed by Asquith, a Liberal, was replaced by another Coalition, formed from the same three parties, and headed by another Liberal, Lloyd George.[1]

The war was not going well and there was considerable dissatisfaction both in the country and among the politicians. To Lloyd George and to some others, it seemed that a main fault lay in the absence of firm direction from the War Committee caused partly by the indifferent chairmanship of the Prime Minister, Asquith. Lloyd George wanted direction handed over to a smaller War Council, with himself as chairman and three other members: Asquith would continue as Prime Minister. This was proposed (to simplify the story), first accepted by Asquith, and then (apparently in a fit of anger at a newspaper attack on himself) rejected. Lloyd George resigned: so did the Unionist members of the Government. Various people were mooted as Prime Minister, but in the end Lloyd George succeeded in forming a Government.

This episode—analysed at length later[2]—will be used in this chapter to illustrate the types of rules which make up a political structure. These rules concern the five following subjects.

First they define what the prize shall be—a cup, a laurel wreath, a position in a league table, some honorific symbol, a position of power and responsibility like the Prime Ministership and so forth. They also say what actions or qualities shall be deemed to have merited the prize—goals scored, runs counted, first to the tape, two falls or a knock-out, ability to form a government, and so on.

Secondly they specify who is eligible to compete for the prizes; there are junior and senior athletic championships; women may not be professional footballers or boxers; men and women do not compete against one another in swimming; major competitions are open only to those who have demonstrated excellence in lesser qualifying competitions. In 1916 only Asquith, Lloyd George and Bonar Law himself were possible contenders for the role of Prime Minister. When they were discussing the possible members of a War Council, Asquith made it clear that he would not agree to Carson (a Unionist) being admitted, partly because there were other Unionists senior to him.

Thirdly, there are sets of rules about the composition of competing teams. The normal situation in Britain is for the Government to be formed from the members of one party. But in wartime, to symbolize national unity in the face of the enemy, a coalition government may be formed.

Fourthly there are directions about how the competition shall take place; in particular, there is a stringent division between fair and unfair tactics. It was alleged, for example, that Bonar Law, having agreed with his Unionist colleagues to convey a rather confused message of support to Asquith, in fact gave the opposite impression: which, if true, was a clear foul in the rules of British political in-fighting. Such principles are normative and cover an ever-changing corpus of pragmatic rules about how to make the most effective use of normative rules. In professional soccer, if brought down by a foul, feign agony *in extremis.*

Fifthly, and finally, there is a set of rules to be followed when a rule has been broken. In particular certain roles are created to deal with this situation: umpires, referees and judges.

A political structure, then, contains rules about prizes, personnel, leadership (teams), competition and control. The last three of these subjects will be analysed in detail between chapters three and seven. In the rest of this chapter each category of rule is briefly discussed and illustrated through examples.

PRIZES AND VALUES

In both games and politics a prize is culturally defined. It is a value like honour, power or responsibility. To analyse a particular structure, these general terms must be broken down into *roles* (e.g. Members of Parliament, Prime Minister, President etc.) which in that structure are defined as having responsibility or power or honour. Prizes are such that there is never enough to go round. A prize which everyone wins is not a prize. Honour has meaning only when some people are without honour; power and wealth are got at the expense of other people. People compete only because the prizes are in short supply.

The prize is always normatively respectable. One identifies a prize by seeing what kinds of ends can be publicly proclaimed to justify competitive behaviour and to denigrate opponents. Lloyd George put forward the new smaller War Council as a step towards winning the war; others (including Asquith) saw it as a step towards replacing Asquith with Lloyd George, a matter of personal aggrandizement.

[handwritten margin note: Normative values expressed for prag. purpose / ends]

Values both create and regulate political competition. The restraint upon manoeuvre which distinguishes a competition from a fight entails that the contestants have some values in common: they agree not only about prizes but also about legitimate tactics. These shared rules pass ethical judgement upon conduct which is not an end but a means. In our own culture honours bestowed in the name of the monarch in return for contributions to the funds of the ruling party rate lower than honours bestowed for public service, especially those given for an act of valour in wartime. To 'buy' a knighthood is a breach of an ethical rule which prescribes appropriate behaviour in the competition for knighthoods. In pre-Independence India Gandhi ruled that the roles of terrorist and of communal (i.e. religious) agitator were unethical in the competition for nationhood. The final break between Asquith and Lloyd George came, normatively at least, because the latter was supposed to have broken the rules by 'trafficking with the Press'.

Values are symbolized. This maintains and strengthens them. Indeed, if they are not constantly tended and re-invigorated, they fade. Consequently rites and ceremonials dramatize fundamental political values and associate them with such non-political values as health or fertility or prosperity or with God.[3]

[handwritten margin note: Reagan]

Besides this positive support the values of a political structure are protected by rules saying what is to be done when these values are disregarded, or, if nothing can be done, what divine retribution will fall upon the transgressor. (Just as honour can exist only when there are some people without honour, so also transgressors are necessary to define and publicize values.)

Values, within one structure, are a constant and treated as an unshifting guide for conduct. Nevertheless it would be naïve to assume that every leader or every member of a political community has thoroughly internalized its normative rules. Most leaders certainly manipulate normative rules in a pragmatic and cynical fashion to achieve prizes. Indeed, the prizes themselves may be pragmatic as when a position of honour carries with it substantial material perquisites. For example, in the Mexican community of Durazno, described by Friedrich[4] the three elected civil officers are paid one peso a day, but this 'is amply augmented by bribes [and] by "the bite" (*la mordida*) on taxes. . . . .' The four officers who control the communal lands receive no pay but 'about 20,000 pesos may be divided annually among [them] . . .'.

That being said, it is probably again necessary to lay the ghost of cynicism. The discussion of prizes has been carried on as if people were solely concerned with getting into office, with achieving positions of power, or in some way advancing themselves. Are they not also concerned with *policies*? Of course they are: at least some of them are, some of the time. I am sure that Lloyd George, Asquith, Bonar Law and the rest of them were very much concerned to find the best policy to win the war; and they quarrelled with one another partly because they disagreed about this policy. Indeed, normatively this was the whole of their quarrel.

But in practice you can only implement a policy if you or one of your team occupies the role or roles from which the policy can be implemented. If Lloyd George's 'powers of drive and energy' were to be used in the prosecution of the war (which is a matter of policy), then he must be shifted from the relatively impotent post of War Secretary to the role of Chairman of a new War Council or to the Prime Ministership (these are roles). Lloyd George's personal ambitions need not necessarily enter into our analysis of the rules of political competition. The manoeuvres of gaining support for oneself and undermining one's opponent's support are used in much the same way whether one is going in for self-aggrandizement or trying to make a particular policy prevail.

PERSONNEL

Every political structure has rules about personnel, which say what qualifications a man needs to occupy a political role. These qualifications vary: age, sex, colour, caste, experience in politics, wealth, education and many others. Age or sex or colour seem to be natural attributes like height or weight or measurement round the waist, but in fact they are more. They are indicators of roles, which are assumed to be compatible or incompatible with political activity. The long ban upon women in politics in our culture implied that a woman's domestic role as a housekeeper and mother unfitted her for a role in public affairs. Personnel rules, therefore, define compatibility between political roles and roles which exist in other structures, or between two sets of political roles.

Most structures identify at least the following three categories of personnel:

(a) The *political community* is the widest group in which competition for valued ends is controlled. Beyond this point the rules do not apply and politics is not so much a competition as a fight.

(b) The *political elite* are those within the community entitled to compete for honours and power. The boundary between members and elite is not always sharp, and the elite may contain within itself many grades.

(c) A political structure also has rules specifying broadly how those who are active in politics should organize themselves into *political teams*.

When analysing a particular structure the first task is to describe the boundaries of its *political community*. This is done by identifying rules which mark off members from outsiders. In modern nations this situation has been tidied by lawyers. Where the rules have not been codified, one may ask whether, when two individuals are matched against one another, they are agreed about the rules.

This right to 'fair play' is linked with other roles. Sometimes they are themselves political: allegiance to a ruler or residence in a particular territory. Those roles can also be non-political: professing the right religion; being born into an ethnic group, class or caste or even membership of a kinship unit. These criteria are not necessarily exclusive.

The people who operate in the roles must have some way of communicating (and themselves apprehending) the role that they are playing. This communication is done by symbols:[5] uniforms, ways of speaking and comporting oneself, and demonstrations of respect towards ritual objects (flags, crosses, thrones, *khadi* cloth).

Not every political community has a common focus of symbolic unity. In other words, not every political community is based upon a sense of community. The British Empire was not: nor (see *Good Soldier Schweik*) was the Austro-Hungarian empire. Such communities exist because roles are played out under duress.

The neat codification of boundaries between our own nation states is not found in every political structure. Some structures operate with sharp boundaries; others are less concerned with keeping people in or out. The boundary, also, may be quite precise, but incorporate devices which allow flexibility.

In short, the questions to be asked about a political community are these:

(a) What political roles constitute membership of that community? *achieved or ascribed alliance*
(b) What other roles (political or not) qualify a man to play membership roles? *birth etc*
(c) What are the symbols of the political community? Are they accepted by the whole population within the community?
(d) Are the boundaries closed or open? If open, how is this achieved? What features in the cultural and natural environment make for an open or a closed political boundary?

The *political elite* are those within the community who are qualified by the rules of the political structure to take an active part in political competition. Exactly the same questions as those listed above may be asked, substituting 'elite' for 'community'.

An open boundary (of community or of elite) depends upon whether roles are ascribed or achieved. Ascribed roles are those into which a man is born or into which he grows, whether he wants to take on the role or not. Caste roles are ascribed: so are roles allotted according to age or sex and played by everyone of the prescribed age and sex (male adult, female adult, elder and so forth). Roles are achieved insofar as they can be attained by acquiring the appropriate qualifications: an elected leader, a palace favourite, a dictator are all achieved political roles. The non-political roles which qualify for elite membership may also be achieved or ascribed: birth into the ruling class is an ascribed qualification; education, political experience, or wealth may be achieved roles qualifying a man for membership of the elite.

The ratio of ascribed to achieved role qualifications for elite status will be a measure of flexibility at the boundaries of the elite group. A lack of flexibility at this point combined with certain demands from the environment can break a political structure.

Political contestants mobilize supporters: that is, they find themselves *a team*. The rules of games are precise about size. Contestants in a game must, within limits, be evenly matched. In politics victory is usually defined as going to the side which is believed to command the largest number of supporters, but even then there may be rules which ensure that the teams are sufficiently balanced for competition to take place.

To discover the principles on which teams are recruited in a particular political structure, the same set of questions which appeared earlier will serve, substituting 'team' for community. Insofar as recruitment is *achieved* through political performance (that is, through type (a) roles), team membership is flexible and the approximate balance of resources, which ordered competition requires, can be achieved by subversion: that is, by a transfer of membership from one side to the other. But if team membership is based on social roles which are ascribed, then the balance of resources must be sought in some other way: perhaps through alliance, or through a referee and a system of handicapping.

A team recruited through achievement criteria is called an *association*. Political associations are also specialized: that is to say, the members co-operate only or mainly for political activity. There is a division of labour between those who go in for politics and those who handle—let us say—economic affairs or religious affairs. The separation is relative, since by definition every political structure has an environment and every political man has non-political roles. But those political structures which do achieve some degree of separation from their environment (that is, some degree of specialization) are capable of handling more complex and more ambitious political operations than those in which political roles have hardly been differentiated from other social roles.

The converse of an association is a *multiplex group* or an *unspecialized* group. Recruitment to groups of this kind is done through roles of type (b): for example, clan elders and clan priests and clan leaders may be the same men performing one undifferentiated role.

Notice, finally, the similarity between communities, elites and teams. To a certain extent we can ask the same *personnel* questions of all of them, because so far as recruitment is concerned they are the same kind of phenomenon appearing at different levels. At each level we are designating complexes of political roles under the heading of 'community' or 'elite' or 'team' and asking what other roles are considered qualifications for community membership, elite status or team enrolment.

We have moved from the widest circle of the political community more narrowly to an elite, we have focused yet more closely on a team and finally, we will come to the most selective unit of all, the leader. There is an evident continuity: a leader is part of a team and a team is part of an elite and an elite is part of a community. In practice elites usually have many levels, so that particular structures are likely to exhibit many more steps than these four on the way from the common man to the president.

At each different level there will be distinctive role qualifications, so that the life history of a leader will be marked by his attainment of various degrees of elite status before he is qualified to enter the competition to become a leader. This process of climbing the latter is analysed, with reference to mobility in the caste system, in Chapter 6.

LEADERSHIP

[handwritten marginalia: in what the hell use sense do we use allocate]

Rules allocate authority within a team. They may prescribe
qualifications for leadership, procedures for appointing leaders,
methods of consultation between leaders and followers, other
rights and duties between leader and follower, and specify
circumstances in which a leader may be deposed. Sometimes
such rules are not written but must be read between the lines of
men's actions.

Administrative and procedural rules of this kind anticipate
contention and the ever-present danger of disorder and fights.
Rules for qualification and procedures for appointing a leader
are designed to ensure that the competition between rivals for
the leader's position remains orderly (standards of orderliness
varying, of course, from one culture to another). In the same
way rules which define the leader's rights against his subjects
and his duties towards them also anticipate the danger which
lies in the antagonisms inherent in any 'command' relationship.

Some kind of leadership role will be found in any political
team, but the variations are immense. Seen from outside the
team, its leader is a competitor supported by followers and other
resources. From inside the team, the leader is the man who
makes decisions and settles disputes. The position may be occupied by one man or by a number of men. The role may be
institutionalized, given a name, equipped with elaborate
mechanisms for appointing an individual to the role, and
marked with ritual and ceremonial usages. On the other hand
it might be merely the man or men who have the biggest fists or
the most persuasive tongues. Leadership roles may be exercised
spasmodically: or the leader may be fully occupied in taking
decisions and settling disputes.

Another important variable is the power which a man has
relative to the power of those who support him. The range may
run from superiors to whom he is a subordinate ally to allies in
the strict sense who are his equals, down to many grades of
followers who are subordinate to him, but whose subordination
may vary from near-equality down to a low level where the
human follower is almost as tractable and undemanding as a
material object, a mere instrument. In effect this classification
of support is made by asking how great are the resources which

Key element to analyses boundaries & their flexibility

the followers command in their own right and retain under their own control.

Another distinction is that between groups united around an ideal or morally committed to a leader, and mercenary groups where the follower makes a contract to support the leader in return for some favour or service. The former are 'moral teams' and the latter are 'contract teams'. The distinction between moral and contract support affects the process of conflict to be discussed later, where it will be shown that people transfer their membership more easily between contract groups than they do between moral groups. *Note however that this distinction is an analytic one, and when actual political teams are examined one asks to what extent are teams of one kind or the other.*

core or following distinctions

Contract support is relatively easily persuaded to change sides: moral support is not. A group of the latter kind of followers is called a *core*: the former (subversible) support is a *following*. Asquith's defeat occurred when an apparent core of Unionist ministers turned out to be a following. The ratio of core to following is likely to affect the tactics which the leader can employ. (Note that we are again concerned with the boundaries of groups and their degree of flexibility.)

COMPETITION

There are also rules in any political structure about how the competition should take place. These rules both directly constrain the behaviour of the contestants and promote orderliness by making it possible for messages to pass between the contestants. Each move in the game is a message which tells the opponent about the mover's strength in resources and about his intentions. There is a limited range of possible counter-moves and very often both contestants know what this range is. The game remains orderly in part because the contestants understand what is happening. Such messages across the arena are called *confrontations.*

At Bonar Law's arrival Churchill promptly launched into a great oratorical tirade against the Government. He spoke as if he were addressing a mighty audience rather than a small group of political friends and acquaintances. Bonar Law . . . began to show signs of irritation. Finally, when Churchill came to a pause in his allocution, he said, 'Very well, if that's what the critics of the Government think of it—we will have a General Election.'

[Churchill was silenced and] afterwards declared that this suggestion to hold a General Election in the midst of war 'was the most terribly immoral thing he had ever heard of'.

Whether or not it was immoral it was undoubtedly a formidable threat. For a General Election in which both Bonar Law and Asquith appealed to the country against Carson and the Tory Diehards could have had but one result—an overwhelming victory for the Coalition.[6]

A competitor confronts his opponent by making statements (either in words or actions) about his own command over resources (both human and material) in order to intimidate an opponent. Bonar Law reminded Churchill that the Coalition commanded popular support. The Pathans do this by calling their followers together or by parading them as for battle.[7] Each culture has its own language for confrontation. The messages can be subtle and elaborate, involving bluff and counter bluff. Confrontation is also found to some extent in fights, but there communication is rudimentary and messages easily misconstrued: as when a man fails to scare off a dog by waving his stick, because the dog has never had a beating and so cannot understand the message.

A confrontation may result in an *encounter* through which both contestants publicly agree about their relative strength. Sometimes this arrangement is only reached after a combat, men being killed and property destroyed, in cultures which go in for violent political games. In other cultures the contest is played out through law courts when fortunes and reputations are destroyed. But a 'showdown' (encounter) may also take place without too much expenditure of material resources, as when the votes were counted after Harold Nicolson's election.

Destruction of people, property or reputations is likely to affect other social structures in the environment of the political structure, because they too depend on these resources. For this reason no political structure can permit destruction to be carried beyond fairly narrow limits. The importance of the devices of confrontation and encounter should now be clear: they may enable competitions to be settled without the destruction of resources on which the whole society, not merely the political structure, depends.

In political structures where contract groups predominate and it is consequently not too difficult to change sides, a confrontation may cause followers to change to what they think will be the winning side. Indeed, since political contracts of this kind usually include protection, the followers would be foolish not to shift their allegiance away from a man whose strength is in doubt. Desertions snowball and there is, so to speak, a run on the political bank, and (to treble the metaphor) the game has been won and lost. This process is called *subversion.*

Political competition, therefore, will be analysed (in Chapter 6) through the three processes of subversion, confrontation and encounter.

CONTROL

Those who are active in politics are usually convinced that their activities are supremely important. Most cultures grant high honours to politicians, at least to those who are successful. Conversely, those who are excluded from entering the political arena may be degraded and without honour. Yet exclusion from politics can be a mark of objective importance: some roles are too important to allow them to become fouled and confused by political competition. Referees are in this position. So also are many non-political roles. The codes of ruling classes, especially those which make a mystique of the military life, often exclude peasants from political competition. Peasants may not seek honour: but neither may they be destroyed. Victory over a rival is not got by laying waste his kingdom, but by deposing him from the throne, seating upon it your own nominee, and continuing to collect the revenue. No political structure could survive if it permitted the systematic destruction of personnel in 'reserved occupations'.[8]

Political structures are vulnerable at this point. Would-be leaders who cannot recruit followers within the rules are tempted to bend the rules and enrol people previously disqualified. The arena then becomes a field and the competition becomes a fight. This, as will be seen, is the story of Bisipara and of other villages in India. Exactly the same dangers exist in the making of new alliances, as when the Bisipara Untouchables make use of their ties with the Congress party and of their status as the favoured wards of government to upset the structure of village politics.[9] This too is presumably why the political establishment of 1916 regarded 'trafficking with the Press' as an heinous offence.

A second set of devices tends to keep teams evenly matched. A man may fight one day with his brother, but become his brother's ally against a cousin, and becomes the cousin's ally against a cousin more remotely connected, and has the support of all his relatives against non-related persons.[10] Rival British political parties join together to form a Coalition against the Germans. At best, however, this kind of behaviour is true only of some societies, and even there one sometimes suspects that the analysis is very much of what people ought to do and remote from what they actually do: in fact brothers may bring in outsiders as allies against one another. Nor do ranks always close in the face of external opponents. King George, hearing of Asquith's resignation, wrote gloomily in his diary: 'I fear it will cause a panic in the city and in America and do harm to the Allies. It is a great blow to me and I fear it will buck up the Germans.'[11]

In contract groups followers may change sides. But such structures have a built-in safeguard against everyone joining that one team and so putting an end to the game. A man adheres to a leader in a contract group because he expects a material return for his loyalty. The environment seldom provides enough for the leader to satisfy everyone's wants. Indeed, the art of leadership lies in judging whose hand may be safely rapped when it reaches for the pork barrel, so that there will be enough to satisfy those whom it is not safe to exclude. Therefore not everyone will be satisfied, if they all join the same side. An analogous principle works for alliances, where it can be shown that it pays someone holding a balance to ally himself with the *weaker* side.[12] In these and other ways political structures which do not provide for a government yet have (in the mechanical sense) a governor.

Finally, there are roles wholly or partially excluded from particular political competitions so that their holders can mediate or adjudicate between contestants. This can happen in two ways: through cross-cutting ties and through 'authorities'.

Those who are opponents in one situation are allies in another, and so are discouraged from whole-hearted and single-minded opposition.[13] Political opponents in one situation may be political allies in another: or they may be linked in some way that does not concern politics. Tallensi bowmen, about to shoot it out as rival clans, were said to shout to their brother-in-law in the opposite group to get out of the line of fire.[14] Many novels have been built around this conflict of obligations. The Gunpowder Plot was discovered because one of the plotters had kinsmen in Parliament and felt it right to warn them to stay away on November 5th.[15] In the 1916 Parliament Bonar Law was a member of the Government: Carson was its most outspoken critic: but both belonged to the Unionist party.

Authorities are roles or sometimes mystical devices like oracles. Through them restraining values are brought to bear upon political competition. Ideal 'authorities' have two characteristics: they are neutral between the contestants; and they command their obedience. But in many structures they do not even at the normative level command obedience: they are merely facesaving devices for communication between the contestants and may mediate (i.e. *suggest* compromises) but cannot authoritatively arbitrate (i.e. *impose* settlements).[16]

The game-politics analogy is now stretched, for while there are undoubtedly roles and institutions in politics which do the job of a referee (the law courts are an obvious example), very often the political referee is in an ambiguous position. In games the referee is clearly and unambiguously *not* one of the players: he can never win the prize. But in politics the position of the referee can sometimes be itself one of the prizes. One player may claim to be the referee, while the other disputes this claim. Referees may be drawn into a contest because someone is trying to eliminate the very game which they are claiming to referee. Finally, even apart from such revolutionary situations, there are political structures which operate without a referee, and yet do not descend into a disorderly free-for-all.

CONCLUSION

A political structure, like a game, operates within limits set by agreed rules, which specify prizes, say how teams may be formed and led, lay down lawful and unlawful tactics, and sometimes appoint a referee with authority to see that rules are observed. To analyse such a structure means, in the first instance, to say what these rules are; later, to complete the analysis, one must say how the rules are applied to particular situations, how they are adjusted to meet changed situations, or how they fail to become adjusted and so fall out of use.

Much of this analysis can be applied to revolutionary situations too: to political fields. It can be applied wholly *within* a revolutionary group, for if such a group is to be effective, order and co-operation must exist and there must be agreed and relatively orderly ways of settling disputes and competing for leadership. Furthermore there are always pragmatic restraints (one might say *constraints*) in the contest *between* revolutionaries and their opponents. Finally there are likely to be, even in the most desperate situations, some normative restraints. You may have defined the Redskins as outside your political community and proclaim that the only good Redskin is a dead Redskin. But you may also believe, as the Fougasse cartoon normatively insists, 'never shoot a *Sitting* Bull'. That would not be sporting.

NOTES

1. These events are very complicated and at certain crucial stages there is dispute about what actually happened, and there is extensive dispute about the motives of the actors. For reasons given in the introduction I have not tried to find out what 'really happened' and I have used only the account given by *Blake*. Other accounts are given by *Beaverbrook, Chamberlain, Lloyd George, Newton, Spender* and *Asquith*.
2. A fuller analysis of Asquith's fall is given in Chapter 6.
3. See *Fortes and Evans-Pritchard*, Introduction.
4. See *Friedrich*, p. 201.
5. See *Gluckman* (2), pp. 26ff.
6. The quotation is from *Blake*, pp. 301–2.
7. See *Barth* (2), pp. 119–22.
8. In one American town in which I lived a change of party control changed the entire personnel in the municipal garbage collecting department, with the result that many people found it necessary, at least for a time, to employ private contractors.
9. See Chapters 8 and 9. A fuller account is given in *Bailey, F. G.* (2).

10. A clear exposition of this principle in action is given in *Evans-Pritchard* (1).
11. Quoted in *Blake*, p. 335.
12. See *Barth* (1).
13. For an explanation of this principle and its varied application see *Gluckman* (1). An excellent account of the principle at work in an actual dispute is given in *Colson*, pp. 102–21.
14. From notes taken in a lecture by Professor Fortes in 1949. The social structure of this West African tribe is analysed in his two monographs, *Fortes* (1) and (2).
15. See *Feiling*, p. 443.
16. See the incident described below at p. 64.

3

Leaders and Teams

POLITICS AS AN ENTERPRISE: LEADERS, RESOURCES

There are teams, both in politics and in games, which seem to work effectively without leaders. One contribution by anthropology to the study of politics has been the meticulous examination of political structures which contain no rules for the appointment of leaders.[1] This means, of course, that there are no *normative* rules for allocating authority. It is an assertion that the culture in question holds, as a major value, that all men are equal and should have equal amounts of political power: this is a contradictory use of the word 'power' which can only mean that men are not equal; the contradiction is neatly underlined by Orwell's famous joke 'some are more equal than others'. The fact that in every society, even the most egalitarian, some are indeed more equal than others, only means that the absence of normative rules allocating authority or even the presence of rules explicitly rejecting authority leaves room for pragmatic rules which enable some men to coerce or influence others (without, of course, giving them the moral right to leadership).

At the other end of the scale are cultures which proclaim, as does India's caste system[2] or any other elitist ideology, that all men are not equal and that the chosen few have the moral right —sometimes the divine right—to rule. In between these two extremes lies a range of societies, or groups within societies, which vary according to the value which they set upon human equality. But every society, if only at a pragmatic level, shows at least some traces of leadership roles and I shall therefore build the discussion of co-operation and team-making in politics around leadership. This will not inhibit our understanding of relatively leaderless groups, of the ways in which they concert their action and of the conditions under which they can do so effectively.

Leadership is an enterprise. To be successful as a leader is to gain access to more resources than one's opponents and to use them with greater skill. To attack an opponent is to try to destroy his resources or in other ways to prevent him from having access to them or from making effective use of them.

Although it sounds a paradox, the opposition which exists between two political rivals also exists in some degree between a leader and his followers. This relationship, too, can be visualized as one of relative access to resources. Insofar as a leader is able to influence and direct his follower's actions, he does so by the expenditure of resources. What passes between them is not so much an interaction as a transaction,[3] and this applies not only to mercenary groups but also to groups the members of which see themselves as fighting for a 'cause'.

It should be made clear at once that this is not a statement about the motivation of individuals. This is not a claim that every social interaction is motivated by thoughts of reward, and that the morals of society are nothing but the practices of the marketplace. No-one can deny the fact of altruism; that men will die for their family or their country, because they see this as a moral imperative, without question as the right thing to do, although it is not apparently in their own personal interest to do so. Indeed a major analytic distinction in this chapter is between a following recruited on a mercenary basis and a following gathered on a 'moral' basis.

Nevertheless, as will become clear, there are advantages in translating even moral interactions into the language of resources. It is not a fruitless question to ask under what conditions is the deployment of those who follow a leader whom they regard as a manifestation of God the use of a high-cost or a low-cost resource. One is not straying far from reality if one imagines a leader asking himself whether to intimidate an opponent by staging a mass rally of the faithful or whether it would not be cheaper to hire an assassin and eliminate the opponent. In other words a moral resource is nonetheless a resource, and therefore open to questions about relative cost.

But, further than this, there is also a sense in which the support of those who act from a sense of moral conviction is a transaction between leader and follower, just as is the support of avowed hirelings. A duty performed imposes an obligation on the beneficiary. In the case of the hireling the return is direct. The 'faithful' (those who follow out of a sense of righteousness) make their gift to the cause, and so impose upon the leader the obligation not merely to serve the cause, but also to shine forth as an exemplar of its ideals. The politician who makes family and home a normative theme is discredited if caught in adultery.

Finally—and rather obviously—the leader of the faithful in practice must expend resources to keep the lamp shining brightly and into the eyes of his followers. Communication—or propaganda, to use a harsher word—has its costs, and the word of God can reach further if one hires a loudspeaker.

In short, in this chapter we are going to look at leaders as men who have limited resources with which to gain their ends, and who must choose between the different manoeuvres or counter-manoeuvres which are open to them according to their estimate of the relative costs. I should emphasize again that this mode of enquiry does *not* deny the existence of altruistic action or the fact that men have ideals: but it does deny that such action is cost-free. At the very least the faithful must be fed, both literally and spiritually: neither type of food is free.

The distinction between the hirelings and the faithful is an important one and I examine it in more detail in the following section.

HIRELINGS AND THE FAITHFUL

A relatively well-to-do household in Bisipara, a village where I lived in India, can be used in a metaphorical way to point up the difference between a moral group and a group based upon transactions: what earlier were called moral teams and contract teams. The Indian joint family, in which a man and his married sons, or a group of married brothers and their wives and children own and manage a farm jointly and share one hearth where the cooking for the whole group is done, is rare in Bisipara. But it is not uncommon for several brothers and their wives and children to live around a common courtyard and share many domestic tasks with one another, although each man has his own land, and foodstore and cooking-hearth.

From the point of view of any one married man in this group, the domestic scene is filled with players who stand around him in circles, the nearest of which have a moral relationship with him and the furthest of which are connected with him more through transactional ties. With his wife and his small children the relationship is, ideally at least, highly moral and hardly at all transactional. Services are exchanged—or in the case of children, given to them without thought of return—for love or out of a sense of duty. This does not mean, of course, that the contract element is entirely absent from the marital relationship. The people of Bisipara know a good wife from a bad one, or a good husband from a bad one, and they make the distinction in terms of services rendered or not rendered, and beyond a certain level of dereliction, the contract breaks and the marriage can be ended. There are also specific ideas about the services which should be rendered by and to sons and daughters, once they are of an age to learn. Nevertheless, in this relationship— and to some extent in the marital relationship—there is an idea that the relationship consists of something more than an exchange of services; there is also some mystical bond which gives to the divorce of a spouse or the disowning of a child a colouring of tragedy which is absent in the, for example, peremptory dismissal of a man hired to do a day's labour on the farm. The people of Bisipara would understand E. M. Forster's Gino speaking of his baby son: 'And he is mine; mine for ever. Even if he hates me he will be mine.'[4]

The tie between brothers is of the same kind. Brothers quarrel because they are rivals for the inheritance and the villagers have a bitter proverb: *bhai shatru*—'Your brother is your enemy.' But such a quarrel is a tragedy, because the relationship should be one of love, innocent of material rivalries. Some trace, ever diminishing, of this insistence on moral solidarity persists through the line of kinsfolk, but at each remove[5] the hard element of the transaction increases. The element of love, of duty, of services given because it is right to give them and wrong to anticipate the return, survives even into the relationship with farm servants and retainers who are addressed in kinship terms and whose bond is felt far to transcend the purely economic.

Beyond these circles are people with whom one has transactions, in relation to which any sensible man will consider first where the balance of profit lies: men hired to work the farm from the pool of casual labourers, shopkeepers from whom one buys kerosene or sugar or borrows money, government officials who give orders, strangers of all kinds with whom one interacts, and so forth. With all such people the cost is to be counted, when contemplating interaction: the relationship must be made to pay. Of course, even in these cases, a moral weighting is frequently present: once a man becomes known through regular interaction, then he ceases to be just the object of a transaction, a mere instrument, and begins to take on the status of a moral being: it can happen even with government officials. Indeed, the weaker party to a transaction will try to better his position by claiming that this is a moral relationship, not a transaction.

One of the best-described cases of the use of transactional relationships to build up a political following is to be found in a book by Fredrik Barth *Political Leadership among Swat Pathans*. These people live in a valley in the mountains of Pakistan. They are followers of Islam but, like the Hindus, they are divided into castes. Full citizenship, so to speak, belongs only to the Pakhtouns, a landowning caste. They alone sit on the council, which is a forum for political manoeuvre; they alone become leaders (*khan*); they alone have the right to compete for political power. Men of other castes take part in politics, but they do so as the dependents and followers of Pakhtouns. The only exception to this are the people whom Barth calls Saints.

Pakhtouns have an ethic of egalitarianism, so far as other Pakhtouns are concerned. But it seems to be not so much equality as equality of opportunity: men can try to win power so long as they have land and are Pakhtouns. Some Pakhtouns are leaders and some are followers, and there seems to be nothing to prevent strong Pakhtouns humiliating the weak Pakhtouns, except in certain prescribed fashions in prescribed situations: for example, the forms of equality are preserved in council discussions. Elsewhere you, as a Pakhtoun, show your superiority over another Pakhtoun in any subtle or unsubtle way you choose, so long as you think you can get away with it.

The contest is between strong men in the Pakhtoun caste. Each leader gathers a following around him in the men's clubhouse which he controls. Some of these men will be his tenants or men who have houses on sites owned by him: others will be in debt to him. Occasionally marriages are used to bind in a follower. The rents for farmland, usually taken in kind, are high and many men can only survive on the largesse which a *khan* hands out to the men who regularly present themselves in his clubhouse and thus indicate that they are his followers.

This relationship is a transaction. The members of a clubhouse get charity from the leader in the form of feasts and presumably other material goods: but, most importantly, to belong to a clubhouse is to be safe. The *khan* is your protector. If another man attempts to take your land away or in some other fashion threatens you, and if this man is too big for you to handle, then your *khan* will give you protection. Indeed, he must do so: for if he does not, he loses points, so to speak, and is in danger of becoming known as a leader who cannot protect his followers and therefore no leader at all: his honour is at stake in your protection. The client, for his part, when the *khan* calls, must present himself, gun in hand, at the clubhouse: he gives service in return for protection. A client who fails to give service will be punished. A leader who fails to protect loses his reputation for honour and valour, and with that gone, he cannot keep followers and so does not have the means to stand up to his rivals. Most importantly, he cannot then protect his land. The Pakhtoun *khan* whose honour and valour is in doubt is like a banker whose credit is in doubt. Such a man is faced with what we can call a run on the political bank. If this happens, then, the Swat valley being a violent place, it is probably sensible for the bankrupt *khan*, too, to run.

No disgrace attaches to the man who changes sides. There is no thought that this is dishonourable: it is merely the sensible and rational thing to do. When shopping around to sell your allegiance where the best protection can be bought, no-one disapproves of a man who makes the best bargain. Presumably those who stay on the losing side when they had a chance to join the winners are written off as politically inept. Business is business.

The men of Bisipara handled certain of their political relationships in just the same way, and I will describe them briefly because they illustrate very well how close a transactional relationship is to opposition and enmity.

Bisipara lies in a backward area. For many years under British rule, and even after Independence when the region was administered by Indians, and even nowadays when the forms of local government and representative democracy are being created, the gap between the villagers and the administrators was and is immense: a gap which remained at colonial proportions even after the colonial regime was finished. Consequently the channels of communication between the rulers and their subjects are few and, such as there are, not efficient. From one point of view this gap is a measure of the peasants' ignorance of how the government works, of what their own rights are, and of the right procedures for claiming those rights. Even under the modern representative democracy, these difficulties of communication persist, for distances are great and communication resources are meagre, and—at its simplest—few peasants can read and write.

Consequently there has existed for many years a category of men who make a profession of bridging this gap between the peasants and the administrative and political elite.[6] For the peasants these are the men who know where to get a licence for a shotgun, how to get a real injection in the hospital instead of distilled water, how to get the file of a court case moved from the bottom of the list to the top or how to keep the file out of the court's hands until one of the litigants gives up in despair or runs out of money, and a variety of other ways of 'fixing', virtually all of which are normatively forbidden in the rules of the bureacracy, being considered corrupt. Indeed, money changes hands: the village broker, as he may be called, claims, quite truthfully, that no clerk will risk his job by interfering with folders in the official file unless he is paid for it. Even where no transgression is being solicited, since everyone at this level in bureaucracy works to rule and the rule is exceedingly complex and the work consequently slow, money has to be paid even to get a licence to which a man has every right. The broker too wants a share for the time and trouble that he takes, and, indeed, as a return upon the expertize which is his stock-in-trade and which cannot be built up overnight.

In the area in which I lived and in many other areas in India these brokers and fixers had become one means through which politicians solicited support from voters. Each broker held a bank of potential voters: people beholden to him for favours done in the past and others hopeful of services in the future.

From above, where the politician stands, the broker looks like a small patron with an attached fringe of smaller clients; a chief with his followers. Indeed he is a man disposing of political resources, and willing to deploy them where he judges most profit will ensue.

But the 'followers' regard this 'chief' with utter distaste. The distaste, which certainly has a strong moral element in it, arises because the brokers—at least those whom I knew—are born men of the village and yet have chosen to become partial outsiders: they are, in effect, a kind of traitor or renegade. But the attitude towards dealing with and through this man is not quite the same. The deal itself is stripped of any moral connotations. Questions of right and wrong, of cheating and fair play, do not arise. The test is efficacy and all judgements are pragmatic: the measurement of success is profit and the relationship is not at all altruistic. The clients may feel 'beholden', as I have said, to the broker, but they do so in the sense that a man feels bound to someone from whom he expects to borrow money next week. If they can cheat the broker or the official and not suffer for it, they cheat: and they expect to be cheated. Indeed, they would hardly think the word 'cheating' appropriate, any more than a man who snares a partridge can be said to have cheated the partridge.

It must already be clear that a moral relationship between a leader and the faithful has a very different set of components. It is not done to reckon up the price, even if in cultures like our own the pervading commercial ethos leads those who act for the greater glory of God into asserting that their reward will come in the life hereafter. In the truly moral relationship the service is its own reward: whether for humanity at large, or for one's nation, or race, or class, or school or university or youth or sport or any of the other countless institutional forms under which the public weal is discerned, whether sanctified in a frankly religious way or through a secular political ideology. In such a situation the leader's task is to keep himself identified with whatever mystical object provides the focus of the peoples' worship. Sometimes, as in the phenomenon of charismatic leadership, he is able in his own person to be the object of worship and the symbol of whatever it is that is valued. In all cases there is some transcending object of mystical adoration—race, nation, God, humanity—which subordinates both the leader and his followers.

Insofar as both leaders and followers are servants of the same cause, some sense of equivalence between them is created. The rule may in fact be autocratic, the discipline may be ferociously sanctioned, and even if the leader symbolizes his position by a display of ostentation and extravagance far beyond the reach of his followers, yet both leader and follower are called 'comrades' or 'brothers'. If the leader lives extravagantly, he must also be seen to be extravagantly generous. The language of common action in such a group is the language of love.

Services given 'for love' are services given without charge. But, as I have already argued, in fact the use of such resources is not without cost: by using them the leader accepts obligations; he must feed the faithful and he must also, through adequate propaganda, nourish the cause itself. Nevertheless there are differences between these costs and the costs incurred in making use of hirelings.

The reward for the faithful is an easy conscience. They do their duty and this is itself their reward. But a feeling of satisfaction, like an attitude of mind, or a piece of news, or a cold in the head, is something which can be transmitted without being lost to the giver. The giver, then, is like Jesus who feeds the five thousand on five loaves and two small fishes: the treasure chest, so to speak, is automatically filled as it is emptied.

Undoubtedly political groups do grow in this way, and with a speed far beyond that which could have been predicted on the basis of resources apparently available to the leader. Crusades and other holy wars, millenarian movements, extremist political parties with flaming ideologies and war 'fever' spread like epidemics. Must we then say that the leaders of such movements, although they may have to feed the faithful and expend resources to keep the cause itself burning, yet receive gratuitously that increment of power which corresponds to the devotion of the faithful? The hireling wants his keep and a salary besides: the faithful want only their keep.

Certainly this is a difference, and, other things being equal, the leader of the faithful has this as his advantage over the manager of an army of hirelings. But the difference is not, I would argue, one of kind: it is one of degree. It would be wrong to claim that while the economic analogies are appropriate for studying a band of hirelings, they miss the mark entirely when applied to moral groups. The difference in fact is this: *the leader of a moral group has a higher credit-rating than the leader of a band of hirelings.* To pursue the analogy, if your credit is good, you can borrow at low rates of interest over a long period: but an unsecured loan carries a high rate of interest, and is lent for a short period.

This is no more than a very simple scheme for classifying leader-follower relationships according to the fiduciary element, and it rests on the ineluctable fact that ideologies themselves, which provide the credit for moral teams, can become bankrupt. In other words such bankrupt ideologies are sets of rules for regulating political behaviour which are ill-adapted to their environment. For example, one could make out a case that parliamentary democracy is just such a bankrupt ideology in the environment of most of the developing nations. The Fourth Republic came to an end because a majority of Frenchmen no longer believed that parliamentary democracy was an adequate form of government: this was made inescapably clear by its failure to control the Algerian situation.

CORE AND FOLLOWING

Some family relationships exhibit ambivalence: at one and the same time they contain both hatred and love. In just the same way political relationships between leaders and followers are more complex than I have yet allowed. So far our discussion has been about 'ideal types', but actual relationships between a leader and his follower are likely to contain both a moral and a transactional element. Indeed, in the history of any organization one could chart the rise and fall of these two elements, balanced against one another: and there have been several anthropological studies which show how rituals which symbolize and re-inforce common religious values are performed when men are beginning to show too much concern for their own personal interests and to quarrel with one another over the distribution of material benefits.[7]

Under certain conditions, when his followers are beginning to look too closely at the balance-sheet of their relationship with the leader, it is a sensible tactic for him not to use his resources to reward the dissatisfied followers, but to stage a ritual of collective solidarity, which, hopefully, serves to renew his long-term credit.

When one looks not at the individual relationship between a leader and a follower, but at his relationship with the whole team, a similar distinction can be made. The pattern resembles that drawn earlier of a man in Bisipara surrounded by circles of kinsmen and others, the element of morality intensifying as one moves towards the centre of the circles and the transactional element decreasing. To keep the picture simple, a leader may have an inner circle of retainers whose attachment to him is moral, and outer circle of followers whose attachment to him is transactional. The former are called his *core*: and the latter his *following*. For a word that covers both categories I will use 'supporters'.

Just as it is in the interest of a banker or a businessman to have a good credit-rating, so it is in the interest of a leader, in certain circumstances, to enrol as many supporters as he can into his core. One of the difficulties which Mendès-France endured as Prime Minister between June 1954 and February 1955 was of this kind. The popular support which he enjoyed among the electorate was not reflected in a sufficiently dependable parliamentary backing. He had a small core (in the sense given above) of left wingers in his own Radical party, who backed him on all issues. But majorities in important divisions had to be mobilized on a transactional basis and according to the question at issue; those who supported him on one issue might oppose him on another.[8]

Faction leaders, who by definition have only followers and no core (this will be discussed later), must spend much of their time and energy in keeping the fabric in repair. To return to the economic analogy, loans must be serviced or re-negotiated very frequently. Furthermore, building up a transactional team of this kind is work for craftsmen: each link must be constructed by hand and often to a different pattern. If one thinks of such a group as a machine then seven-eighths of its output are spent on its own maintenance and only a fraction remains for political activity. There are no economies of scale. This is one reason why faction-fighting is regarded as wasteful of social resources.

The size of a clientele which can be recruited for political activity on a transactional basis is limited. Actual contending groups, actual teams, can only grow beyond this limit by changing their nature, either by becoming identified with a cause or by stiffening themselves with a bureaucratic organization and a bureaucratic ethic, which is itself a kind of ideology. We come back later[9] to these processes by which the core element in a team increases at the expense of the following, and turn now to asking what can be said about the basis of a core beyond the fact that it rests upon an ideology, upon love for the leader either directly or more often as the representative of some transcending ideal, and, metaphorically, that it is based upon long-term political credit given by the supporters to the leader.

The people of Bisipara are divided into castes, among whom the Warriors, about a fifth of the population, are—or were—dominant. The pattern which I am about to describe is one which Warriors say used to exist and should now exist, although they recognize that political and economic changes in the larger world beyond the village has almost totally altered the former distribution of power. In former days the Warriors owned the main productive resource of the village, the land. Men of other castes received a share of the produce of the land, but only by virtue of being the dependants of the Warriors. Some provided special skilled services: priests, herdsmen, barbers, washermen, street sweepers and scavengers, and so forth. These specialists each received at the harvest a proportion of grain fixed by tradition and occasionally adjusted by the village council: and they were paid smaller amounts, also in kind, each time their services were used. In addition each Warrior household had attached to it one or more households from the caste of Untouchables, whose members were farm labourers. They received their food each day from the Warrior kitchen and they received customary presents of clothing, and a share of the grain at harvest time. A few were also given fields to cultivate for themselves in their spare time, perhaps using the master's plough cattle. In this relationship the Warrior master was called *raja* (king) and the servant *praja* (subject).

Political rivalry lay between Warrior households. In this respect the Warriors were like the Pakhtouns: they alone were full citizens entitled to enter the competition for honour and prestige. At the present time, for reasons described elsewhere,[10] this competition is virtually in abeyance for the Warriors are being forced increasingly to close ranks in the face of a revolution from their Untouchable castes. But enough has survived for us to find out how leaders recruited their supporters for the competition, which is called *doladoli*.

At the present time there are two such factions (*dolo*). When I first enquired about this, it seemed as if the two teams were recruited through kinship. Virtually all the Warriors in Bisipara were descended from a common male ancestor, but the two leaders represented different lines of descent and were each, so it seemed, supported by close kinsmen and opposed to more distant kinsmen. Closer investigation showed that this was not quite the case, and there were several examples of people changing sides and of close kin (an uncle and his nephews) being in opposed factions. Furthermore, there were ways of symbolizing alliance which were independent of closeness of kinship tie. When there is a death or a marriage, and at certain other crisis rites, it is customary for kinsmen to make contributions towards the expense. These contributions are fixed by custom, and one gave a slightly larger amount to a household in one's own faction than to a household in the enemy faction. These gifts are publicly counted and a record is kept of them, so that this custom in fact serves as a way of making known a change in political allegiance.

The point is that political allegiance was here being compounded with kinship ties and with ritual obligations. Later, when I was given an old genealogy written many years before, I realized that sections of the genealogies which I had recorded had been re-written to meet the realities of present day village politics. It is the idiom of brotherhood and the ritual obligations with give the political relationship its moral flavour. The re-writing of genealogies had the effect of giving normative respectability to alignments first arranged on a pragmatic basis.

Relationships of this kind, which cover more than one activity, are called multiple or multiplex. The metaphor is that of a rope in which several strands are bound together lending strength to one another and making it difficult for a man to separate out one strand and cut it, without damaging the others.

The relationship which a Warrior master has with his Untouchable *praja* was also of this kind. They are tied economically as employer and employee. But the competitive potential of such a relationship is muted both by ritual and by political obligations, and the morality of the bond is symbolized, for example, in the terms of address used: the servant calls his master 'father' and is himself addressed as 'son'. The *praja*, like the followers of the Pakhtoun *khan*, is expected to fight for his master, and himself expects to receive protection from him: if the *praja* wants to lay a complaint before the village council, he can do so only through the grace of his Warrior patron. But, unlike the follower of the Pakhtoun *khan*, the relationship is rendered moral by multiplying the ties which bind patron and client together. In our folklore the employee who marries the boss's daughter, has thereby removed the transactional hostility and insecurity of his former relationship, and the element of trust is increased. 'I hear that in the gown trade it is so bad that they are sacking the sons-in-law.'

We are now able to say more clearly what is the sociological meaning of long-term political credit given by the faithful and withheld by hirelings. The simplest form of relationship between leader and follower is the transaction based upon calculations of interest and profit: here the credit is short and the terms are harsh. But if this relationship is supplemented by, or even replaced by a bond of religion or of kinship or of both, the tie becomes a moral one, is less easily broken, and commands much more generous terms of credit. You can petition to have a defaulting debtor declared bankrupt: but it is less easy to do so if he is your brother-in-law and a deacon of the church to which you belong.

In this context neither 'kinship' nor 'religion' must be narrowly interpreted. It would be a mistake to think that cores come into existence only when the leader has sufficient daughters to marry all his henchmen or when everyone is fixated upon some transcending mystical goal. The same process is taking place when men use even the idiom of kinship, or when they can use the language of love for a leader or a cause without exciting derision. The man who says that because he is a civil servant he must observe scrupulous honesty and show no favours is making an essentially religious statement: he is stating a supreme and absolute value, which requires no further justification, least of all on the grounds of expediency. He is morally committed to the organization which employs him, so long as it continues to exhibit the standards of honesty and probity which he values.

In short, the core are those who are tied to the leader through multiplex relationships: the bond with a follower is transactional and single-interest.

UNSPECIALIZED GROUPS

I have been arguing so far about political teams, groups whose members co-operate in order to compete more effectively for prizes. In theory there is no reason why such a group should not consist entirely of a core, everyone being morally committed to support the team and all bound to one another by multiplex ties. But this very fact that the members share an interest in several different fields of activity suggests that the possibilities of political manoeuvre will be more closely restricted than is the case with more specialized political groups and that such groups cannot respond easily to changes in their environment. We suggested in the preceding section that inasmuch as a core gives a leader better credit facilities, it will make him a more formidable opponent in the contest. We now look at the opposite argument: that a core can in some circumstances be a millstone around the leader's neck. Less picturesquely, core-based groups tend to be less able to make a rational adaptation to environmental changes, especially when they are brought into contact with more specialized political structures.[11]

In an earlier chapter I mentioned the clans of the Konds, a tribe who live in the hills of Orissa in India, where Bisipara also lies.[12] The members of these clans co-operate for three kinds of activity: they own a tract of land in common and it is their duty to fight to keep it safe from intruders; the sons and daughters of the men of the clan regard one another as brothers and sisters and must find their spouses from other clans; and, thirdly, they co-operate in a large array of ritual observances which centre upon the Earth (*Tana penu*) and which are thought to ensure fertility and prosperity for clan members. These three sets of activities are notionally interlinked so that, for example, to mate with a clan sister or to shed the blood of a clan member pollutes the Earth and requires that everyone should join in rituals designed to remove the danger to the common prosperity and fertility.

This many-stranded relationship makes the clan a moral group. In theory at least there are no followers, for even those who leave one clan and join another as the result of the demographic imbalances described earlier, must accept all the obligations and enjoy all the rights of membership in their new clan. They cannot have the land and the protection unless they also observe the rule of exogamy and join the Earth congregation. (Perhaps this should be in the past tense, for the Kond tribal structure, like Bisipara's caste hierarchy, is becoming vestigial.)

A structure of this kind, on the argument of the previous section, should have provided reliable support for political leaders. Yet these clans had no leaders. There must have been in the past, as there are today, men of influence who exercised pragmatic leadership, but there was certainly no office of clan leader to be filled: and even the unofficial leaders no doubt were constrained by the Kond belief that Konds are brothers and therefore equals. There were clan priests, but these were technicians rather than leaders. Even to-day the visitor is struck by the demeanour of cocky independence which marks the Kond off from his hierarchically-minded Hindu neighbour.

The absence of normative leadership in this instance goes with multiplex grouping. The Konds had no specialized political leaders because they had no specialized political groups to be led. This, of course, is a tautology. But it is not tautological to go further and say that political groups had not evolved because the political tasks set by the environment were not overwhelming: and, at the same time, the environment did not provide sufficient surplus to support political specialists.

This is only the hint of an argument about the way in which political specialization can occur. Our interest at this point starts from the other direction: given that an unspecialized structure exists (i.e. a core) what constraints does it set upon a leader.

Leadership, as I will argue later, consists among other things in taking decisions. In unspecialized groups these decisions are routine ones: when to sow and when to reap; how to deal with an incestuous couple; how to negotiate with an enemy clan to find a bride for one's son or a husband for one's daughter; and so forth. The suggestion from this is that the leader who commands a multiplex group has little control over the running of large areas of its activities, and, perhaps more importantly, cannot easily siphon off his supporters' time and energy from these activities and invest them in political manoeuvring. In other words, he not only has to expend resources in keeping bright the ideology, he may have to allow that this ideology is the supreme value and find himself serving it, rather than the ideology serving him. One Oriya senior politician, whom I knew, claimed to spend six hours a day in prayer and meditation: in fact he probably had time enough for his politics, since the count of his average day's work, on his own description, came to over 40 hours. In short, the political leader whose supporters form a core may find that much of his resources must be spent on activities which are peripheral to his political interests. The situation is analogous to the leader of hirelings who also, but for different reasons, finds maintenance costs high.

The second point is that core-based groups find it more difficult to re-deploy themselves to meet some change in their environment, because such re-alignment may require corresponding adjustment in the associated fields of activity. This is both a simple proposition of the kind that the rich in Bisipara cannot form a class because they are ritually divided from one another by caste, and the more general proposition that most ideologies tend to inhibit political expediency. This comes out more clearly when one looks at factions, which lie at the opposite end of the spectrum from core-based groups.

FACTIONS[13]

The word 'factions' is strongly pejorative. Faction-fighting is thought to be socially destructive and while there are people who will, without shame, describe themselves as politicians (because they are too modest to call themselves 'statesmen') no-one will glory in being a faction-fighter. It is always the other side which goes in for faction-fighting.

Although, as we will see, it is no accident that the word has this pejorative meaning, we must begin by proposing a neutral, formal definition of what a faction is, and postpone or avoid making any value judgement about whether factions are good or bad. Such judgements are inappropriate: factions are 'bad' in just the same sense that adolescence is 'bad'—that is to say everyone concerned has to put up with some discomfort, just as when the weather is 'bad'.

There are two connected characteristics which mark out a political group as a faction: firstly the members do not co-operate because they have a common ideology which their co-operation will serve; secondly they are recruited by a leader with whom they have a transactional relationship.

The members of a faction do have a shared ideology, insofar as they would all subscribe to the political variant of the saying, 'Business is business'. But this, of course, does not unite them: it sets them in opposition. The point of unity, if that is the appropriate word, is the leader, the man with whom they each separately have their own transaction. The leader of a group of hirelings defines the group: without him there could be no group. Groups without leaders must always be moral groups. Every faction has a leader, whether it be one man or a clique (core) of several men, each with their own followers.

A faction is also a specialized group: its *raison d'être* is political competition, and, indeed, one pejorative connotation of the word is that factitious people go in for politicking just for its own sake and not to win legitimate prizes. This does not mean, of course, that the practitioners ever acknowledge that this is what they are doing. They appear under a variety of normative disguises and one of the ways of recognizing a faction is to notice that the same set of people fight at one another's side through a series of engagements, while displaying a cavalier disregard for the ideological consistency of the causes they support. If Faction *A* in an Indian village supports the Congress then that in itself is sufficient reason for Faction *B* proclaiming themselves Communists.[14]

Yet, if one looks at the circumstances in which faction alignments appear, the process is not at all frivolous. It is, as I said, like adolescence: a rejection of past allegiances and a fumbling, haphazard and—to an outsider—desperately selfish searching for new ways of arranging social interactions. Factions may arise when the environment provides some new kind of political resource, which existing groups cannot exploit.[15] Lineages, for example, are ill-adapted teams for winning spoils in state elections: they are too small and some larger grouping is required. Party agents come down to the villages to work among people who are quite unmoved by the appeal of party ideologies. Consequently the benefits of party allegiance are communicated to them in material terms, sometimes via the brokers whom I described earlier. Here and there the message gets through to individuals in different lineages, especially to those individuals whose faith in the mystical values of lineage brotherhood is not strong. These men constitute a following for the politician or broker and they can sometimes be persuaded to act against the interests of their own lineage. Therefore they are branded by the traditionalists as self-interested and immoral: deviants who pursue their personal interests to the detriment of the common good.

In a sense this is an evolutionary process. The actors are not tied to any group for mystical or sentimental reasons. The leaders who prove most skilled at exploiting the new resources pay the biggest dividends and attract the ablest followers: the fittest survive, the fittest being those best adapted to the new environment. I would suggest too that periods of faction-fighting, like adolescence, precede maturity. The faction which is most successful in the competition for new resources develops a core and in time the core expands to the point where a new kind of group, which is no longer a faction, has come into existence.[16]

It was suggested earlier that any continued series of trans-actions between the same partners will tend to engender a moral relationship. This, indeed, is the dilemma of a bureaucracy. Bureaucrats should treat their 'clients' in a completely universa-listic fashion: as members of the public and not as friends or enemies. But continued transactions create friends and enemies among this public, and the bureaucrats become improperly obliging or disobliging, making room for forms of nepotism and even corruption. In the same way the impersonal universalistic standards of ability can much more easily be used to throw out a graduate student, who fails an exam, at the end of his first term than is the case if he fails the exam after six terms: for by then his teachers know him, have developed a moral relationship with him and feel the tragedy involved in forcing through the consequences of his failure.

So it is with the leader and followers who make up a faction.

The longer they hold together as a group the longer they are likely to hold together. If at first the sole bond of allegiance lies in the pork barrel, later the credit built up by continued successes will carry the leader through one or two failures. When that point is reached the faction is already developing a core and has ceased to be purely a faction.

In situations like this, morality is a matter of keeping in step. While there are a few deviants experimenting with new ways of playing the political game, they remain out of step and are considered deviants. But the faction that continues to prove effective in getting men security or whatever it is they want will grow in size, until there are so many people marching to the new pace that they can no longer be called deviants. The new way of doing things, from at first being merely the effective way, now becomes the right way: from being a pragmatic device it gains, by degrees, normative approval.

By the time it gains normative approval, the 'hireling' structure of the faction is likely to have been changed in two main ways. Factions, as I said earlier do not advertise themselves as factions but try on various kinds of normative clothing. Sometimes these are serious attempts to find a normative identity: sometimes they may be cynical manoeuvres parading one's own righteousness to discredit an opponent. But, sincere or not, one of these normative identities may be found appropriate and become the symbol of the group's new found morality and a means of augmenting and later replacing the transactional basis of recruitment.

The second possible development is a consequence of size and depends upon the nature of the political structure's environment. This development is the growth of a division of labour within a faction and the emergence of a bureaucratic structure and, with it, a professional ethic. The faction in the raw, so to speak, is a segmentary structure: the ties which the leader has with his followers are all independent of one another. This, indeed, is one of the factors that creates factional instability, for desertion is the ending of that one transaction and has no ramifying consequences. In a sense, each participant is master of his own affairs, and self-sufficient. But a division of labour and an allocation of specific tasks to different people within the faction completely alters this. The hierarchy is no longer one of men *if common interest goal develops then the faction stabilises into pol grp.*

who are jacks-of-all-the-political-trades, able to hive off as complete units on their own and perhaps form another faction, but men specialized in finance, or legal affairs, or in propagandizing the group's ideology: cogs in the machine, the loss of which may wreck the machine but which also have no existence outside it. The faction is then transformed from being an aggregate of like and loosely-joined units to being like an organism.

CONCLUSION

We have in effect been tracing a hypothetical evolution of specialization and solidarity in a political group. We began with unspecialized groups in which political activity is an aspect or incident of other kinds of social interaction. The simplest kind of group specialized for political action is that which consists only of a following, in which relationships between leader and followers are entirely transactional. A more complex pattern is found when a group, which has political action as its *raison d'être*, makes use of other kinds of social interaction—religion or kinship, for example—as a means of recruitment and maintenance. The distinction between this kind of political group, which we called moral, and the unspecialized group (which is also, of course, moral) is hard to draw, and I suppose it is not unknown for supposedly political groups to dissipate their energies in other activities: this, at least, is a complaint which party activists make about workingmen's political clubs. Nevertheless, moral groups are certainly less open to fission than are factions. The highest level of solidarity is achieved when the group is organized as a bureaucracy, the members of which have an interest in the corporate continuity of their own organization (like moral groups but unlike factions), are specialized for political action (like factions but not like unspecialized groups), and provide for their own continuance (unlike factions which are in difficulties when the leader is removed).

In conclusion, there are three points to be made, which indicate that the task of analysis is hardly yet begun. We are still dealing very much in terms of ideal types. Actual political groups are likely to be a mixture of all kinds so far discussed: of cores, followings, and bureaucracies in varying 'mixes'. Secondly, and following from this, it would be a mistake to think

No shit

that political groups evolve necessarily from the simpler to the more complex forms. The development can go in any direction. Bureaucracies can be diluted by a dose of another kind of 'morality', losing their specialist purity and becoming particularistic, as has happened to some extent in ex-colonial territories. Moral groups may lose their fervour and become tamed to a transactional arena or a less fervent morality. In April 1947 de Gaulle formed his RPF (Rassemblement du Peuple français), a movement to which people might affiliate without leaving their parties, a transcendent organization which soon became a centre for those opposed to the Fourth Republic. The RPF was a 'rally', having as its central normative themes constitutional reform in the direction of a presidential system and the modification or abolition of the existing party system. The RPF did well in the municipal elections of October 1947 and in the general elections of June 1951, but as early as 1952 its deputies were adjusting themselves to the ground rules of party manoeuvring in the Fourth Republic. The votes of some of them helped to invest the Radical Pinay as premier in March 1952 and the Conservative Mayer in January 1953. Some of them became ministers in the Conservative Laniel government of July 1953 and later in the Radical Mendès-France and Faure governments (June 1954 and February 1955 respectively). They were now called Républicains Sociaux, a name adopted in 1953. De Gaulle, recognizing that his movement was being domesticated from under him by the Fourth Republic, dissociated himself from them in May 1953. Thirdly, the introduction of any new political resource is likely to bring on a period of factional experiment, which may last long enough for one to be tempted to say that some political groups, like some people, fail to get beyond adolescence.

The different structures outlined in this chapter—unspecialized, transactional, moral and bureaucratic—are all sets of rules regulating competition for political prizes within political groups. They are, of course, ideal types: actual structures must be understood not by asking which type they are, but rather what are the proportions in which the different types are drawn upon. But every structure, whatever its 'mix', is in a process of continuous adjustment with its environment. If we are to understand why one 'mix' rather than another is found, then the answer must lie in the environment. A general example of this process is the suggestion that factions arise when new kinds of political resource become available in the environment. A particular example is the post-war difficulty of France. Decisive action was required on many fronts, but the *immobilisme* which resulted from the structure of the Fourth Republic, prevented such action and parliamentary rule gave way to presidential rule. Before this can be carried further, we need to look at other parts of the political structure and we continue in the next chapter, to examine the tasks which the leader of a political group must perform within his group. Later chapters will discuss his competitive activities outside the group.

NOTES

1. One of the earliest and best known examples is *Evans-Pritchard* (1).
2. The literature on caste is extensive and much of it confusing. A general idea of the ideology of caste may be got from *Karve*, *Bouglé* and *Dumont*. To understand the caste system in operation, consult monographs by *Mayer* (1) and *Bailey, F. G.* (1), collections of essays by *Srinivas* (2) and (3) and an essay by *Bailey, F. G.* (5).
3. For a discussion of attitudes towards leaders in peasant societies and elsewhere see *Bailey, F. G.* (7).
4. The quotation is from *Where Angels Fear to Tread*, 1947, p. 155.
5. This is a matter not only of degree of kinship but also of geographical proximity and frequency of interaction see *Mayer* (1), Chapter 8.
6. For a fuller description see *Bailey, F. G.* (4). See also *Bailey* (7).
7. These examples which come to mind are the Great Festivals of the Tallensi (*Fortes* (1), p. 243), the ritual hunt of the Lele (*Douglas*), and the 'social drama' of the Ndembu (*Turner*, Chapter 10).
8. This, as in the case of other references to French post-war politics, I owe to Bruce Graham. See *Williams*, pp. 45–6 and 127.
9. See pp. 53–5.
10. See Chapter 9 and, for a fuller account, *Bailey, F. G.* (1).
11. The extreme case of this is that of those societies which anthropologists call acephalous: that is, they lack normative rules for leadership. Political groups were not specialized and their political structures were quite unable, unaided, to adapt themselves to colonial rule. Macpherson (see Chapter 9) had perceived that

this was so with the Konds. For an account of the grafting of leadership institutions onto one such society see *Evans-Pritchard* (2).

12. The full description is in *Bailey, F. G.* (2), Part 1.
13. For a discussion of the way in which this word is used in social anthropology, see *Nicholas* (3).
14. See *Nicholas* (1), p. 36 and (2), p. 31.
15. *Nicholas* (3), pp. 57–8 makes a similar point. See also *Gallin*.
16. There is an analysis of a fraction maturing in this way in *Graham* (3), pp. 16 and 23.

4

The Leader's Tasks

UNCERTAINTY AND DECISIONS

If everyone has enough land to grow the food to feed his family, if the rains come when they are expected, if there are no marauding enemies about, if there are tried and accepted and effective ways of dealing with trouble-makers within one's own community, if everyone is healthy, then there will be less work for a leader. Even if there is not enough land, if enemies attack, if the rains do not come and if there is sickness, there will still not be much scope for leadership, providing that all these crises have been encountered and survived before. In other words, leadership is called for particularly in conditions of uncertainty and when there is a need to take decisions *which are also innovations*.

Uncertainty means conditions under which people cannot find a rule to guide their reactions. They cannot easily assimilate their present condition to some similar condition in the past, and use this as a precedent for making a plan of action. Sometimes this uncertainty will arise not because no precedent exists, but because there are many precedents, each counselling a different course of action, and all of which to some degree seem to fit the present predicament. Rules by their very nature are general, while situations are particular. When there are several possible decisions, then each can have its own supporters, and what begins as a debate can grow into a dispute, a competition and even into a fight.

The French Fourth Republic faced such a crisis when the Algerian uprising broke out in November, 1954. There were three courses of action possible: all-out war; a political settlement with the F.L.N.; or the development of Algeria through social, political and economic reforms to deprive the insurrection of popular support. But this was the period of instability, of changing governments, of *immobilisme*. The Mendès-France

government, in office when the war began, might have followed
any one of these three courses with a reasonable chance of success. But its successor governments found themselves less and
less able to control the Algerian situation. The Mollet government (January 1956–May 1957) marked the period when the
civil authorities in Algeria became openly unresponsive to directives from Paris and when the army, dissatisfied with the direction of the war, began to formulate not only the means but also
the ends towards which policy in Algeria should be directed. By
the second half of 1958 de Gaulle was able to step in as arbitrator, make up the French mind, and, after protracted manoeuvring, bring the war to an end in 1962. By 1958, too, he had won
the fight to replace parliamentary government with presidential
rule.

Even if there are no partisans, it may still be necessary to
select one course of action and reject the rest in order to avoid
disaster. In short the effective working of a political team
requires some means of taking decisions, whether judicial or
administrative, within the group; and this is one of the duties
which make up the role of a leader. This, it is said, was Asquith's
failing as chairman of the War Committee.

A leader's other duties are of two main kinds. One is the
recruitment and maintenance of his group, a task which we have
discussed at length in the preceding chapter. Essentially this
consists of binding in followers by the use of two kinds of
resources: material and moral, that is, by rewards and by propa-
gating an ideology, both of which, we concluded, can be visualized
as the leader's credit-balance with his followers. This credit-balance is also affected by the leader's success or failure in carrying
out judicial and administrative tasks within the group. A
skilled performance of these tasks increases the leader's credit:
mistakes and failures must be countered by bribery or by
intensifying propaganda.

The leader's other range of tasks concern the world outside
the team, especially that part of it which constitutes the arena
in which the team is competing. The need to make decisions and
to take action, to deploy and redeploy resources arises from the
actions of other competitors in the arena. Indeed, one of the
distinctive characteristics of political competition, is that
actions are intended to produce uncertainties and disputes

within the opposing teams. Carson probed the nerve of ideological differences in Asquith's coalition.[1]

The present chapter concerns judicial activity and the taking
of administrative decisions by leaders within their own teams.
It goes beyond the structure of formal political rules and asks
how these rules are applied. These formal political rules are, of
course, normative: publicly-stated right and proper ways of
reacting in specified situations. When we go beneath these and
ask how they are in fact applied, we arrive at pragmatic rules.
These are part of the actor's cognitive map of his situation no
less than are the normative rules. They tell him not what is the
right or the good thing to do, but what will bring him the biggest
pay off as leader of a team.

JUDICIAL TASKS

One of the essential skills in leading a band of hirelings is judging
how far they can be deceived. The clever leader, when he con-
ducts the initial transaction through which a mercenary is hired,
indicates that this payment is a mere token of what can be
expected in the future. Indeed, the opposition inherent in such
a relationship, to which I have referred earlier, arises because
each partner is trying to make the other one be a creditor: each
wishes the other to give services in return for a promise of future
repayment. The house servants whom we employed in India
generally manoeuvred matters so that they always had an
advance of wages: but servants employed by villagers, who were
more astute than ourselves, received their pay in arrears.

From time to time the leader of a transactional group has to
pay off some of his political debts to his followers. If he has
raised their expectations too high, then those who are disappointed may decide to cut their losses and find another leader.
But before this happens, the followers are likely to anticipate
that a handout of spoils is due, and to put pressure on the leader
to give them their due share, even if this means that some other
follower will go short. In other words, within the team competition arises between followers to increase their own share in the
distribution of scarce spoils, and the leader is then forced to
adopt a judicial role.

The Congress government of Orissa in 1959 found this aspect

of leadership particularly difficult. Work on the new steel plant at Rourkhella was impeded because those who were displaced from their homes by the plant were represented in the Assembly by a small party (Jharkhand) whose six members kept the Congress government in office with their votes. Again, when it was announced that a new medical college would be sited in a hill district, two members from a coastal district, which had also bid for the college, announced that they would refuse the whip. (In fact the coalition overtook them and Congress was able to refuse them the whip and expel them.)[2]

Leaders of moral groups can find themselves in similar difficulties. Their subordinates may compete with one another for precedence. They may accuse one another or their leader of treason or of ideological infirmities. They may also, of course, debate on a relatively rational basis about the best line of action in a particular situation.

Such schisms are not uncommon. At the time of writing Harold Wilson has intermittent trouble with the left-wing of his party because they consider that he has sold the pass on such issues as Vietnam. In Orissa and in India generally a number of senior Congressmen left the party in the years after Independence because they felt it had lost is socialist ideals and had become a party of patronage and transactions, in spite of Nehru's efforts. No-one succeeded in holding together the Indian Communist Party, when the differences between Russia and China became acute and when China turned on India. India since 1964 has had two Communist parties: one 'Russian' and one 'Chinese', one 'right' and one 'left'.

In other words both kinds of team, moral and contract, may turn itself into an arena, requiring the leader of the group to become a referee. Other rules of behaviour within an arena form the subject of a later chapter: here we ask what forms the role of referee may take. It is, in most but not all situations, in the interest of a leader to get these disputes settled as quickly as possible: for they use up resources which he might otherwise have had at his disposal in the competition with other teams. In this chapter we are looking at the situation from the point of view of the referee and not through the eyes of the competitors, and we shall be asking how the different judicial roles which are open to the leader vary in cost.

There are two kinds of cost involved. In the short run the least expensive course of action is to sit still and hope that the matter will sort itself out; but, in the long run, failure to take a decision may prove very costly. Proverbs about nipping quarrels in the bud and stitches in time saving nine are part of the home-spun wisdom of our political world, which makes the not unreasonable assumption that people go in for political competitions in order to win and not in order to have a quiet life. Calculations of this kind are no doubt part of a referee's estimate of the situation, but in this chapter we are interested rather in the different costs of the actual judicial processes rather than in the wider question of when it pays to let things drift or to take a quick decision.

The least expensive role which the leader can adopt is that of mediator. He offers to hear both sides of the case and then to suggest a suitable compromise. But that is the extent of his commitment: he offers his opinion, which the disputants may accept or not accept, as they like: but, as a mediator he does not enforce his decision. The disputants must accept it, as we say, of their own free will: and, in another sense, the process is free for the mediator insofar as he does not have to commit resources to sanctioning the decision and forcing it upon the losing party or upon both parties, if neither happen to be satisfied.

Under what conditions is the leader likely to act as a mediator? Firstly, since the mediation is only effective if both parties agree to the compromise, there is the risk that they will not agree and the dispute will not be settled. Therefore, other things being equal, the leader is likely to mediate, if he judges that the long-term costs of continuing the dispute are not going to be serious: if he considers that the matter is trivial. Secondly, mediation will occur and be successful when the leader perceives that both disputants, being unsure of victory, want a compromise arranged so that they can withdraw without losing face. It may be that in such a situation the astute leader will improve his own standing by pretending that what is in fact a mediation is his authoritative decision.

The third situation, together with the comment made in the last sentence, suggest that mediation is in some cases an abdication of leadership. It is clearly sensible to insist that you are mediating, if you know in fact that you could not enforce your decision upon an unwilling disputant. But to say that a leader is in this position is to say that his political credit is low. This, of course, does not apply if the leader is seen to have decided that the dispute is too trivial to merit the expenditure of resources involved in the other kind of dispute settlement: arbitration.

A neat illustration (already briefly mentioned) of the difference between mediation and arbitration is given by Barth in the story of the Pathan Saint who whistled. The Saints, as the English word chosen for their name suggests, are men of especial religious standing. They are men of peace: their homes provide a sanctuary and their persons are inviolate: their demeanour is gentle and persuasive in contrast to the *khan*, who should be rough and assertive. One such man, dressed in the white turban which is the badge of his sanctity, was mediating between two rival gangs who were drawn up under their *khans*, one side unarmed but the other, contrary to their promise, armed and ready for battle. He suggested his compromise, but the belligerent *khan*, who evidently thought that matters should come to a fight because he was going to win it, prepared to brush the Saint aside and open fire. At this the Saint whipped off his white turban (thus desacralizing himself for the occasion), stuck his fingers in his mouth and whistled. Out of the bushes around, set ready in ambush, arose the Saint's own men. The reluctant *khan* was thereupon compelled to accept the Saint's decision and what began as mediation ended in arbitration.[3]

For the leader arbitration is an altogether more serious and costly process than mediation, and, other things being equal, he will arbitrate when he judges that the long-run costs of leaving the dispute unsettled will be high. The very act of announcing that the leader will arbitrate, rather than mediate, mortgages resources which have to be held in readiness for enforcing the decision, should that prove necessary. This does not, however, mean that the leader is always reluctant to arbitrate and does so only when he fears that continued disputing will break up his team. He may also judge that the time is ripe to make an assertion of his leadership and to show that he has the resources to enforce his will, if that proves necessary. In other words, an arbitrated decision is not merely a means of keeping order: it is also a means of broadcasting messages that the leader's political credit is good.

For example, the United States effectively arbitrated and brought an end to hostilities in the Suez Campaign of 1956 and so reinforced a claim to world leadership. De Gaulle, too, from 1958 onwards was able to arbitrate between the French extremists and the Algerian nationalists in a way that no other French leader in the preceding four years had been able to do. This demonstrated the strength of his political credit and so reinforced it. To take a contrary example, the long record of failed arbitrations and failure to arbitrate discredits any claim which the United Nations might make to a position of world leadership.

The actual costs of enforcing a decision are not all of the same kind. The most obvious expenditure lies in providing people who will act as policemen and force the disputants to follow the decision, which is, of course, where the weakness of the United Nations lies. But also, short of this crude material extreme, there are various forms of moral pressure which are in fact arbitrated and enforced decisions, although it may sometimes appear that the reluctant disputant has concurred of his own free will. The confessions before the Peoples Courts, which occurred in Communist countries, were arbitrated decisions of this kind. Clearly hirelings are not going to behave in this way, but the members of a moral group may do so. The process is not cost-free, although the expenses are not of the same kind as when enforcement personnel are used. In the first place, some personnel have to be used—someone's time has to be spent—in brainwashing (that is what the process amounts to) the disputants. Secondly the arbitrator who works by this method puts at stake the ideology, just as any leader stakes his credit in an arbitrated settlement. It is a gamble of varying degrees of uncertainty: a win sees the ideology or the leader's reputation vindicated and strengthened; but a failure to enforce the decision tarnishes both.

In certain kinds of moral teams leaders avoid this danger of personal involvement by having God decide. There are many forms which this may take. It may merely mean that the leader announces that he has prayed for guidance, or has seen a vision: then it is God's wrath which the recusant risks, not the leader's. The same effect is achieved by the use of various mechanical devices for ascertaining the divine will: ordeals for the litigants; oracles; drawing lots; and so forth.

The point of these devices is that they make it inappropriate for the disappointed party to harbour a grievance against the leader: or indeed against any person, for the source of his discomfort lies beyond his reach outside the human world. An analogous secular restitution is the 'adjutant', part of whose job it is to take the blame for mistakes or unpopular measures and so preserve the myth of the leader's infallible wisdom and kindness. Such devices draw our attention to a fact which successful leaders know: their judicial task is not primarily to see that justice is done, but to control dissension within their group and ensure that their supporters will co-operate with one another, when that is necessary. Mediation is cheap, for one reason, because if it is successful both parties consent and, in theory at least, are ready to co-operate from that time onwards. Arbitration, insofar as both parties are invited to state their case, has some element of this, but there is in the end a greater risk that one litigant will be disappointed, will resent being forced to carry out the decision, will withdraw the political credit that he had given to the leader and, if he can, leave the group.

We have given a simplified account of why a leader should adjudicate and of the relative costs and risks of different forms of judicial action. The leader's aim is both to keep his group strong and his own position secure with the least possible expenditure of resources in doing so. This, of course, is oversimplified because these aims sometimes contradict. Leaders will be found stirring up dissensions among their followers and perhaps so arranging things that some disgruntled follower will leave the team in disgust. This kind of activity shows that he is not trying to maintain the whole group intact, but rather to maintain his own position as leader even at the risk of losing some of his followers. These kinds of activities will be considered in the context of an arena in a later chapter.

DECISIONS

In October and November, when the work in the fields had slackened before the December harvest, and when the occasional shower of rain made the ground soft, so that tracks could be seen and followed, the men of Bisipara used to go hunting. They would wait for reports of wild boar or deer seen raiding outlying fields, and then follow the tracks until they thought they had come upon the stretch of jungle where the beasts were hiding. The headman led the party and when he decided that they had located the area where the animals could be found, he positioned the four guns to wait in ambush and sent off the twenty or thirty beaters to work round in a wide circle and drive the animals downwind towards where the guns waited. Sometimes the beaters, thumping at tree trunks with their long axes and letting out irregular staccato cries, would flush an animal and allow the guns to get in a shot. Eventually the beaters, now shouting more regularly so that they would not be mistaken for an animal moving through the thick foliage, reached the guns and everyone would gather in a clearing and smoke and talk and rest and later move off to a new stand.

In a day's hunting there were three kinds of decision to be observed. The headman would talk over with other experienced men where the animal could have gone and what stand should be taken next: he would then say where they would go next and, this decision taken, the discussion would give way to idle chatter until the time came to make a move. The move from a rest position towards a new beat seemed to be spontaneous. Someone would get up and stretch and say 'Let's go.' Some time later someone else would do the same until most of the party were on their feet and stubbing out their leaf cigarettes, and all saying, to no-one in particular: 'Let's go. Let's go.' Then they would go, setting off in single file through the trees, led by no-one in particular; everyone knew the way. The third type of decision was quite different: it arose in response to an emergency. Occasionally the beaters would raise a leopard or a bear, which would cut out sideways between the guns and beaters. At once the operation would change from being a sport to a military operation: the headman took charge and directed both guns and beaters where to go with swift laconic commands, which were instantly obeyed.

This vignette illustrates three kinds of situations in which decisions are taken and three kinds of decisions. First there are commands which arise as instant responses to an emergency, in which it is important for the leader to ensure that action is initiated quickly. Whether the members of the team understand and agree with what they are being told to do, is less important than that they should do what they are told. This, as everyone knows, is the situation in wartime in our own countries. Secondly, there are decisions in which speed of action is not so important that it leaves no time for debate about what is the best action to take. This is the situation in which the hunters debate about which stretch of jungle should next be drawn. Then it is much more important that both guns and beaters should understand what is proposed, and the reasons for it, and should go along with the decision and co-operate with it. In the third situation, that of moving off after rest, the decision is of quite a different kind. It is entirely consensual: it is taken by no-one in particular. It does not matter whether the rest is of five or ten or fifteen minutes' duration. One feels almost that the occasion is taken to emphasize that they are all hunters together, relaxing as equals, and that no-one is in command. It is, indeed, difficult to think of the move after a rest as being the occasion for a decision at all.

It seems from this that a leader, when taking a decision, must balance the need to act swiftly against the desirability of ensuring that his team knows why the decision is being taken and acquiesces in it. This again is a question of cost. The consensual decision requires no enforcement, does not put the leader's authority at stake, and, insofar as it is consensual, should leave no-one disgruntled. But the swift unexplained command can provoke resistance, even hatred and does require sanctioning: unless, as in the case of a well-drilled army or a group of fanatical supporters, they have been specifically trained to accept authoritarian actions. The feebler the means of sanctioning his decisions at the disposal of a leader, the more trouble he must take to ensure that his supporters both understand and acquiesce in his decisions.

When a leader takes a decision, he must have the ability to envisage certain constraints and guide lines and to find a way between them. First there are a number of normative rules which might be relevant to the situation. Even if the leader does not accept any one of these as an absolute guide, as a matter of conscience, nevertheless he risks losing supporters if he cannot afterwards point to one of these rules and claim that it guided his decision. Secondly he must have some idea of the resources that will be expended in implementing that particular decision, and whether in fact he can command these resources. Thirdly, he must think pragmatically about the consequences of his decision, supposing it is implemented. Will it, in fact, satisfactorily deal with the variation in the environment, which is the occasion for the decision in the first place? What will be the effect of expending resources in this way on his ability to implement other decisions which will arise in the near future? Questions of this kind can be multiplied amost indefinitely.

In point of fact decision-takers do not have to function like computers, taking in and making sense of a great number of variables. Social life is possible because most decisions have the agony taken out of them by being routine. Even emergencies, like the leopard springing up before the beaters, become routine and although the reaction must be swift and the situation may be dangerous, it has all been done before. This, I suppose, is the whole design of rank-and-file military training: to render all possible emergencies matters of routine and so minimize the occasions when someone has to take a decision which has never been taken before.

Such a decision can be the truly expensive one. For the most part leaders try to meet new situations by forcing them into the categories of familiar situations, or by making minimal adjustments to well-tried plans—what political scientists call incrementalism. When the outcome is clearly unsatisfactory, then the leaders are driven to make an innovating decision. Such a decision is expensive, firstly, in the way that any gamble may turn out to be expensive: one is never sure that the return expected will in fact come. Secondly, the rank-and-file are being asked to do things which they have not done before, and this requires, if not training, at least a degree of thought and care which a routine action does not.[4] Thirdly, the resources diverted to make the new way of action possible may alter the pattern of resources available for other activities, so that the new decision may have quite unintended and unanticipated consequences. All this does not of course mean that innovating decisions must always be disastrous. Far from it: the returns can be great. But it does explain why innovating decisions are made with reluctance and sometimes only in response to dire necessity. As we will see later, political competition is kept short of fighting partly because people go on taking the same kinds of decisions in the same circumstances, and so allow their opponents to anticipate the next move, to understand what is going on, and to make a relatively sophisticated and economical use of social resources for purposes of political competition.[5]

CONSENT AND COMMAND

Decisions are called for in conditions of uncertainty: when no rule can be found to guide action or when there are several possible rules and a choice has to be made between them. For the leader there are many economies in selecting a known course of action, and in the short run he risks least by choosing such a course and making minor adjustments to meet the particular situation. One reason why this is a less expensive way of using political resources is that the supporters who have to implement the decision and take the consequences, understand what they are being asked to do, and, having done it before, are likely to be confident about the outcome and to this extent they accept the decision.[6]

For the leader a main question is always what will be the effect of his actions upon his political credit. First he has the choice of taking action or of sitting quiet and doing nothing. He must decide about the consequences of action or no-action upon his political credit. The price of no-action might be an escalating dispute within his own team, which will eventually destroy it, or it might be destruction by an enemy or by some natural force, if steps are not taken to avoid this fate.

Once he has decided to take action, the the leader must take short-run decisions about the administrative costs of different types of decision. The least expensive are those which withhold the exercise of leadership by seeking a consensual decision, although these do in practice cost the time spent in persuasion and may often in fact be a normative cover to a series of behind-the-scenes transactional arrangements which persuade the reluctant to withdraw their opposition. This can be true both of consensual administrative decisions and of mediated settlements. The most expensive decisions to implement in the short run are those taken through a command, without previous consultation. In judicial situations arbitration approaches this extreme, but there is some prior consultation. These decisions are expensive because resources have to be expended either beforehand in training people to carry out orders without question or afterwards in forcing the reluctant to do what they are told.

NOTES

1. In the Nigeria debate: see pp. 102–103.
2. These examples also show that 'transactional' does not simply mean 'self-regarding'. In both cases spoils were being sought for constituents and both were justified in strongly normative terms. Nevertheless, on these occasions the members evidently regarded their connection with the Orissa government (Congress party membership in one case and a parliamentary alliance in the other) as transactional. For more details see *Bailey, F. G.* (4), pp. 6–7.
3. *Barth* (2), p. 99.
4. This topic could be explored further. Some cultures build up the idea of youth, newness, vigour and innovation as a normative theme. Actions are acceptable insofar as they can be presented as innovations. This is usually the case in post-colonial or post-revolutionary societies. A great deal of this is in fact a normative façade, a language of claims and confrontations. What I want to do is in accordance with the spirit of the revolution. What you want to do is reactionary: even if in fact both courses of action were commonplace before the revolution. Secondly, it seems not to last long: particular sets of innovative policies quickly ossify and are given, so to speak, the status of perpetual youth, like Peter Pan. Thirdly, the main point still holds: any policy which is genuinely new must initially be expensive (even if it ultimately shows a profit), because it requires new kinds of training, and causes people to fumble at doing what they have not done before.
5. I owe some of the points in this chapter to a discussion with Bernard Schaffer. My analysis, however, no more than touches the fringe of a complex subject. See *Schaffer and Corbett*.
6. There is an illustration of this in *Barth* (3), p. 10. He is talking of herring fishermen: 'It is for the skipper to take the decision of choosing the vessel's course; but he does so in the context of important transactionally determined constraints. There can be no doubt that a vessel's chance of finding herring is greater if it strikes out on its own than if it follows other vessels. Thus the purely technical and economic considerations should favour such a course. But if a skipper, without special information to justify the move, decides to go elsewhere than where other vessels go, he demands more trust in his transaction with the crew. They are

asked to respect his judgement, as opposed to that of other skippers; they are thus asked to make greater prestations of submission than they would otherwise have had to do. The skipper also risks more by not joining the cluster: if a few vessels among many make a catch, the crew and the netboss can claim that it might have been them, had the skipper only given them the chance. If the vessel on the other hand follows the rest, they are no worse off than most, and the onus of failure does not fall on the skipper.'

5

Strong and Weak Leaders

Some years ago I spent an evening interviewing a Minister of a government, the identity of which, for reasons that will shortly be obvious, I shall not reveal. The interview was perforce an unstructured one since in the first half hour the Minister shifted sufficient whisky to increase greatly his desire to communicate but also very much to lower his ability to follow a coherent line of exposition. He was much possessed by the thought of his own power and of the responsibility of his position, and, indeed, of the happy chance of high birth which made him fit to be a leader. All this was interspersed with gossip about his colleagues, routine denigration of the opposition, anxious invitations to visit him in his constituency, and *obiter dicta* about ballroom dancing, folk culture and other small matters of the moment.

Later in the evening we were joined by a man who made profuse aplogies for disturbing the Minister, but indicated that some urgent matters had arisen as a result of the day's business in the House, and the Minister must take certain decisions which could then be implemented in time for the question hour next day. This man, a civil servant, had brought the file so that the Minister could study the questions, before taking a decision. But *in vino veritas*: all the Minister said was: 'Where do I sign?' A pen was then produced by the civil servant, the places for signature were indicated, and, with more apologies for the intrusion and great signs of deference, the visitor backed out of the room.

In his performance in other contexts, this Minister did not acquit himself too badly: but, if the clues are taken only from the incident I have described, then the Minister had only the forms of power and the real power was exercised by the civil servant, who had clearly taken the decisions and drafted the required documents, before he set out for the Minister's house that evening.[1]

At the other extreme it is not difficult to think of people who hold no formal office but exercise great power. Barth describes how a young man returned from work outside the Swat valley, wearing an elaborate wrist watch in which he had invested his earnings. He was showing it proudly to other men in the club-house when the *khan* said, tersely: 'That will be your present to me.' This was done, it seems, not because the *khan* coveted the watch, but solely in order to demonstrate his power over his followers, through an act which can be likened to the conspicuous consumption of political resources.[2]

This chapter asks questions about strong and weak leadership. But it should be made clear that this is not the same as questions about strong and weak development of political office. There are societies which have no formal leadership roles: they have no idea of an office for which someone must be selected. The Nuer are an example.[3] Other societies may have such offices but not attach must importance to them because the list of rights and duties which constitute the office is not thought to confer the right kind of honour or prestige on the incumbent. In several parts of rural India, when the British instituted administrative headmanships for villages or localities, it was the practice for local notables to ensure that this office went to a junior person.[4] At the other extreme are societies which have highly institutionalized and specialized leadership roles, marked by elaborate rituals of induction and enlarged by ceremonial, in which it is made clear that the office itself is more valued than the holder. 'It's not the man you're saluting', the recruit is told, 'it's the uniform.'

The fact that a political office is specialized or that it is reinforced by ritual observances certainly is not irrelevant to the power which the incumbent can exercise. The office itself is one of the resources which he can use in the exercise of power over his supporters. But, as the examples are intended to show, it would be wrong to confuse the scale which anthropologists construct between tribes-without-rulers and centralized states with the range of weak to strong leaders. The questions are independent of one another, to some extent, and to confuse them is to ignore the distinction between normative and pragmatic rules.

We already have a variety of synonyms for strong and weak leaders. The strong leader commands: the weak leader asks for consent. The strong man has men at his disposal like instruments: the weak leader has allies. The former's political credit is high: the latter's low. The strong man has ready access to political resources: the weak leader does not. Notice that questions about a leader's control over his team are questions about the relative size of his political resources as measured against the political resources independently controlled by his supporters. We are asking why a leader is strong within his team, rather than, at this stage, why one leader is stronger than another leader: the two questions do, of course, overlap with one another.

TRANSACTIONAL GROUPS

Contract teams, it will be remembered, are groups in which the followers do not feel themselves beholden to the leader or to any cause as a matter of conscience, but evaluate the relationship with the leader on the basis of profit or potential profit. They have invested their services or their money with that leader in the hope of dividends. The metaphor suggests that the leader's control over any of his followers will depend upon the relative importance to each of them of that investment. The follower who has invested only one-tenth of his political capital with the leader does not stand to lose much if he severs the tie. The man who has invested everything and no longer has channels open to rival leaders is in the opposite position: he cannot so easily withdraw from the team. I noticed in Orissa several instances in which the sons of a middle-class family had diversified the family interests. In the case of which I am thinking one brother was a senior civil servant; another was a politician—not very successful—in the Congress party; the third was a full-time worker for the Communist party. I asked if this was an accident and was told that families were pleased if things turned out this way, especially during the Independence Movement, for then the family could never be entirely on the losing side.

From the leader's point of view an investor who has provided half the stock is, other things being equal, a follower to be persuaded rather than commanded, the more so if the investment is only a small part of the investor's fortune: indeed, such a leader is in danger of becoming a follower himself. Against this, the tiny investment that represents a fortune for the investor indicates a follower who is close to being a mere instrument.

This capital which is invested and the dividends which are handed out from time to time to the followers, can take several forms. One of these is material goods: money or food or clothing. The Pakhtouns provide an example. Very close to this is a category of spoils which are titles giving access to material goods: contracts or licences in a controlled economy are examples. This, so the cynical politicians of Orissa said, was the fuel which drove their political machines. At a further remove from this are titles of honour which in turn shade into what one might call 'moral' rewards, like the satisfaction of serving the cause: but that takes us beyond the range of transactional groups and will be discussed later in this chapter. Besides transactions involving material goods, contract teams often are formed around the exchange of services. These too may take many forms. The Pakhtoun *khan*, for example, provides protection for his follower's person and possessions. The clients of the village broker, described earlier, benefit from his special skills in opening the backdoors of the Administration. In neither case could the follower have provided this service for himself.

It should be stressed that in spite of the materialistic basis of transactional groupings in politics, successful leadership is a matter of skills rather than just of possessions. Being rich is not enough: it is not even necessary. The skill required is a thorough knowledge of, and ability to apply the pragmatic rules through which other people's resources can be tapped and through which these resources can be converted into a political following.

It is a matter of creating confidence. The transactional leader works to create a kind of legitimacy for himself: to make other people expect that he will do what he says he will do. In other words the gang of hirelings, no less than the moral group, is pervaded by faith: that the leader can deliver the goods. This faith is reinforced when the leader does in fact deliver: but in addition to this each political culture produces an elaborate system of pragmatic rules which tell a leader how he should signal his own trustworthiness and which tell the followers how to read the signals. The village broker—and I take the example of the man I watched many times at work in Bisipara—must make the villagers believe that he can communicate with and manipulate clerks and officials in a way that the ordinary villager cannot. He dresses like a clerk or like a minor official in the Congress party. If asked about some procedure in administration, for example how to get a Government loan to build a house, he delivers an authoritative, if mystifying and unhelpful, lecture, the message of which is that he alone might make the arrangement but the questioner could not. He values being seen with officials and takes care to be present when they come to the village: this, of course, serves a double purpose, for the broker also wants to convince officials that he is their sole means of effective communication with the villagers. The broker in fact had a complex task in presenting himself to the world, for he wore a normative mask of devotion to the public weal, which had, however, to be sufficiently transparent to allow clients to see his skill at manoeuvres which were normatively condemned. His livelihood depended, as it were, on pretending to be a policeman in such a way that everyone would recognize him for a criminal.

Let us go back to the question of relative control. The Bisipara broker, at least when I knew him, was a small man with a clientele which he discovered was much smaller than he thought when he himself stood for election. The problems of control are more easily discussed in the context of larger and more complex groups: those which contain smaller groups inside them. In such a case the leader does not have direct access to everyone in his group: his contact with at least some of the rank and file is mediated through subordinate leaders. These leaders are, at least potentially, rivals of the main leader and the relative size of their political credit will determine his control over them. Let us now look at the tactics open to a leader who wants to strengthen his control of the group. It will be easier if we limit the discussion to human resources, that is followers, and take for granted what has been said earlier about the material goods and the skills, which are, in a transactional structure, the means of attracting and holding followers. Let us also simplify the picture by stipulating that only transactional ties between leader and follower are allowed: the strategy of creating moral ties or building bureaucracies will be considered later.

Other things being equal, the leader is strongest when all links run directly to him, with no intermediary leaders. The simple logic of this is that intermediary leaders are like intermediary rent-receivers: they 'taste' the revenue on its way up and so diminish the amount available to the person at the top. Therefore one tactic is for the main leader to try to attach the followers of intermediate leaders directly to himself. But there are two difficulties. One is that the intermediate leader will certainly consider this a violation of their contract and will, if he is in time and is not strong enough to put up a fight, cut his losses and go elsewhere. The other difficulty arises because the intermediate leader may turn out to be necessary in realizing the political rent from his band of followers: the main leader may find it technically impossible to communicate with the extra followers. In other words the cost of such a takeover is not only a payment of spoils to the followers set against their services, but also the cost of the 'managerial' functions carried out by the deposed intermediate leader.

Sometimes the leader can see the writing on the wall and holds back. In 1921 non-co-operation movements were mounted by the Congress in India. In the United Provinces they were able to exploit agrarian discontent. But, in their turn, the British administration encouraged local resistance to the disorders and were much helped by a class of subordinate allies, the landlords (called Taluqdars). These landlords were exceedingly privileged and their exactions no doubt contributed to the agrarian troubles, which aided the Congress. For this reason— and, I suppose, for reasons of natural justice, since tenants in neighbouring areas were much better off—the U.P. Government introduced legislation to trim Taluqdari power. But in fact the Taluqdars were able to get, through negotiation, more than they had given up. In spite of pressures from the Government of India and from local Liberal interests, the U.P. Government forced the bill through. 'Butler [the Governor] believed that action to alleviate peasant discontent which was not acceptable to or condoned by the landlords would produce disaffection and an additional threat to provincial stability among the class which was the main safeguard of rural order.'[5]

A successful takeover is achieved by undermining the political credit of the intermediate leader. The pragmatic rules for doing this vary from one political structure to another. There are some straightforward cultures like the Pathans, the gangsters and racketeers of the American cities, or some totalitarian nations of our own day, where the job can be simply carried out by murder. Or, somewhat less violently, the leader may bring new personnel into the arena or create roles for existing personnel, making them depend directly on himself and cutting out the intermediate leaders. This is one way in which one could construe the Red Guard violence in China at the present day. Other cultures prescribe less crude ways of lowering public confidence in a rival. He may be harassed or attacked directly and ruined financially through litigation, a tactic favoured in the politics of village India since the British introduced their kind of law court.[6] A more subtle tactic is to 'entrust' the intermediate leader with some task at which he will probably fail, and to let it be known that this has been done. If he refuses to undertake the task, he declares himself a small man: if he tries and fails, he uses up resources and loses reputation and credit. The only risk which the main leader runs is that he may have misjudged either the man or the situation, and be embarrassed when the intermediary successfully completes the task.

A well-known tactic for coping with an ambitious subordinate is 'divide and rule'. In quantitative terms, the problem of control is keeping the political capital of subordinates smaller than one's own. One way to diminish a growing subordinate is to cut him in two pieces: to play off one of his subordinates against him. This, too, has its risks. Badly played, a group with one leader and a subordinate becomes an arena with three groups and the likelihood of the weakest, if he holds the balance, allying himself with the next weakest.[7] Even short of this point of disaster for the original leader, by covertly encouraging internal competition he allows resources to be lost, so to speak, through avoidable friction, and thus cuts down his potential level of political 'production': that is, he diminishes his ability to compete with other teams.

Still following the question of how a leader can increase his control over supporters, we turn now from transactional groups towards those which also contain a core.

DIVIDING THE WORK

One of the difficulties in building up transactional political teams (and one reason why the word 'faction' carries connotations of smallness) is that each link has to be made separately and kept in repair separately. Furthermore, since one man might be bound in by the loan of a field, another by a supply of cartridges for his gun, a third blackmailed by your knowledge of some fearful secret in his past, and a fourth because he is expecting your help in getting his son a place in the High School, and so forth—given this diversity which is the characteristic of transactional teams—there is no one set of pragmatic instructions which will serve to maintain every strand in the rope: each one has to be serviced in a separate way. This must be part of the reason why a succession of conflicts in the Swat valley did not in the past terminate because everyone was on the winning side. Teams could not be maintained beyond a certain size: above that size leader-supporter relationships gave way to alliances, to rivalries and to splits. The soaring Khan, if not shot down by a rival, eventually fell to the ground under his own weight.

From the point of view of the leader of a transactional team, the danger is that subordinate leaders are images of himself, doing just what he is doing but on a smaller scale. They are self-contained and they are capable of growth up to the point where they can hive off. One solution is for the leader to divide up the work not according to areas or groups of men in which the subordinate leader carries out all the jobs of leadership, but to divide up the job of leadership itself and allocate them to different people, himself alone being competent in all fields of leadership. In other words, he introduces specialization into politics.

If this is done, the leader benefits in two ways. Firstly he has removed the possibility of a challenge to his own rule, for while officials may be experts in tax collecting, or judicial affairs, or religious matters none of them are experienced in looking to the whole matter of government. By centralizing certain activities especially tax-collection and military matters both of which are crucially important in developing political capital, the leader has removed the possibility of any subordinate leaders who may have survived setting themselves up as rivals. A segmentary pattern has been transformed into an organism: a set of inter-dependent parts, like a man's body, no one of which could live an independent existence.

Secondly, specialization solves the problem of size in a way that is impossible in a transactional group. This does not mean that bureaucratically organized groups can grow indefinitely: as is well known such organizations, if grown beyond a certain limit, also suffer from diseconomies of scale. Nevertheless the rational procedures which are part of a bureaucracy simplify and routinize the tasks of recruitment, maintenance, dispute-settlement, decision-taking and deployment of resources.

The discussion so far has been conducted in a somewhat programmatic fashion. But this simplified outline is not a fan-tasy, and it is not difficult to find actual societies where the political structure suggests this transition from transaction to bureaucratic modes of team-building. The Rajputs were the dominant caste of warriors and landowners in that part of north-western peninsular India which bears their name: Rajputana. To simplify somewhat, they were divided into kingdoms and each kingdom was divided into chiefdoms and so forth, resem-bling the pattern of main leader and subordinate leaders which has been discussed in this chapter. Each of these chiefs had charge of his own tract of land and people, and the superior chief had no direct contact with subjects except those on his own estate. He was, in fact, and in Rajput theory, not so much a ruler but one Rajput among others, *primus inter pares*. This situation was very unstable. Leaving aside the devastation caused by wars against outsiders, Rajputs fought for precedence among themselves, and the man who was first among his equals at one period, would find himself down among the equals (or dethroned or killed) at another time.

Bhai shatru—the Rajputs had and their descendants still have a strong normative ethic of brotherhood,[8] yet a man's enemies and the men who could threaten his position of leadership were his clan brothers; for they, like himself, were born to chiefly rank. From men of other castes the rulers had nothing to fear, for they could not set themselves up as rulers. In this respect at least they were trustworthy and could be given positions of responsibility. Consequently in those kingdoms where the ruler

was sufficiently in control to want to plan consolidation, he did
so by organizing an embryonic civil service, recruiting for this
purpose not Rajputs but Brahmins. Even without the safeguard
of specialization the Brahmins were loyal firstly because they
could not aspire to replace the ruler and secondly because they
owed their preferment to that ruler: if he went down, so did
they.[9] The same system keeps a large number of minor functionaries—dog-catchers, gaolers, garbage-collectors and the like
—loyal party members in smalltown America.

Systems of this kind—personal bureaucracies, so to speak—
are clearly one stage behind the fully developed legal-rational
system in which the civil servants owe their allegiance not to
particular political teams, but to the team which is in power,
and, beyond this, to the regime; or, beyond this still, to a set of
normative rules of bureaucratic behaviour. Such men are loyal
to the system itself, and to the leader only so far as he remains
within the rules of the system. No rival will arise from among
them, as in a transactional team: but if sufficiently provoked
they can become collectively a rival, deposing particular leaders
and outlasting all of them. We have come back to the Minister
whose directives were written for him by his civil servants.

MORAL TEAMS

What has just been said about bureaucracies can also be said
about any group which is held together by a shared ethic.
Accordingly it applies to the leader of any core. Support is
gained at the price of conformity, at the price of renouncing
(or at least seeming to renounce) any tactic which could offend
the normative values of the group. But the same handicap, of
course, is placed upon any would-be rival within the group.

The main political capital of the leader of a moral group is his
monopoly, if he can establish it, of the right to communicate
with or to symbolize whatever mystical value it is that holds
the group's devotion. John Middleton,[10] in his book about the
Lugbara of Uganda, describes how the elders of lineage seek to
discipline ambitious subordinates, especially those who have
ambitions to hive off and become elders in their own separated
segments. Lugbara believe that elders may invoke the dead
ancestors of the lineage to punish with sickness those who give

offence. So, if an elder should fall ill, his rivals are most anxious that the divination held to determine the cause of the illness should indicate that *their* curse and invocation was the cause of the illness. For if this is so, it is taken as conclusive proof that they are in touch with the ancestral spirits and that their claim to leadership is validated.

Spiritual or moral leadership in political groups is a matter of manipulating symbols. When he gained power in 1958 de Gaulle took care to present themes which favoured presidential rule and discredited parliamentary rule. French radio and television were noticeably biased in his favour. The Fourth Republic, it was said, had weakened the state by allowing parliamentarians to play 'sterile games'. Presidential rule created a new responsible party in the UNR, made it possible for effective decisions to be taken in the interest of the nation as a whole, and allowed the President to restore the honour of France. National honour, national effectiveness and responsible leadership were the themes symbolized. Control of these symbols and of the means of counteracting them constitute political capital.

The leader who monopolizes such symbols has two ways of protecting his position. The obvious one is to deny their use to subordinates and rivals as de Gaulle did. This is also the way the Indian caste system works: there is an elaborate apparatus of ritual disqualifications, marking more and more degraded positions in the hierarchy. One part of this concerns ritual services by specialists: for example, low castes are not entitled to certain services from the Brahmin priests. But if nowadays, some rich low caste man pays enough he might find a Brahmin willing to carry out the service. By making this arrangement the low caste man is laying claim to one of the symbols of high status. Having failed to keep him from using the symbols, the high castes have a second line of defence: they pronounce the symbol worthless. They say that the Brahmin was not a real Brahmin, or, alternatively, that he has now polluted himself so that his services do not symbolize any longer that the recipient is of high status.[11]

CONCLUSION

Actual groups, as I have said before, are not either moral or transactional or bureaucratic: leaders may make use of all three principles. The 'moral' discomfiting of the upstart low caste man just discussed, may involve some very transactional relationships to pressure other Brahmins and the public in general to ostracize the offending Brahmin. His caste-fellows expel him not only because he is polluted, but also because their own purity is spotted and they risk loss of livelihood by continuing to associate with him.

Nevertheless, although three kinds of pattern can be found, it is possible to see the relationship between a leader and his supporters in all three either as capital (the political resources, either material or moral, which he and they actually have) or as credit (the resources and potential resources which his supporters believe that he has and vice versa). Relative access to political capital and political credit distinguishes the leader who is weak among his supporters from the leader who is strong.

NOTES

1. Many of the politicians to whom I talked in 1959 in Orissa complained that civil servants were too powerful: they were the real rulers. Even some of the Ministers said this—about other Ministers not themselves. Orissa is not alone in this: from time to time political journalists in Britain sort out those Ministers who are in charge of their Ministries from those who are not. Normatively the Minister always has the power: he decides what shall be done and his civil servants work out how it will be done. Pragmatically, however, the civil servant is also powerful, for experience and knowledge of how the system works make it easy for him to say that there is no way of implementing the chosen policy: it will be necessary to choose another one.
2. See *Barth* (2), p. 91.
3. See *Evans-Pritchard* (1).
4. See for example Eric J. Miller, 'Village Structure in North Kerala' in *Srinivas* (1), p. 51. The reasons are complex and vary from one case to another. This could be one way of ensuring that no notable gets an edge over any other notable through monopolizing new resources. It is also a way of expressing contempt for the imperial rulers and of ensuring that men of consequence do not have to get too closely involved with the foreigners. The junior appointee serves as a long spoon. See the discussion of middlemen, pp. 167–76.
5. See *Reeves*. The quotation is from p. 272.

6. See *Cohn* (2), p. 90.
7. See *Barth* (1).
8. See *Hitchcock*. This article is, among other things, a splendid demonstration of how normative themes are manipulated for pragmatic purposes. The ethic of brotherhood (*biraderi*) provides a normative cover for the acceptance of settlements in disputes which the contestants see no advantage in pursuing further. *Bhai shatru* means 'Your brother is your enemy': see p. 38.
9. The main source of information on traditional Rajasthan is *Tod*. I have also made use of *Dutra* and an undergraduate dissertation written by Diana Hailstone.
10. See *Middleton*.
11. This is discussed in more detail in Chapter 6. Bernard Cohn describes how the ambitious untouchable Chamar caste in the village of Senapur took on more and more of the attributes of the high Hindu caste, the Thakurs. They were moving into 'a culture vacated by' the Thakurs, who were increasingly 'westernizing' their behaviour. The Thakurs allowed them to do this, presumably, because by that time the religious attributes of Hinduism were no longer symbols of political power. See *Marriott*, pp. 53–77.

6
Contests

There is a leaning in politics towards intellectual disorder, towards a calculated lack of clarity. Different cultures have different styles for doing this. De Gaulle spreads his arms wide and tells the French nation, 'I have understood you' or, when elected President, 'As the leader of France and the head of a republican state I shall henceforth exercise supreme power in its full meaning, and according to the new spirit which has given it to me'. It is obscure and contradictory; but it sounds good. In Britain we seem to favour a bumbling rambling reasonable-man style which is sometimes used quite deliberately to take the edge out of a situation and obscures lines of division and enmity until no-one quite knows what the trouble was about. Henry Fairlie describes R. A. Butler taming a conservative conference on the issue of corporal punishment in just this way. The art seems to be that of uttering highly acceptable generalities (i.e. normative themes) in such a way that each member of the audience can give them the particular meaning which most pleases him.[1]

Some Pakhtouns were met in council and two leading Khans were attempting to outmanoeuvre one another. The proceedings were punctuated by intervals in which one or the other of the rivals retired behind a haystack and endeavoured to enlist support for himself and detach supporters from his opponent. A was having the worst of the confrontations. Suddenly, when a minor supporter of B was speaking, A rose to his feet and rudely told this supporter that small fry like him should keep their mouths shut in the presence of greater men. Whereupon, Barth reports, the meeting broke up in disorder, for this was a gross violation of the Pakhtoun ethic that in council all men are equal and all Pakhtouns have the right to express their point of view.[2]

The manoeuvre is not unfamiliar to those raised in our own culture. There are occasions in committees when someone, who despairs of carrying a particular point, will prevent the other side from winning by raising a point of order in such a way as to throw the whole discussion into confusion. Pakhtoun *A* raised his point of order in a paradoxical way by grossly violating an established procedural principle, but it comes to the same in the end.

This incident illustrates a point which needs to be emphasized: politics more than any other kind of legitimate social interaction, encourage calculated deviance from the normative rules of proper behaviour. Pakhtoun *A* must have known very well that he was about to commit a normative outrage: but he must also have been guided by a pragmatic rule that his offence would bring an end to the meeting and so save him from the loss of political credit involved in being on the losing side. He evidently judged the normative discredit got through his breach of good committee manners a price worth paying.

Our understanding of politics will be incomplete if we confine ourselves to the normative rules through which order is maintained. To do so is to take the point of view only of the authorities. Their concern is to keep the society intact, despite the troublesome fellows fighting with one another and making a nuisance of themselves down below. But down in the dust of the arena, the concern is to beat the other fellow despite the constraints and restrictions which the authorities seek to impose. One of the great gaps in anthropology is that we have been too much interested in the 'system' and although we know that people live half their lives finding ways to 'beat the system' we tend to take serious notice of them only when they are caught out, brought to trial and punished. In fact of course sometimes people do 'beat the system' without being punished; that is how systems change. The pressures of competition in politics drive them to find ways to win without actually cheating, or to cheat without being caught out, or, in the extremity, to fight to sweep that system away altogether and find one that suits them better.

We shall not come quite to this last extremity in the present chapter, although the story of Lloyd George and Asquith has an element of this. Our interest is in competition short of the point where an open attack is made upon the rules. Competitive moves between teams can be categorized into challenges and decisive combats, which will be called respectively *confrontations* and *encounters*. Secondly we shall look for regular *sequences* in the different kinds of move. When it is necessary to refer to competitive interaction in a general way, the word used will be *arena*.

Certain questions will not be asked in this chapter. For the most part the competition which takes place within a team, discussed in the preceding chapter, will not be considered, except in the important context of subversion. Secondly a discussion of control institutions will be reserved for a later chapter. My illustrations will come principally from three sources: my own material on Bisipara, Barth's analysis of politics in Swat and a biography of Bonar Law.

DOLADOLI

'*Dolo*' and sometimes the English word 'party' are used by the people of Bisipara to refer to contending groups which we, in a loose way, would call 'factions'. As the word 'faction' carries a connotation of disapproval, so also does '*dolo*'. The scrapping (that word also has the right connotations) which goes on between *dolo* is called *doladoli*, and although it is entered into with zest and is a subject of burning interest both to those engaged and to those who merely watch, it is also deplored. 'The trouble with this village', they sometimes say, 'is that there is too much party.'[3] They mean by this that so much time and energy is spent on disputing over minor issues and scoring points that the public interest is neglected. This, of course, happens at all levels. In 1959 when the Congress government in Orissa had a very narrow majority, such an expenditure of time and energy and such ingenious subterfuges were required to keep the government in office that little time was left to 'implement the plans': this situation was called 'instability' and by some considered one of the graver defects of parliamentary democracy and its tolerance of Oppositions. The French Fourth Republic, for much the same reasons, suffered from *immobilisme*.

The composition of these *dolo* has already been briefly described. They formed around two prominent men in the Warrior caste. Most Warriors belonged to one agnatic lineage, and the factions largely matched descent divisions in that lineage (the genealogies, at least, being adjusted to make it appear that this was the case). A few renegades were known to have changed sides (one man being matched with more distant agnates against his brother's sons) and both factions included supporters from other castes beside the Warriors. Faction membership was symbolized by a modification of the ritual duties of agnatic kinship. A man made bigger contributions to wedding and funeral expenses for houses in his own faction than for opponents. Each faction also had its own *jati puo* (which means 'caste son'), a Warrior living in the village but not of the dominant lineage, who cooked during the short period of most intense pollution following a death, when those closely related to the dead person were ritually disqualified from preparing food.

The leader built up his credit partly by protecting his supporters from attacks by outsiders and men from the other faction and partly by scoring points off the leader of the rival faction.

These confrontations usually took place in the *panchayat* (the village council). They consisted of impassioned verbal attacks upon or defences of the honour (*mohoto*) of the leaders of each faction or their principal henchmen. They accused one another of gross breaches of the normative rules of public behaviour: of embezzling village funds; of failure to contribute to common tasks; of sowing dissension in the village to serve their own selfish ends. These accusations were hotly debated in a quasi-judicial manner, with the accusers asking for fines to be imposed and the defendants firing back counter-accusations. But since consensus is a rule in the village panchayat and no decision can be reached unless everyone agrees that it is the right decision, the council seldom, if ever, reached a decision in this kind of affair.[4] The confrontation would end in hot air and ruffled tempers; one, or sometimes both sides would stalk out in anger; and the affair would slip back to the more covert competition of gossip and backbiting.

Then, sooner or later, there would be another confrontation of just the same kind, followed by another period of gossip and slander, and then by another public confrontation: and so on. The sequence extended backwards to some reported beginning when the ancestor of one of the leaders displaced from the headmanship the ancestor of the other leader. This, so far as I know, was the only time when there was ever an event which could be called a defeat or a victory: this apart, there were no tales of great battles or decisive encounters. One bickering and indecisive confrontation followed another.

What stood out was the recreational quality of *doladoli*: the game was played very much within the rules and the contestants exercised considerable self-restraint. One would not have thought so watching them in action in the *panchayat*, faces contorted with fury or fixed in a mask of bitter contempt. It is true that the rancour was indeed great: there was no pretence of reconciliation, as we have when contestants are expected to shake hands after the battle is over. In a sense, the battle never was over; even in non-arena situations, the leaders of the opposing *dolo* were watchfully and coldly polite towards one another; never friendly. Nevertheless many holds were barred. Neither side committed substantial resources to the conflict. They did not try to impoverish one another or in other ways to inflict substantial and material damage upon a rival's political capital. They closed ranks rapidly in the face of external opposition, when a real tragedy struck, or when a common and urgent task had to be completed. Nor did they take their quarrels outside the village by bringing suits against one another in the Government courts. In short, although everyone loudly deplored *doladoli*, in fact—at least at the time when I observed it—these internal dissensions were not allowed to damage the public interest of the whole community.

This was a battle of words: and words, unlike sticks and stones, do not break bones. The contest was conducted through an endless series of confrontations, with never an encounter. Challenge and assertion was met by counter-challenge and counter-assertion. Each side goes on flinging gauntlets down at its opponent's feet until, as it were, the pile is so high that the would-be combatants could not get at one another even if they wished. Points are scored by the quality of the gauntlet and the dexterity and style with which it is flung down. In spite of appearances there is no real 'brinkmanship' in *doladoli*: there is no danger of this contest escalating from a 'slanging-match' into a fight.

Another way of looking at the umbrella of normative restraint

under the shade of which *doladoli* is conducted is to notice that
the process is essentially one of communication. Both sides know
the same language: they know the meaning of the combative
symbols used. But they also share a set of rules about permissible tactics. In other words, to the extent that confrontation
is the principal mode of interaction between opponents, to that
extent they are playing a game and both are interested in keeping the structure of that game (i.e. the rules) intact. They are
also concerned with keeping down the expenses of the game;
keeping the stakes low.[5]

PAKHTOUNS IN CONFLICT[6]

Pakhtouns compete for control over people and over resources:
that is, over land. But one can also say that Pakhtouns are
fighting one another not about land, but about honour. Pakhtouns themselves say this: and men even impoverish themselves
in their efforts to maintain their honour. But these two prizes
are not alternatives: honour and land go together. When a
Pakhtoun is outfaced and loses his honour, his followers will
come to feel that he can no longer protect them and they will
join a different clubhouse, headed by a stronger *khan*. Without
followers the weakening *khan* cannot protect his land. He becomes like a banker whose credit is in doubt. Therefore, whether
we say that Pakhtouns fight for honour or for land, it comes to
the same thing in the end.

Given this objective, what moves can a combatant make in
order to win? One regular move is simple and straightforward:
you maintain your honour and you remove another man's
honour with the least ambiguity by murdering him; there was
one successful Pakhtoun politician with over two hundred
murders to his credit. But murders are the extreme form of
competitive interaction: they constitute encounters which form
the punctuation marks in a series of competitive interactions.

There are certain moves beforehand, which either lead up to
murder or which may bring victory without the final drastic
action. These moves consist in taking followers and allies away
from your opponent, by undermining his political credit or outbidding him in the various ways discussed in an earlier chapter,
and attaching them to yourself. When you think you have the

edge, you communicate this fact, in various stylized ways, to your opponent: you make a challenge. The next move is his. If he thinks you are wrong, he may merely communicate this fact to you by issuing a counter-challenge. The stage is then set for rapid re-appraisals and then either a rapid withdrawal from the brink by one party (there are institutionalized ways of doing this, to be discussed in the next chapter) or an encounter in which the estimates of strength are put to the test. If the opponent thinks that you may be right in your estimate of your own strength, but that the disparity is not too large, he may attempt to turn the tables by finding himself more allies or more followers, preferably by detaching them from you. It is then your move. And so the process goes to and fro until one side has reached, and publicly admits that it has reached, the limit of its resources. Then follows the run on the political bank, to which I referred earlier, and the flight or sudden death of the banker.

One of the arts of subversion lies in being able to work out which one among your opponent's followers or allies is ripe for an offer, perhaps because he is himself becoming a rival of your opponent. Lesser fry, presumably, may be detached by the normal inducements of protection, a house contract, a land contract and so forth. If this is done to a sufficient degree, your opponent is brought to a critical threshold at which desertions occur without further prompting by you—the take off point, so to speak—and you have only to sit back while his remaining supporters lose confidence in his ability to protect them and join another clubhouse.

In Bisipara's *doladoli* very few people changed sides: no-one was shot or driven off his land or in other ways ruined. It is not difficult to envisage this game, other things being equal, being played in perpetuity. But the Pakhtoun game is different: one can see ways in which the players could put themselves out of business.

One way to destroy a social system is to destroy the people who operate it. One energetic Pakhtoun had scored forty-one murders. Yet, against this, the Pakhtoun competition is so designed that not every contest has to end in wholesale slaughter, although, evidently, murder was not a rare event. Firstly, the device of confrontation is a way of convincing one side that to fight is to lose; and, at the same time, it, together with subversion and the fact that these were largely transactional teams, is a way of ensuring that most people have the chance to be on the winning side, even if there is a fight. There are also (to be discussed later) Saints, who are mediators and whose actions enable one or both sides to climb down without too great a loss of face. All these are devices for keeping sufficient pieces on the board for the game to go on.

Given the critical threshold mentioned above, the fact that at a certain stage desertions may snowball to the point where virtually everyone has joined the winning side, there is a danger that the game will no longer be played because it has run out of not people, but groups. Why does not one leader wipe out all the other leaders, his last successful contest putting an end to the game?

There are several answers to this question, some of them general and some peculiar to Pathan culture. First there is a simple actuarial point: forty-one murders notched on his gun butt would make a man a bad life-insurance risk in any culture. Murder makes a man an object of revenge, and the more murders he commits, the more enemies wait for the chance to cut him down in a revenge killing.[7] Secondly, the process builds enemies faster than it builds friends. Each victory brings a man to the notice of those who will be his next opponents and they may want to squash him while they can: alternatively they may join with others in order to suppress him. Thirdly a man's team lasts only for his lifetime. Leaders need land as a resource to provide grain to feed members of their clubhouse. If a leader has more than one son, the estate is divided and with it the standing of the leaders. Finally there are the technical difficulties of maintaining a contract team when it grows beyond an appropriate size: this was discussed in an earlier chapter.

In discussing the ways in which the potential destructiveness of Pahktoun competition is kept within bounds, we have touched upon some restraints which are not part of the rules of the game, whether normative or pragmatic, but which are the consequences of these rules. For example, the pragmatic rules which regulate the building of contract teams make it impossible for teams to grow beyond a certain size and unthinkable that one team should ever monopolize all political resources. This is of a different order from the normative convention in Bisipara's *doladoli* that one does not go outside the village, by, for instance, taking an opponent to court.

We have now discussed two modes of competitive interaction: confrontation and subversion and we have mentioned a third, encounter. At the level of ordinary discourse there is no difficulty in distinguishing between a confrontation and an encounter. A confrontation is a message about one's own strength to an opponent or to potential opponents: it can also be a challenge. An encounter takes place when the challenge is accepted and the competitors may set upon one another and continue until one has won and the other is defeated.

In *doladoli* the exclusive use of confrontations and the form which the confrontations take makes the competitive interaction cheap. But this clearly need not always be so. Some confrontations make their point by their extravagant use of resources. In village India one finds big men issuing a generalized confrontation by building themselves a grand house, or excavating a reservoir for the village thus demonstrating, among other things, that they are persons of consequence.[8] Creating political credit can itself be an expensive process. In just the same way direct confrontations can also be ruinously expensive: the several 'arms races' which have occurred in this century have been expensive. It may, of course, be that in fact they have been cheaper than wars which followed. Nevertheless, the fact remains that it is possible to go politically bankrupt through a series of challenges without, so to speak, a shot ever having been fired.

It is not possible, therefore, to make the distinction by saying that confrontations tend to use up less resources than encounters, although this is certainly testable and possibly generally true. Nor, I think, is violence the best criterion: in other words, an encounter can take place without 'a shot being fired'. The difference between confrontation and encounter is, I suggest, analogous to the difference between a debate and a decision. Confrontations are messages and claims (including, of course, bluff) about command over political resources, about political credit: an encounter occurs when both sides agree on a version of what their relative strength is. This may occur through an actual battle, either literally or in the form of a vote or in whatever other mode is characteristic of the culture concerned; or it may be brought about by the withdrawal of one side, conceding victory to the other; or, finally, it may be the result of a mediated settlement. In other words the flow of confrontations is punctuated by encounters which have the effect of letting both the players and the audience know what is the state of the current market in political credit, which teams are weak and which strong, and—most importantly—what kinds of teams seem best able to show a profit in current conditions.[9]

If the flow of confrontations is divided into episodes, one may then ask about the sequence of episodes. Does this too reveal patterns? I now consider this question through a hypothetical reconstruction of the ways in which a caste low in the Bisipara hierarchy raised themselves during the first half of this century to a position near the top of the hierarchy.

CASTE-CLIMBING

Owing to the curiously inept policy of the Administration about strong drink between the years 1870 and 1910, the Distillers of Bisipara became exceedingly rich.[10] Prohibition was introduced in 1910, but by then the Distillers, with forty years of windfall profits behind them, had more wealth per head than any other caste in the village. Their money was invested in the village in land, which they farmed with the help of labourers, and, in economic status at least, they were all square with the erstwhile dominant caste of landowners, the Warriors.

Distilling is not a respectable occupation among Hindus, and, so I was told, so long as they were both poor and occupied in distilling liquor, the Bisipara Distillers were above the line of untouchability, but not very far above it: they would accept various prescribed forms of food and water from most of the clean castes, none of whom would take food or water from the hands of a Distiller. But farming is respectable, especially if you are a rich farmer, so that after the British had inadvertently helped to make them rich there was something anomalous in the position of the Distillers. Those members of superior castes who were employed by Distillers, or who borrowed from them money or grain, would be in a particularly embarrassing position, for the ritual of caste enjoined them to display the symbols of a superiority, which, at least in the sphere of economics, they did not possess.

The Distillers, probably even before 1910, set about altering this position. First they assumed, so far as they could, the attributes of a respectable caste. Farming, as I have said, is respectable. The actual distilling, I was told, was done by hired employees, probably Konds, and after 1910 dropped altogether. Nowadays the good Distiller does not touch strong drink. They have not gone so far as to ban widow-remarriage, although it is frowned upon; but their women do not work on the land and they wear the long *sari* like the Brahmin women, and not the knee-length *gamucha*. They do not keep chickens; they sport the sacred thread; in fact they tend to make a parade of being a good deal holier than the next man, even sometimes than the local Brahmins. In the field of interaction too, they exaggerate in a manner which first led me to suspect that they were not, so to speak, to the mantle born. All other castes in Bisipara, even the Brahmins, will accept meat butchered by a Kond: but not the Distillers, and if they are to be honoured at a wedding, they are given a goat which is still on the hoof, so that they can butcher it themselves. They will not accept food or water from anyone but the Brahmins, although the Warriors will take water from a Herdsman. All these manoeuvres have brought results, and although people of other castes sneer behind the backs of Distillers and sometimes tease them in subtle ways,[11] it is generally felt that they are somewhere up around the top part of the caste scale: not, certainly, where they claim to be, above the Warrior and second only to the Brahmin, but somewhere just below. Herdsmen, for example, whom most people rated one notch below the Warriors, thought that Distillers came just below Herdsmen.

When, in 1954, I first wrote about these events I thought I had said all that needed to be said about Distillers and their progress.[12] They had taken on the attributes of a respectable caste; they were making claims to higher status in the field of interation by refusing to take food from the hands of other castes generally recognized as higher than Distillers; some individuals in these castes accepted food and water from Distillers; therefore they had progressed from near the bottom of the clean castes to a position near the top, albeit a disputed position. This statement is correct, but it leaves unanswered a number of questions which seem to me to be the essence of politics. If this is a contest and the Distillers are one of the protagonists, who is the other protagonist? Is it the Distillers versus the rest of the clean castes, banded together to keep these upstarts down? Or is it the situation like that in the Swat valley, or in the world of professional boxing, where the road to the top is marked by a line of trophies, indicating a succession of victories over ever-more-formidable opponents? Again, our description is not explicit on what the Distillers are fighting for. Is it a kind of honour in the local Hindu idiom, resembling the Pakhtoun ideas of honour? If it is honour of this kind, can we relate it as we did for the Pakhtouns, to control over men and resources? Thirdly, our description appears to be wanting in the detail of how the Distillers actually manoeuvred so as to get certain people to take food and water from their hands. Let us now consider these and other questions, speculating about the way in which a Distiller could have advanced himself, by constructing a model for the game of caste-climbing.

The objective in the game is to maximize purity at the expense of someone else: that is, the object is to maximize the kind of political credit, which is symbolized in the idiom of the caste system. Purity is expressed in two ways. Firstly it is symbolized in the deferential services which the village specialists give. If payment is made in cash for these services, the recipient admits relatively low status: but his status is high if he can pay through a *jajmani* arrangement, making an annual payment in grain at harvest time. Secondly, purity is symbolized in the giving and accepting of water and cooked food: to accept these in certain prescribed forms is to acknowledge either equality with, or inferiority to, the giver.

The Distiller who wishes to break into the ring of those who receive *jajmani* deference from the village specialists can do this in four steps. Clearly it would not be in his interest to destroy this ring: he merely wants to cut himself in on the profits, so to speak. Firstly he 'buys' the specialist, by getting him into debt, by threats of violence, or by any other method which his superior wealth makes possible. Secondly he compels the specialist to provide his services in return for cash: this carries no status implications, for many of the specialists offer their services to all comers (except Untouchables) in the market-place. It is a transaction pure and simple, without symbolic importance. The third step is to compel the specialist to accept a *jajmani* arrangement, and, fourthly, the Distiller may then be able to establish with the specialist the same commensal relationships that the Warrior or Brahmin enjoys.

Let us first identify the teams in this competition. If Leader One (the Distiller) wins, then the rest of the Distillers benefit, for one of the normative rules of the caste system is that status adheres to the group and not to the individual. The other Distillers, therefore, constitute a core. (Emperically there could, of course, be backsliders in this core, and a more sophisticated model than I can construct would have to allow for this.)

Leader One's potential following is the specialist whose services he is trying to subvert.

In practice it is not always easy to identify Leader Two, except to say that he must be one of those whose monopoly of the specialist's deferential service has up to that point kept the purity-rating of the Distillers low. The difficulty of identifying him may arise because Leader One may be allowed to get through a round by means of a 'bye', Leader Two having decided that it is not worth his while to take action. If, of course, he does take action then the difficulty of identifying him disappears.

The first two steps which the Distiller takes—getting the specialist into his power and buying his services—constitute subversion. But they do not add to the Distiller's political credit until he can bring off the confrontation which is implied in the second two steps. These are claims to purity, as prescribed in the normative rules of the village political structure. They are a challenge to the incumbent monopolists of that specialist's services to acknowledge Distiller equality or to dispute it. If Leader Two allows a bye and does not dispute the claim, then an encounter has taken place and Leader One has gained an increment of political credit.

If Leader Two does enter the arena he may do so at the pragmatic level by getting the specialist out of debt or by directly harassing Leader One to make him give up the attempt. Alternatively he may allow that particular specialist to give deferential services to the Distiller, but render these worthless by proclaiming that the specialist has defiled himself by serving a Distiller, is no longer to be counted as a source of political credit, and will be replaced by another specialist who does not serve Distillers. This is a zero-sum game: Leader One can only win to the extent that Leader Two loses. If Leader Two introduces new resources into the game (if he patronizes a different specialist) then the subversion cannot be turned into a successful confrontation and Leader One (the Distiller) has lost that particular encounter.

It is to be noticed, by the way, that there are no normative rules for caste-climbing. Pressuring the Washerman and buying his services are pragmatic rules. There is no Oriya word for caste-climbing, and competition between castes can only be made orderly by pragmatic rules. Both Leader One and Leader Two agree in their definition of what the prize is: that is, on the meaning of symbols which indicate political credit. They also have a tacit agreement about the pragmatic rules involved, for no-one raises public objection to the Distiller lending money to the specialist, until he tries to use this debt to claim political credit.

The sequence in *doladoli* consists of a repetition of episodes (hardly even that, for they are not marked by encounters), each duplicating its predecessor. But the sequence in caste-climbing is cumulative. If the Distiller succeeds in his first episode—perhaps with the Washerman—he is then qualified to apply the same pressures to a Barber or a Herdsman. Each successful encounter is a qualification to aim higher, until in theory the ambitious Distiller has achieved the same credit-rating, so far as concerns the service of specialists, as the dominant Warrior.

One may ask, therefore, why the Distillers cannot cut the whole process short by subverting the Brahmin, the highest category of specialist. If they succeeded, they should then, by the rules of the game, command the deferential services of all the other and lesser specialists. One might think that a sufficiently high material offer would do the trick. But why should a higher offer be necessary? It costs no more to get a poor Brahmin into debt than it does to buy up the debts of a Washerman.

The crucial variable, which makes this impossible, is the accumulated balance of political credit at the Distiller's disposal. This can be seen, in a matter-of-fact way, as the number of people who have still to be squared in addition to the specialist under attack. If Leader One makes his attempt upon the

Brahmin without having gone through the qualifying rounds with the Washerman, Barber and so forth, he has to contend with the whole hierarchy. He does not have sufficient credit to do this and the only result, if he buys over a poor Brahmin and uses him to make a confrontation, will be to have that Brahmin disqualified by the Warriors and outcasted by his fellow Brahmins. This removes whatever political value that Brahmin might have had for the Distiller.

ASQUITH AND LLOYD GEORGE

Making hypotheses about the way in which the Bisipara Distillers 'must have' or 'could have' made their way from near the bottom to near the top of the clean-caste hierarchy is relatively easy because we are not dealing with any one particular case. If we had evidence of how the Distillers triumphed, for example, over the Barber caste or the Potter caste, then it would at first have been more difficult to discern the structural principles underlying the actions of the people concerned. This is because rules (i.e. structural principles) are general whereas situations are particular. To state the rules of political manoeuvre—or any set of rules—is to leave out many variables concerned in an actual situation: for example the Barbers might just at that time have been easy victims because they had recently been involved in an expensive law case, or because their leaders were not resolute in character, or something of that kind. This applies also to our account of *doladoli* and the Pakhtouns, for these also were general statements of the rules of political manoeuvre in those situations and not particular cases.

General rules are got by looking at a number of particular situations and extracting what is common to them. In this way one arrives at, so to speak, the essence of such situations. For example, in caste-climbing one would expect always to find the pattern of confrontation and encounter and of episodes and sequences (and in other kinds of political manoeuvre too); but we might only on that one occasion find the loser already weakened by a law case, and therefore we would have to regard the latter as accidental.

These sets of rules or principles can be used to understand particular situations, for through them one can sort out the essential from the accidental features. We shall now see how this works on Blake's account of the fall of Asquith in 1916.[13]

One last word of introduction: the words 'accident' and 'essence' are unfortunately value-loaded—they imply that the essence is somehow important while accidents are merely accidents. But this is true only for particular disciplines or approaches. If we chose to look at the fall of Asquith from what might be called the 'Freud-Bullitt' point of view,[14] making use of the concepts of Freudian psychology, then the rules and regularities of politics would be the 'accidents' while the states of mind of the protagonists, which in this account are pushed aside as accidents, would constitute the essences. What is accident and what is essence depends on the discipline concerned.

At the beginning of the story Asquith's cabinet was made up of 14 Liberals, 10 Unionists and a Labour representative. The immediate cause of Asquith's fall was that the Unionist Ministers resigned and sufficient of them later agreed to serve in Lloyd George's Coalition. The latter's most resolute Unionist supporter was Bonar Law, but at the beginning both he and virtually all of his Unionist colleagues in Asquith's cabinet, distrusted Lloyd George. If we can work out how they came to change their mind, we are on the way towards understanding the contest in which Asquith fell from power.

Once again it must be said that we are not pursuing the 'real' reason of why each of these ten men changed sides. We cannot trace out the personal history of each one of them and discover the experiences which formed their attitudes towards authority, on class issues, towards Welshmen, and all the many personal clashes and petty enmities which, from Blake's account, seem to have influenced their actions. That is work for the historian. Generalizing sciences like politics or anthropology are looking rather for the cultural idiom in which they acted and described and justified their actions. We are seeking first the public and ostensible reasons, which were in use in 1916 in the United Kingdom, for such political manoeuvres; and we are looking for a kind of grammar which lies behind this language.

The language of this kind of political game consists, at the highest level, of a number of normative themes.[15] The Pakhtouns changed sides to be secure and for other similar materialistic reasons, which a man could use to justify his conduct. In *doladoli* the normative themes are different: the winner is the man who can show that he has acted honourably, or in the public interest, while his opponent has been selfish and dishonest. Georgian culture (and its Edwardian and Victorian predecessors), like *doladoli*, favoured the idiom of public service.

The dominating normative theme at that time was victory in the war. On every occasion on which someone justifies a change which would either remove Asquith or take the direction of affairs out of his hands, the normative justification is victory in war: Asquith is too tired or too indecisive or too tolerant of discussion to make an active and incisive leader. The counter-theme is that Asquith is indispensable because everyone trusts him: he can 'hold the country together'. Lloyd George's opponents mirror these themes: Lloyd George might be incisive and dynamic but he lacks 'the one thing needful—he does not inspire trust . . .' He is ambitious for himself and not for the general good and therefore he does not have the political credit to make people follow him and to hold the country together: therefore the war cannot be won under him.

Victory in war is, so to speak, the trump card in this pack of normative themes: there is nothing which counts for more. But it is not the only card. Just as Harold Nicolson nailed the flag of honesty to his electoral staff, so, in the protracted intrigue which brought down Asquith, Bonar Law several times expressed concern that he should do nothing 'disloyal' towards Asquith. Asquith himself, in rejecting Carson's name as a possible member when first a War Council was mooted used two themes: first, Carson was not sufficiently senior; secondly, his appointment would indicate that Asquith's Government lacked the courage to withstand Carson's opposition and therefore, as a coward, Asquith would lose the confidence of his colleagues.

Whether or not these normative themes are the 'real' reasons for action is not, I repeat, our concern. We are interested in the way in which they are used to demand support and to proclaim one's own political credit-worthiness. Early in November the House debated on the sale of enemy businesses taken over in Nigeria. The Government favoured an open auction to all bidders: Carson put down a motion saying that such businesses should be sold only to British subjects. Here there is a straight clash of normative themes: Liberal Free-Trade as against

Conservative (Unionist) Protectionism. Carson had at least two birds for this particular stone. One was the Coalition Government, which would of necessity be reminded of old differences of principle, temporarily and uneasily in abeyance. The other target was Bonar Law, leader of the Unionist party, but also a member of the Government (Colonial Secretary) and therefore voting with the Government in the interests of Free Trade and having to wind up the debate on their behalf. Carson's motion says very clearly that he (Carson) better upholds Conservative principles than does the leader of the Unionist party, Bonar Law. In other words, this motion is a bid for Unionist leadership; a confrontation. Indeed, the challenge was even more direct insofar as Bonar Law had, on entering the Coalition, announced that he would remain in the Government only so long as his own party (the Unionists) had confidence in his actions. Even if Carson's motion were defeated, Bonar Law could only be secure if a majority of Unionists voted for the Government.

Bonar Law, as Colonial Secretary, spoke last for the Government and I quote part of his reply with bracketed and italicized emphasis of the normative themes he used:

'This is a motion of want of confidence in the Government, moved—and this I must say I do regret—with a violence which to my mind is hardly in keeping with the serious situation in which the country stands . . .'

(Carson is not as interested as he should be in *winning the war*)

'I, at least, will never question the sincerity of the motives by which my right hon. friend (Carson) is actuated . . .'

(His motives are his own *personal ambitions* to get me out of the Unionist leadership)

'and I hope and believe that our personal friendship will stand the strain of political opposition and even of such speeches as that to which we have just listened . . .'

(I am *magnanimous*. I doubt if Carson is, judging from the way he's just behaved.)

There could hardly be a clearer example of the way in which normative themes are used to discredit an opponent and to build up credit for oneself in order to gain support.

In the event 73 Unionists supported Bonar Law and 65 supported Carson. Bonar Law's biographer sees great significance in the narrowness of this majority for it made Bonar Law realize that in his own party there was strong opposition to Asquith's Coalition, the continued existence of which depended on his (Bonar Law's) support.

To identify the normative themes is only the first part of an analysis. One knows by that stage (to quote Harold Nicolson again) that those 'clover-shaped cards' are in fact clubs. Or, to change the metaphor, to know the normative themes is to know the vocabulary. The next step is to play the cards or to use the vocabulary in communication with friends and enemies. This is done by means of confrontations.

A confrontation is a message which the receiver has no option but to receive and to act upon. For some time before the events in the Autumn of 1916 which culminated in Asquith's fall, the newspapers owned by Northcliffe (which dominated both the popular market and the 'establishment' through the *Daily Mail* and the *Times* respectively) had conducted a continuous campaign against Asquith's leadership. But Asquith ignored them and disdained to reply, just as, in the rules of chivalry, a man of rank disdains a challenge from a man of markedly lower rank.[16] Under Asquith's rules, newspapers were not admitted into the arena: most of his colleagues, too, in both parties condemned 'trafficking with the Press', with their lips at least, if not in their hearts.

Bonar Law, until the very last stages when Asquith burnt his boats and put a stop to negotiation, wanted Asquith to remain as Prime Minister, while Lloyd George directed the war through a small War Council. Some time after the Nigeria debate Bonar Law learned that Lloyd George and Carson were acting together to bring about the creation of a War Council and he agreed to meet with them and discuss their plans. But first he told Asquith what was afoot. Bonar Law's biographer, no doubt correctly, says that this shows his determination to do nothing behind Asquith's back. But Asquith must also have read a message about possible changes in his pattern of support: his most trenchant critic (Carson), the leader of the Unionists in his Coalition (Bonar Law) and his own most powerful rival in the Liberal party (Lloyd George) were acting in concert. Apparently he was not enthusiastic, but did not raise any objection to the discussions. In other words, he chose not to interpret Bonar Law's conversation as a confrontation.

Five days later Bonar Law, Lloyd George and Carson produced a memorandum, which contained the draft of a plan establishing a War Council under the chairmanship of Lloyd George and the Presidency of Asquith. This was presented by Bonar Law to Asquith, who took it down to the country for the weekend and on Monday wrote to Bonar Law, rejecting the plan and giving careful normatively-acceptable reasons for doing so. Lloyd George does not 'inspire trust'; Carson is too junior; to give in to Carson and Lloyd George would be to weaken the confidence of his other colleagues; etc. Pragmatically, what the rejection said was that Lloyd George and Carson did not command sufficient support between them to make him (Asquith) take their confrontation seriously. Indeed, it seemed he was right for when Bonar Law told his fellow Unionist members in the Government what was going on, he found them extremely hostile. They thought that Bonar Law was being bamboozled by Lloyd George, and they called the affair an 'intrigue'.

After he had received Asquith's rejection, Bonar Law suggested that Asquith and Lloyd George should talk directly together about the new War Council. Lloyd George then wrote to Asquith, again suggesting the new council but this time leaving the Prime Minister without any position on it. Asquith rejected the plan and put forward counter-suggestions which were not acceptable to Lloyd George. The latter at once wrote to Bonar Law, telling him what had happened and saying 'The life of the country depends on resolute action by you now.'

This last phrase, of obvious normative significance, means pragmatically that Lloyd George could do nothing more until the rest of the Unionist members of the cabinet had been brought into line behind Bonar Law and against Asquith, to support the creation of a new War Council

They were called to a meeting on Sunday, December 3rd. On both the Saturday and the Sunday newspapers carried rumours that Lloyd George might resign and printed stories about his desire for a new War Council. These had been leaked by a Conservative back-bencher and confidant of Bonar Law, Sir Max Aitken (later Lord Beaverbrook) who, owning a newspaper, seems not to have been inhibited by the code against 'trafficking with the Press'. One presumes that Aitken intended to make a generalized confrontation on behalf of Lloyd George and Bonar Law by showing the extent of their support among 'the people'. It apparently had the opposite effect on the Unionist Ministers, who again felt that they were being pushed along by Lloyd George, whom they believed responsible for the leak to the Press.

It seems to have been a very confused meeting and resulted in a rather ambiguous resolution to be conveyed to Asquith. This called upon him to resign, and said that they would themselves resign if he did not do so. It seems that some present at the meeting wanted Asquith out and probably replaced by Lloyd George: others thought that the situation was now so disturbed that Asquith could only re-establish his authority by resigning, allowing others (e.g. Lloyd George) to try for the leadership and fail and then successfully reforming a government, presumably without Lloyd George. But, whatever their motives, the call for Asquith's resignation sanctioned by the threat of their own withdrawal, was the clearest of confrontations.

The actual confrontation occurred when Bonar Law conveyed this resolution to Asquith. Once again history is clouded and there is a debate about whether or not Bonar Law made sufficiently clear the supposed friendly intentions of some of the Unionist Ministers. In the event Asquith interpreted the threatened withdrawal of support as anyone else would, promptly climbed down and promised to see Lloyd George and negotiate with him.

This meeting took place on Saturday afternoon. In the evening and on the Sunday details of the compromise were worked out, more or less in Lloyd George's favour. Asquith would not resign but would reconstruct his government, as he had done once before in 1915, to make the War Council possible. But by Monday evening Asquith had repudiated the agreement, and on Tuesday Lloyd George resigned and his resignation was accepted.

The normative reason given for this change of mind was yet another article in *The Times* attacking Asquith in the course of outlining the proposed reconstruction. Asquith believed—it seems wrongly—that this article had been inspired by Lloyd

George. The pragmatic reason for the turnabout was that Asquith's support now appeared to him stronger than it had on the Saturday. His Liberal Ministers, on learning of the proposed reconstruction, urged him to stand against Lloyd George; and, it seems, some Unionist Ministers also conveyed their support and their hostility towards Lloyd George. Hence Asquith felt strong enough to issue the firmest of all confrontations by accepting Lloyd George's resignation.

The drama then moves from the main arena back to the group of Unionist Ministers, some of whom felt that Bonar Law had mismanaged the interview with Asquith and had not conveyed the friendly intentions behind their call for his resignation. They asked Bonar Law to attend a meeting to explain his conduct. By then Bonar Law's patience must have been getting thin for he immediately interpreted this as a confrontation, told them he would appeal to the party against them, and that if they wanted a meeting, they must come to him. They did so and a meeting was held: Bonar Law's views prevailed and all the Unionist Ministers resigned. At this, Asquith too resigned, having discovered that after all, he did not command the support of the Unionist Ministers.

Lloyd George, a few days later, succeeded in forming a Government and became Prime Minister.

These events show very clearly the connection between normative themes, support and confrontations. The themes are used to justify or discredit a policy or a person, and they are the publicly-given reasons for support. The contestants confront one another by sending messages about the support they command. It remains now to pick out the one or two encounters which occurred in this sequence of conflict episodes.

When Carson challenged Bonar Law's leadership through the Nigeria debate, heads were counted. The latter turned out to be the winner numerically but evidently not by a sufficient margin to feel himself strong: in a sense this was a victory for Carson not on the anti-Bonar Law front but on the front against Asquith, for it was one factor which moved Bonar Law to support Lloyd George. The other decisive encounter came after Asquith's resignation when Lloyd George succeeded in forming a Government for this showed, unambiguously that Asquith was was not, as it is said he believed himself to be, indispensable:

that Lloyd George in fact commanded the greater political credit.

Of course, this is far from being the whole story. We have looked in detail only at two kinds of political resources which the contestants can manipulate: manpower and normative themes and the connection between them. There are other kinds of resource which go to make up a man's political credit: Bonar Law's reputation for honesty. Asquith's for imperturbability, Lloyd George's for energy. There are also skills like Carson's or Lloyd George's parliamentary oratory. There are also particular roles which have not been systematically discussed: Northcliffe, a resource and a pressure from outside the normative arena; Aitken, a manipulator and behind-the-scenes message-carrier working for Bonar Law and Lloyd George, young and a mere back-bencher but rich and influential. It is possible that such factors would in the end turn out to be accidental, but it seems more likely that analogous structural features will be found in other kinds of arena. Nor, of course, have we discussed the certainly accidental features (from our point of view) of Asquith's fall, such as his long tenure of the Prime Ministership and consequent weariness and the shock of his eldest son being killed in the war two months before Lloyd George's attack began. But factors of this kind are the province of the historian, not of the generalizing social sciences.

CONCLUSION

Competitive interaction between teams in an arena consists of building support and undermining the opponent's support through subversion. Each step is publicly justified through the appropriate normative themes. This is followed by challenges in the form of confrontations. Much of this is, as I have implied, a matter of bluff, for what matters is not the resources that a man actually commands, but what the relevant people think he commands. Cards, so to speak, are held close to the chest. But from time to time this message-sending, this dialogue of claim and counter-claim, is stopped by an encounter, through which claims to political credit are validated publicly, both for the players and for the bystanders, or are discredited.

Some arenas, like *doladoli*, seem never to have encounters, perhaps because everyone knows what the state of political credit is, or perhaps because no-one cares enough about the affair to insist upon a showdown. Others terminate decisively, as in the fall of Asquith. Yet others, like the Pakhtoun arena or the model of caste-climbing, have something like a league table with rules laying down the manoeuvres open to teams according to their position in the table.

Men employ stratagems which are not pronounced upon in the normative rules. They also follow other pragmatic rules which permit them to make calculated breaches of the normative rules. Pakhtouns insult one another in Council and British politicians make covert use of the Press. The situation seems to tremble on the brink of disorder and disintegration, yet in all the cases discussed, there is an overall order and regularity.

In the next chapter we will look at institutions and other devices in arenas, the function of which is to prevent disorder and structural disintegration. Later we will discuss situations in which political structures are changed or in which they disintegrate.

NOTES

1. See *Fairlie*, p. 37. This article eulogizes British Parliamentary institutions and the style of British politicians. I agree with him that British pragmatic deviousness is probably on most occasions good for us all, but Fairlie's message is conveyed with such glutinous fervour that, like peanut butter, it sticks on the palate. Those who admire cynicism should not do so in a style that borders on the religious.

    De Gaulle's utterances are taken from *Werth*, p. 239 and the London *Times*, December 31st, 1958.

2. See *Barth* (2), p. 118.

3. They in fact use the English word 'party', which seems to have even nastier connotations than *dolo*.

4. For a discussion of normative and pragmatic considerations in consensual decisions in councils and committees see *Bailey, F. G.* (6).

5. Since the time of that first, and possibly legendary encounter in which the headmanship changed hands, there have been, so far as I know, no others. Is there, then, a prize? If there is no prize, ought we still to classify *doladoli* as politics?

    There are several possible answers. Firstly, since the British left, the power of the headmanship has declined rapidly. Therefore, although it is still a prize, it might be considered not worth too much effort. Secondly—and this is a better explanation—the prize might be to get oneself acknowledged as having the quality of a true leader and one's rival exhibited as a fake. In other words the prize might not be the specific role of the headmanship, but the more general role of 'responsible leading man'.

6. The source for the whole of the following section is *Barth* (2).

7. *Friedrich*, talking of the Mexican community of Durazno, lists 77 political killings in the past 36 years, 21 of them taking place in a three-year period. Durazno has a population of about 1,500. In 1960 a leader who had dominated local politics for 30 years was shot down in his own doorway.

8. *Hitchcock* has described how the Rajputs of Khalapur do this. Many public amenities—tanks, bathing *ghats* (steps), temples etc.—in Bisipara and its neighbouring villages were provided in this way. Notice that we are making no assertions about motives. The benefactors concerned would probably have claimed that they were in search of religious merit: but the effect of their philanthropy (which was sometimes competitive) was to mark them out as important men.

9. See Chapter 9.

10. For details see *Bailey, F. G.* (1), Chapters IX and X.

11. A piece of government land, on which a house was built, stood in the middle of the street of the Distillers. When the occupant, a Distiller, died, the Warrior headman, in whose gift the land lay, proposed to install a Kond henchman. This was a nicely calculated piece of malice. On the one hand government land could be counted caste 'sterile'. On the other hand the house was terraced onto other houses and the proposal could be interpreted as an assertion that Distillers were down around the Kond level. That is how the Distillers saw it and they made a great fuss.

12. The analysis of caste climbing which follows was suggested to me in a conversation with McKim Marriott.

13. See *Blake*, Chapters 19–21. See also Chapter 2, note 1 of this book.

14. The reference is to a curious article on President Wilson, examining particularly his actions in the peace negotiations after the 1914–18 war. See *Freud and Bullitt*.

15. The term 'normative theme' was suggested by Bruce Graham. These are what I have earlier called 'values'. The word 'theme' is attractive because it suggests that politicians keep harping on them.

16. As Bonar Law's biographer suggests, this was a failure to manipulate a relevant resource. Pragmatically the personal rules of 1916 in Britain did not exclude the Press, which in fact worked hard to tarnish Asquith's image. De Gaulle, another olympian personality, was not so handicapped by the ethos of his time: see p. 83.

7
Control

There is a pervasive—and to my mind persuasive—notion that structures of social interaction are like gardens: if they are not tended, they run wild or wither away. For those who think this way, 'muddling through' is a way of courting disaster and to believe that 'it will all come right in the end' is a piece of stupid optimism. Men must plan and organize according to their needs and their resources: they must anticipate breakdowns and, if one should occur, they must act swiftly to make the repairs: otherwise, as when a small hole in the dyke is left unplugged, the whole structure will be swept away. We encounter this notion of self-accelerating sequences in politics in the idea of a critical threshold at which processes become like explosions, uncontrollable until they are spent of their own accord. To this extent every planner is a pessimist: he anticipates the worst and tries to prevent it.

On the other hand every planner is also an optimist. If he did not believe that there was a chance of controlling human destinies by his own efforts, there would be no point in planning. He may envisage a future state of affairs which is different from that to-day, or he may see the present as good enough and plan to keep it that way, but, whether a reformer or a conservator, he anticipates a future which is, in part at least, his own creation.

There is another kind of pessimist who believes that those who claim to control our destinies are under an illusion. Planned action always has unintended consequences. These pessimists too, are right. Not only may the plan fail to take into account all the relevant natural circumstances: it may be thwarted by the action of those who have a different plan—a situation which is the subject of this book. A well-known example of the man making imaginary deployments of forces which run along their own tracks—like someone thinking he is steering a railway train—

is Tolstoi's General (Prince Bagration), acting on intelligence which is quite wrong and sending out messages and orders which never reach their destination.

It would be hard to deny that much of life is lived in this blind fashion. There are failures which are unexpected and successes which are unforeseen. Yet, in spite of this uncertainty, one cannot believe that all constructive action and planning is a mockery. Even in the stimulated uncertainty of political competition, some degree of prediction is possible. Moreover, even if it were true that conspicuous and purposive action never attained the target at which it is directed, yet men act on the assumption that it will, and we cannot understand what they are doing unless we take this assumption into account. Tolstoi's General, in any case, is not a proof that a calculated direction of a competitive team is impossible: it proves only that some people are not good at directing and perhaps that direction is more difficult in some arenas than in others.

What, then, is the equivalent of the sand or the jungle which wrecks the untended garden? What causes the rules of a structure regulating political competition to cease to be effective?

In several places, both theoretically and through illustrations, we have discussed the part played by the environment of a political structure. Most of this chapter will be concerned, on the other hand, with the *self*-destructive aspect of political structures—the leaning towards disorder discussed at the beginning of the last chapter. But this is never the only factor: the self-destructive elements are, so to speak, helped out by acts of God in the environment. Or perhaps it should be the other way round: structural death is caused by acts of God (i.e. the environment) helped out by the acts of politicians and the rules under which they are operating.[1] Without Indo-China, the European Defence Community debate, the conflict overstate aid to church schools, without the Comintern, without Algeria, without all the other crises, then the structure of the French Fourth Republic might have survived, in spite of the ruinously expensive game of parliamentary manoeuvre entailed by the system of party alliance. Let us take the dominating effect of the environment for granted in this chapter, and ask rather what politicians do which both exacerbates and diminishes environmental dangers.

Firstly they compete for scarce prizes: this puts a premium on invention, on finding a new stratagem which will throw the opponent off balance. The invention may be a calculated deviation from the normative rules of fair play, and effective because the opponent has not guarded himself against a punch in the kidneys delivered on the blind side of the referee. It may also be that the rules do not anticipate all the possible stratagems, so that innovation is possible without offending against any normative rule as in the running battle between accountants and the income tax authorities. Again, rules may be broken through ignorance: the rules governing personnel may be sufficiently lax (or may have been broken) to allow into the arena a competitor who does not understand the rules of competition and who makes outlawed moves, just because he does not know they are outlawed. If these moves are also effective, so that the new-comer wins by cheating, then others are likely to follow suit and only the intervention of a referee can restore the normative rule of competitive behaviour: otherwise the normative rule changes. No one, nowadays, would condemn a politician for 'trafficking with the press'. Indeed, since the advent of television, politicians are admired for their skill at using such instruments of propaganda.

Sometimes there may be a drift away from the normative rules, arising from the actions of individuals, but unintended by them. This, in another form, is the situation of Tolstoi's General A well-known example of such a drift away from normative correctness into pragmatic chaos is the bureaucratic cycle. The rules of a bureaucracy specify impersonal dealings with its 'customers'. But regular customers become known, roles are personalized, and bureaucratic impersonality is endangered. Pragmatic exceptions build up against the normative rule. Then comes a critical point where the bureaucracy is likely to renew and sharpen its normative rules in order to restore the desired impersonality in dealing with the public. Just as a period of debate is terminated and the situation clarified by a decision, or a series of confrontations are summarized and the political credit balance made public by an encounter, so also, it seems, a period of drift away from normative rules into pragmatic devices ends with a stocktaking process which either restores and restates the normative rules, as in the example of the bureaucratic cycle, or announces a set of new or modified normative rules. The cycle resembles the annual spring-cleaning and redecorating with which householders 'set their house in order'.

The arena has to be set in order because, through drift, ignorance, or calculated deviance *new* kinds of resources have come to be employed for political purposes. The competitors may have developed new skills or new alliances. Athletes who compete in such endurance events as cycle-racing or long-distance running may have taken to using drugs to give themselves an edge over their competitors. The boxer may have pickled the scar-tissue on his face. Political parties may discover that they can communicate better with their voters by hiring professional advertisers to do the job for them. About a decade ago the political parties in India awoke to the fact that the new Local Government organization could be a crucial means of influencing the voters, and there was a heated debate about whether or not party politics should be kept out of the villages. The Untouchables of Bisipara have slowly learned that they can manipulate the Administration and the political parties in order to force the clean castes of the village to treat them as equals. All such events raise the question of whether or not the use of these new resources is legitimate. No-one objects to pickling scar-tissue, but cyclists are disqualified for using certain drugs. Party politics do extend now into Indian villages, perhaps because no-one could think of a way of keeping them out. Sometimes, of course, no decision may be taken. Sometimes the employment of the new resource proves ineffective, and it falls out of use of its own accord.

But why is it ever necessary to regulate the use of new resources? Perhaps one could make a case that the best device would be a free market in the use of political resources. If communal hatred or racial antagonism is the best way of building up support, then, on the theory that the people's wish is the politician's guide, teams should be enlisted by such appeals. But there are few politicians nowadays in Britain who will openly and shamelessly be seen to be making use of such devices. (Not but what some do in fact use them.) The usual explanation for such normative restraint would be that it is not in the general interest (the interest of the collectivity) to encourage such inflammatory and destructive prejudices. This is, of course, correct; but it is also part of a wider and vaguer feeling, which I mentioned at the beginning of the book, that resources expended on politics should not exceed a proportion of the society's total resources. This is not so much a question of the cost of administration, which is in the forefront of the minds of those who believe that the best Government is no Government. Administration can be productive, in the economic sense, and turn out to be in fact not a cost but a source of profit. Rather it is a question of the use of resources purely in competitive action: this has to be paid for in the time spent upon it, in comforts and even necessities forgone, even in lives lost. In this sense political competition is parasitic upon other forms of social interaction, and the whole point of having rules of political competition is that they limit the areas of social life which can be drawn into politics. This is the attitude implied when the people of Bisipara say: 'There is too much party in our village.'

The use of new resources in politics, by whatever means they are brought into play, are the occasion when politics may trespass further into other forms of social interaction. At first sight there is no inherent reason why this should be so. The new resource, one presumes, is adopted as an experiment because it is thought that it will be more effective than some other resource: if it proves to be so, then, one supposes, the old resource will be dropped. If in village India it is discovered that one can harass one's opponent more effectively by enlisting the help of the local politicians than, as before, by being a favourite of the Administrators, then in time the Administration will cease to be used as a resource in village politics, because it has been seen to be ineffective for that purpose.

To some extent this is the case: obsolete tools are shed as new ones come into use. But there is still a danger in the taking on of new resources, which comes about just because they are new. The competitors have not learned how to use them skilfully and economically. When a new resource is brought into play the pragmatic rules which state the limitations of this tool and the way to use it effectively have not yet been developed. This can only come about through a relatively expensive process of trial and error.[2]

The orderliness of a competition, as I insisted earlier, depends upon both sides knowing the rules; both normative and pragmatic. Victory in the game depends (among other things) upon creating uncertainty in the opposing team and so disorganizing it. But the game can only remain orderly so long as this uncertainty remains slight. Order is at a maximum and uncertainty at a minimum if it is known that a certain move allows for only two kinds of riposte. (If there is always only one kind of riposte, then it ceases to be a game and becomes a kind of ritual dance.) But if a move is entirely new, then the riposte also must be new. Neither side can anticipate what the other will do next: the choices become very wide. This is the situation in which people overcommit resources to 'be on the safe side'.[3] In other words, the orderliness of a game depends upon effective communication between the competitors, which means that both must understand the language being used.

This can be illustrated by outlining a situation in Bisipara which will be more fully discussed later in the context of change. Since it does concern change I shall use the word 'conflict' rather than 'contest' or 'competition': nevertheless the story will serve to show what I mean about the lavish use of political resources in situations of uncertainty and the consequent extension of politics into a wider area of social life. The conflict was between the clean castes of Bisipara and their Pan Untouchables.[4]

Once the Pans were farm labourers, owning no land, each family being attached to a family of Warriors in a permanent economic and political relationship called *raja-praja* (king-subject). However, over the last four or five decades these Pans have acquired various sources of independent income. They were helped by government policies designed to improve the lot of what then were called the exterior castes. One Pan had been a policeman, another was in the army, several were schoolmasters, one was an agent for the Depressed Classes League and had been a candidate (unsuccessful) for the Orissa Legislative Assembly. Others had made money trading in cattle and, in short, there were some Pans who were as rich as the richest members of the Warrior caste. Like the Distillers, those Pans who made money invested it in land. Needless to say, such men were no longer 'subjects' in the technical sense of the word, and in fact when I arrived in the village in 1952, there were only two men who acknowledged that they were the *praja* of Warrior families: one was the village Watchman and his *raja* was the local chieftain, a Warrior; the other was a messenger, also receiving a government salary, employed by the other local chieftain, again a Warrior.

It would seem from this that the Bisipara Pans were economically qualified to start out on a course of social climbing up the ladder of the caste system, just as the Distillers had done and were still doing. Indeed, they might seem to be in a better position, for the post-Independence Indian governments had done what the British never dared to do: they had passed legislation against the practice of untouchability in addition to intensifying their welfare activities. The Bisipara Pans did set out on such a course: their attempt to gain entrance to the village temple (to be described shortly) was part of a whole series of actions designed to claim a more respectable status in the village. They abandoned their traditional and polluting occupation of flaying dead cattle and eating the meat. They announced that they were teetotallers. They made no objection when their typically Pan privilege of music-making was taken away from them. Several of them grumbled loudly at losing the associated privilege of begging, but they made no collective appeal or protest. The richer Pans put their women in long *saris*. They built a temple in their own street, and one of the schoolmasters officiated as priest, for no Brahmin would serve them. The men took to wearing the sacred thread, and some of them seemed to take on that air of unctuous complacency which marks the village Brahmin in our area. Finally they dropped the name Pan and announced that henceforward they would be called Harijans— the children of God.[5]

These are all symbolic statements about the position to which the Pans aspired (potential confrontations, in fact). The Distillers had followed just the same course. But displays of the attributes of respectability have to be validated by symbolic interactions. You can wear the colonel's insignia, but this means nothing unless people treat you as a colonel. The Untouchable can dress up like a Brahmin, but this is empty unless people can be persuaded to treat him, if not like a Brahmin, at least as no longer an Untouchable. The Distillers, I conjectured, did this by using their economic power to subvert specialists and then staging a series of successful confrontations which translated this economic power into politico-ritual credit. But the Pans were not rich enough and not enough of the Pans were rich: they were unable to cross the immense gap which separated them, as Untouchables, from the lowest of the clean castes. What might have been a limited competition (as in the case of the Distillers) became in fact a series of extravagant and—in the early stages at least—indecisive confrontations.

The first incident which I witnessed in the conflict between the Pans and their fellow villagers took place at a temple which lay about a hundred yards across open ground from where I lived. A procession of Pans, dressed in their best clothes, some carrying brass plates with offerings, and headed by a band of cymbal players and a man with a portable harmonium,[6] came out of the village street and approached the temple. They do this every year, laying their offerings on the ground, from where the priest's assistant comes to take them into the temple. The clean castes—some men, but mostly women—were coming meanwhile in ones and twos and taking their offerings into the temple ante-chamber. Shortly after the Pans reached the temple there was an altercation with the priest and his assistant: the Pans wanted to take their offerings into the temple claiming that under the Temple Entry Acts passed by the Orissa Government, they had the right to do so. The priest refused and sent a messenger for the headman, who lived fifty yards away. The headman came, accompanied by a large body of clean caste men. There was further quarrelling, but in the end it died down and the Pans departed, back to their own street, without entering the temple. The clean castes left several young men standing guard around the temple, armed with battle-axes. In the evening the Pans returned, but this time a police inspector arrived just before them, for they had sent a messenger to the district headquarters, seven miles away. The arguments were renewed, with a deal of sophistry from the clean castes (they claimed to have no objection themselves to Pans entering the temple, provided the police would first organize a referendum of all the clean castes in the sub-division): but in the end the crowd again dispersed, and the inspector, satisfied that there would be no disorder, mounted his cycle and returned to the headquarters town.

Some time later the village council (*panchayat*) to which the

Pans did not have access, decreed that Pan musicians would no longer be allowed to perform at village festivals, and would no longer be allowed to solicit for alms: instead these rights would be given to some Untouchables of a different caste who also lived in the village.

Towards the end of that year (1953) an elderly Pan met a clean caste youth on a narrow fieldpath at dusk one day, and, so it seems, pushed the youth out of the way and headfirst into the mud of a paddy field. The Pan fled across the fields to his home: the youth ran to the nearest clean caste street and there raised an outcry. The council met and a message was sent summoning the Pan, who replied that it was already dark, he was afraid to walk out in the night, and he would attend in the morning along with his caste brothers. But it seems that not all the Pans were afraid of the perils of the night—of encountering a leopard or stepping on a snake—for some of them walked the seven dark miles to the police, and said that the clean castes were rioting and had attacked their street with guns.

When the clean castes arose in the morning, they found the council house occupied by a constable. Later a sub-inspector arrived, listened to both sides, said there was no case to answer, ordered everyone to behave properly, and went away. The Pans appealed to the police again, and the same procedure, with the same result, was carried through by an inspector. They appealed again, and this brought a circle inspector; and so it went on through the ranks of the police up to the superintendent; and then through the civil authorities up to the district magistrate. In the course of these enquiries, the Pans brought off a notable coup in attracting the interest of a minister in the Orissa government who was touring in the area: he ordered another round of enquiries, all with the same result, that there was no case to answer and that everyone should behave themselves. All this took about a year, while I was in England, and I returned just after the magistrate's second enquiry: at that stage the clean castes were debating about holding a levy to raise funds to hire a lawyer, for they had heard that the Pan untouchables intended to institute a civil case: that was in 1955.

There are many facets to this story of change in village India, and we will look later at some of them. Here I draw attention to the Pans' use of the police, the Administration, and the

Congress Government. These were not, of course, entirely new resources: the area had been administered for more than a century, and both the police and the Administration were known and feared, alike by clean castes and Untouchables. For about three decades the policy of the Administration had helped to improve the economic standing of the Untouchables. Yet these outsiders had never before been drawn directly into the village dispute between clean castes and Pans.

For both sides it proved expensive. The Pans in particular behaved as if they had burned their bridges behind them: they kept coming back to the attack with one appeal after another, although it must have been clear after the first enquiry that they were not going to make the charge stick. All this involved them in fees and various kinds of illegitimate expenses, travel expenses and—not least—the difficulties and humiliations which all peasants, let alone Untouchables, suffer in such circumstances. The clean castes too conducted themselves as if in a state of siege, with hours spent in meetings discussing tactics, oaths of secrecy and levies to raise expenses for those who were required to attend the judicial enquiries. They also, in my opinion, grossly overestimated the support which the Pans could get from the politicians and the Administration and were in a state of continuing uncertainty, bordering upon panic. (This, in fact, was the payoff for the Pans, although I am sure that they had not anticipated it: the clean castes emerged not merely with loathing for their Pans, but also with a new fear.)

Yet, despite the fears and uncertainties raised by the use of this new resource in village politics, and despite the violence of the emotions which compared in intensity with race antagonisms in to-day's American cities, there were some voluntary restraints. The poor Pans needed employment as day-labourers on the clean caste farms: and the farmers needed their labour. The labourers continued to offer themselves and to be hired even through the bitterest period of the quarrel. In 1955, when a similar quarrel broke out in a neighbouring Kond village and the Konds announced that they would not employ Pan labourers, this was taken by the Bisipara clean castes as a typical manifestation of Kond idiocy.[7] To this extent at least the clean castes of Bisipara did not misread Pan confrontations: here they knew where to draw the line.

This dispute contrasts strikingly with *doladoli*. In the latter no new kinds of political resource are introduced: the confronting exchanges, albeit rancorous, go smoothly to and fro, and while men frequently seem to lose their tempers, they never lose their heads.

To summarize. We began by asking what can go wrong? Why do political structures tend to break down? The main factor is the environment and the strains it imposes. The answer, so far as concerns the actors, is that actions have consequences which are not anticipated. This is especially so when the environment imposes new strains. Orderliness depends upon anticipation, upon expectations being fulfilled. Yet the paradox of political competition is that the prize goes to the team which can act in a way unforeseen by its opponents, and perhaps unanticipated in the rules of the game. This element of self-destruction is built into any political structure from the moment it defines prizes, which not everyone can win. Moreover, sometimes even the initiators of a course of action do not realize what will be the consequences. All this creates further uncertainty, and the danger in uncertainty is that more and more resources become defined (pragmatically) as available for use in political competition.

This section ended by noticing the restraint which the people of Bisipara observed even in their bitterest dispute. In the next section we look more systematically at this element of collusion, which helps to keep structures intact.

COLLUSION

Competitors collude when they decide to withhold from the arena certain resources which are available to them. To bring these resources into play, they decide, would make the game too costly. Our task in this section is to find out what is meant in this context by 'too costly'. The discussion applies, to some extent, not only to competitions but also to fights and revolutions.

Once again the politicians of the French Fourth Republic will serve as an example. In spite of the rather sorry picture which their actions have left, they seem at bottom to have been concerned with keeping republican institutions intact. There were, of course, exceptions like de Gaulle himself and his followers. France had suffered more than ten years of disorder and disunity, beginning in the mid-thirties with the right-wing rioting in Paris which led to the formation of a Popular Front of Radicals, Communists and Socialists. Then there had been the humiliation of defeat and then the Vichy regime. Experience had taught the politicians a hard lesson in restraint.

In October 1945 a referendum was held to approve the setting up of an Assembly to draft a new constitution and in the subsequent elections Communists, Socialists and a centre party, the Mouvement Républicain populaire (MRP), polled most successfully. The Radicals, a centre right group, and the smaller right-wing parties did less well. A government was formed of the three largest parties, the two from the left-wing and the MRP. Between these parties there were some very acute disagreements, for example about educational and economic policies, but both they and their right wing opponents were concerned to restore a republican form of government and to make no radical changes in the French political system.

To this end a number of pragmatic rules evolved, governing the kinds of resources which could and could not be used in the competition between parties. On the whole, in the early period at least, a damper was kept on such explosive issues as colonial policy, pressure for wage-increases, aid for church schools and so forth. Each party refrained from making full use of these explosive themes in its own interest, in the knowledge that to go all out might wreck the whole system. Furthermore each party, even the Communists at that time, were fairly broadly based in the electorate and could not afford to link itself too closely with only one theme.

The word collusion has connotations of secrecy, deceit and fraud. In fact many acts of collusion are tacit: the competitors will not admit that they are withholding resources. But it will be convenient to extend our discussion to cover those situations in which the competitors admit and even glory in the fact that they are withholding their full strength. They are prepared publicly to justify their actions. In other words, pragmatic collusions and normative agreements have to some extent the same significance: restraint in the interests of stability. Secondly, collusion implies that *both* competitors are restraining themselves. But there are certainly situations in which one man gives his all to the contest, while the other holds back. This is generally done by the stronger man and it follows one of the most general normative rules of competition, that encounters should take place only between those who are more or less equal. Where mistakes in matching have been made, the stronger competitor may decide in the interests of the normative rule of equality not to demonstrate his superiority too openly or too abruptly. An example of this will be given later.

In this way encounters may, so to speak, be mitigated. Collusion also includes those situations in which encounters take place by anticipation of the outcome: in 'deconfrontations' or withdrawals. Challenges may not be accepted, and the weaker party responds to a challenge with a symbolic acceptance of inferiority. A striking, if coarse, example of this behaviour is found among baboons, one of the more aggressive types of primate. The males of a troop sort themselves out into patterns of dominance and subordination. If annoyed by a challenge— perhaps inadvertent—from an inferior, the dominant male will stare fixedly at him: the inferior should then look away. If he does not the dominant male will move as if to charge; the weaker baboon should then cringe close to the ground, turning its head away from the aggressor. Failing that, there will be a charge and a chase: but even then there are ways of communicating withdrawal. The weaker baboon may still save itself being bitten by turning its back, presenting its hindquarters and allowing itself to be mounted, just as a female is mounted in copulation. There could hardly be a clearer way of symbolizing whose political credit is the highest. An encounter has taken place, but it is, literally, bloodless.[8]

Human politicians, who are also primates, do not symbolize their inferiority so explicitly, but there are hints of a similar order of thinking in, for example, that extremity of abuse in the vocabulary of the Bisipara villagers: the word *sola*. This is a word with an absolutely respectable meaning of 'my wife's brother'. As a word of abuse, it is taken to mean 'Your sister is a whore'. But the challenge is in fact more direct: the aggressor is saying that he could dishonour the sister, if he wished, and his opponent could do nothing to prevent it. There are large areas of the peasant and tribal world, particularly those influenced by Islam, where the chastity of maidens and the fidelity of married women is used as one index of political credit.[9] This is not, of course, to say that all ways of confronting an enemy or of symbolizing submission and so putting an end to an incipient battle must carry sexual overtones: each arena has its own rules for grovelling and confrontation.

Grovelling takes place when one competitor regrets having entered into the arena, judges that he must lose heavily in an encounter, and has less to lose by acknowledging his own inferiority. The same symbols may also be used, of course, if an encounter has begun, and the loser feels he cannot stand any more punishment. But there is also a situation of self-restraint, in political competition more than in games, in which *both* competitors draw back from the brink because they are not sure enough that they can win or because, in general, they have come to realize that peace will serve them better than a contest.

When this happens both sides are concerned that the political credit which they have amassed through aggressive posturing should not be dissipated by their withdrawal from the encounter. It may be that the reasons for backing down are entirely pragmatic in both cases: that is, not the kind of explanation which they could issue publicly without losing face. But they are generally likely to symbolize their new posture by a joint statement which gives a normative reason for adopting it. In this way they can save face. For example, in the early months of 1959 the Congress Government in Orissa kept itself in power with great difficulty, being able to hold a majority only by the grace of six members of the Jharkhand party, who allied themselves with Congress.[10] A man sick or a man reluctant to accept the whip on a particular issue drove the government to a variety of stratagems, some of which brought them considerable discredit. Individual members were not slow to sense the power which this gave them, and they put in demands on their own behalf or for their constituents which were patently against the public interest. Then, in the late spring, a coalition was formed with the main Opposition party, the Ganatantra Parishad (GP). The GP could have held out and tried to force an election. But in doing so they risked the suspension of parliamentary government in Orissa, for the central government might declare that

the state should be ruled by the Governor until the situation
became clearer: by accepting a coalition they at least got some
places in the government and, as their opponents said, their
hands into the pork barrel of patronage.

For both sides there were compelling pragmatic reasons for
accepting the coalition: but a share in the spoils (GP) or inability
to discipline one's own rank-and-file (Congress) are not justifica-
tions which one can put unashamedly before the electorate. The
small left-wing parties, and some sections of the Press did, of
course, make the most of this situation and they branded the
coalition as a bourgeois conspiracy to remain in power at all
costs. The leaders of the new coalition issued statements saying
that the prevailing 'instability' was detrimental to the interests
of the whole state of Orissa and that the new government would
be in an infinitely better position to 'implement the Plan'. In
other words, refusal to engage in political competition should
not be taken as a sign of political bankruptcy, but rather of a
joint concern for public welfare. The formula is carefully adjusted so that if it does bring an increment of political credit,
this is shared equally by both sides.

In such an event the competitors are in fact saying that the
prize for which they have been contending (in this example the
right to form a government) has turned out to be of less importance than some other value outside the arena (in this case the
public weal, as symbolized in the current Five-Year Plan). Such
an *external* factor is found in all collusive situations. Indeed, the
external factor is characteristic of all arenas where competition
is taking place: something (for example, sportsmanship or 'the
game') is ostensibly valued more than the prize. Now let us look
at some of the different forms which this external factor may
take.

Analytically there is a distinction between those external
values which are pragmatic and those which are normative. In
the example of the Orissa coalition of 1959 both were present. If
collusion does come to public notice, some kind of *normative*
excuse will be sought. There are, however, some acts of collusion
which virtually defy normative justification and which the
perpetrators are most anxious to keep secret. These are acts to
win those pragmatic prizes which run flatly against the normative rules.

A clear example of this is the boxer who 'throws' a fight, because someone has paid him or has induced him to do so by threats of violence. The pragmatic prize (the bribe) is evidently bigger than the normative prize (victory in the match), and the two kinds of prize contradict one another. This does not mean, of course, that all pragmatic prizes contradict normative prizes in so immediate a fashion. One of the privileges of being a successful professional sportsman is to make money by advertising hair-oil or beer or any other product which is not too incongruously linked with that particular sport. But even such a man is on the edge of that delicate area where he has to make the occasional extravagant gesture to prove that the game and its glories come first and the money-making second.

In the first two elections conducted on an adult franchise in Orissa, there was a good deal of uncertainty about how best to get in touch with the voters. One variable considered important was the 'social base' of the candidate: if a man stood for election where his community or caste were in a majority, then he had a better chance of winning than in constituencies where the electors were not connected to him by such social ties. From this it was a short pragmatic step to counter one's opponent by putting up a 'dummy' candidate to split the caste or community vote. Yet a further step into the abyss of pragmatism was taken when it occurred to some enterprising individuals that there was money to be made out of pseudo-confrontations: that they could enter their names as Independents against a candidate who had the same social basis as themselves, in the hope that he or his agents would bribe them to stand down before the election. Sometimes this happened: at other times their bluff was called and they lost their deposits.

A more ambiguous case was that of certain left-wing agitators. At that time Orissa controlled the purchase of food grains by issuing licences, the holders of which enjoyed an effective monopoly. A peasant might arrive at a shop with a cartload of rice, which he knew was of Grade A, to be told by the trader that this was in fact Grade C rice and he would be paid no more than Grade C prices. The peasant would have to give in or wait idle while the costs of his visit to the market town mounted. Such dishonest traders caused great distress and, very properly, some left-wing politicians, intent upon making a good name for them-

selves, took up the battle. They might arrange to picket the
shop; they might sit down and fast in front of it; or, in a variety
of ways, embarrass the shopkeeper. The latter might climb down
and mend his ways: more often, so the right-wing politicians
said, he paid a sum of money to the agitator who then moved on
to start the next agitation. In such ways, so it was said, the
small parties of the left financed themselves. If these allegations
are true, then this is an example of a pseudo-confrontation,
mitigated because both competitors have their eyes on prizes
outside the ostensible arena of competition.

A similar pattern of interaction may be found also where the
controlling prize, as it might be called, is offered normatively in
another arena. This is the situation of fighting on two fronts,
and there is nothing inherently discreditable about the controlling prize, as there is in the examples of bribery and corruption
given above. Nevertheless, the competitors will sometimes try
not to publicise their dilemma, for it does at least advertise the
fact that they do not have the political capital to compete
effectively in both arenas, and if this becomes known, their
chance of making a face-saving (and resource-saving) withdrawal from the lesser arena is that much lessened. At the time
of writing this, one suspects that the Wilson government in
Britain is in just such a dilemma as between the economic crisis
and the Rhodesian crisis. It is also the dilemma of any politician
caught in a situation of change: for example, one of the Pan
leaders in Bisipara was becoming increasingly active in constituency politics and had that much the less time to devote to
the internal struggles in the village. He was very much concerned not to appear to be withdrawing from the village arena.
It is also, I suppose, the dilemma of any respresentative, who
must from time to time choose between the general interest and
the particular interests of those who elected him: this is an
especially difficult situation for representatives in countries like
India where the electors have a distinctly parochial outlook.

The controlling prize is not necessarily political. Politicians
may withdraw from the arena in order to devote themselves to
their professional or business interests. India, especially since
1947 when Independence was achieved, has seen the retirement
of many politicians, a few in order to devote themselves to
religious contemplation in the manner sanctioned by Hindu

culture, and more to engage in social work, which was (somewhat optimistically) considered to be non-competitive. The man who was Chief Minister of Orissa at the time when I first went there retired from politics to carry out voluntary social service in the Sarvodaya organization and the Bhoodan movement. There were other instances of such withdrawal into 'good works' which seem in some cases not to have been normatively inspired, but rather to have constituted pragmatic refuges where wounded politicians could convalesce and prepare themselves anew for the fray. Indeed, in cultures which set a high value on religiosity, such a move may be a means of enlarging one's political credit.

Finally it should be noticed that some of these acts of self-restraint or withdrawal occur *ex post facto*, so to speak. Although most of the discussion has been carried on as if the actors were totally rational and calculating, knowing that if they put resources into X, they will be short for Y and therefore must arrange a withdrawal from that arena, it also happens that actors can over-reach themselves and discover only when they are drawn up for an encounter that there is no ammunition left. In other words, the restraint in politics may be a latent function of other social institutions: what we at first see as restraints may in fact be constraints. This can also happen within the general field of politics: the 1959 coalition in Orissa is a manifestation not so much of the actors' self-restraint as of the constraints which the situation put upon them.

A very simple example of situational restraint on political competition is that imposed by the agricultural cycle in Bisipara. In July and August, which is the planting season for paddy, and in December–January when it is harvested, village politics are in the doldrums. The men (and women) are out in the fields from dawn until darkness, and they literally have no time to dispute about the big symbolic issues. They close ranks, so to speak, against the common enemy, time and the weather. In the late winter and in the hot months of spring and early summer, when they have a truce with nature, they turn upon one another in a variety of symbolic interactions, some of which are political and competitive. *Doladoli* is for the hot months. Perhaps it was a measure of the gravity of the caste dispute that the encounter of the Pan man and the Warrior youth occurred and was allowed to escalate although the paddy was in the fields and the harvest soon to be collected.

Closing ranks against a common enemy is a form of normative restraint. This, obviously, is a variant of the situation where the contestants realize that peace rather than conflict is in their mutual interest. Insofar as the threat of suspending parliamentary rule and handing over the state to the Governor's administration brought about the 1959 Coalition, this was an example of closing ranks in face of an external threat. Closing ranks is also a case which arises from fighting on two fronts, or from being threatened with that situation, but it poses a less serious problem insofar as both the competitors are in the same situation. Neither has to take special precautions against losing political credit by ending the competition, because both are involved and neither can take advantage of the situation to the other's detriment. The phenomenon is too common to need exemplification, except to say that the conspicuous restraint in *doladoli*, at the time when I saw it, may have been caused by the activities of the common enemy, the Pan Untouchables.

Closing ranks in the face of an enemy is a special case of cross-cutting ties. Those who are enemies in one situation are sometimes required to act as allies in another situation. With an eye on future co-operation, they restrain their behaviour in present competition. A war-time election seemed to Churchill immoral. 'I fear it will buck up the Germans', wrote George V seeing the ranks of his Government opening below him.

Sometimes such behaviour is closely directed towards particular ends and borders upon the pragmatic. In the world of committees it is called 'back-scratching', and within an institution a language of indirect verbal signs develops, the purpose of which is to propose bargains: offering, for example, present support in return for backing on some future occasion, which may or may not be specified. Sometimes committees may be adjourned so that this bargaining can take place in a more direct form. Since all committees operate on the normative rule that they are guided by rational considerations of general interest, such bargains which minister to particular interests and enlist support on a transactional basis rather than on considerations of principle, must be kept under cover: everyone is likely to know about these pragmatic bargains, but they are not recorded in the minutes, which report the normative proceedings of the committee.

On other occasions ranks are closed in a secret and pragmatic fashion, but with a wholly normative purpose. For example, the value of family unity and harmony is maintained by protecting the younger and weaker members in competitive games within the group. Some rules are covertly broken so that on at least some occasions the youngest and least skilled will win. Socialization processes are softened so that beginners are not alienated and made anti-social. Very close to this kind of restraint are the training competitions which take place inside a group. Military manoeuvres are carried out with blank ammunition, and other kinds of precaution are taken to see that no damage is done and no resources wasted.

Restraints may also be observed not so much in the face of an enemy and for the sake of a group to which both contestants belong, but in the interests of the structure itself which is directing their activity. People not merely accept the rules of the competition but go out of their way to protect them. A man who had been a professional boxer of some distinction in his early youth entered a university after the war and was allowed to resume amateur status and represent that university. In competition with another university he found himself matched with a valiant but unskilled novice. He allowed the bout to go for the three rounds, avoided damaging his opponent, and was observed, in the course of a clinch, to lean over the ropes, catch the eye of his second, and wink.

The wink apart, this was good sportsmanship. A requirement of any kind of competition (as distinct from a fight) is that the competitors should not be too unevenly matched. This rule had not been observed in the example quoted. But the boxer's behaviour to some extent concealed this fact. Whatever his motive —kindheartedness or arrogance or laziness—the effect of his restraint was to protect one of the normative rules of the competition.

It is not a tautology to claim that competitors in politics restrain themselves because they respect the normative rules, because, as has been shown, they can also restrain themselves out of self-interest: for pragmatic reasons. But how are they brought to respect normative rules?

Part of the answer is that they may be punished if they do not. We will deal with this question later. The other part of the answer is that these rules are internalized through the process of socialization, and they are kept in repair by various ritual devices and made immediate, almost tangible, to the competitors through symbolic objects.

These rites and symbols bring home to the competitors the fact that they have a common interest in seeing that the rules of the competition are observed. This is the meaning of the handshake which precedes a contest and the embrace which nowadays concludes it. The perpetrator of a nasty foul immediately shakes hands, if he can, with his victim to signal that his lapse was inadvertent and, despite it, he intends to continue to be a sportsman. By accepting the handshake the victim indicates that he too will observe the rules and has no intention of retaliating. The more spectacular all-in wrestlers, who attract the crowds just because they do *not* stay within the rules, symbolize their intention by refusing to shake hands or by turning the handshake into a throw.

Those rites which indicate a common acceptance of normative standards are especially important when these standards are in danger. People who live closer to nature than we do make a direct connection between natural disasters and moral infirmities. If there is a drought, or if more children or more cattle die than usually happens, if a man is lost to a tiger or a leopard in the forest or if many cattle are killed in that way, then the Konds believe that the Earth has been defiled and they look around or think back until they find someone who has committed incest or has attacked a fellow clansman and injured him.[11] In other cultures, the ancestral spirits, if their descendents quarrel, may bring sickness down upon the living to convince them that it is better to live in harmony.[12] Among other people the rites which are thought to assure a successful hunt may not begin until all those present have unburdened their minds and spoken out about every grievance they have against their fellows.[13] Overarching and undisputed values like health and fertility and prosperity are made common symbols and made to stand for the rules which ensure orderly social interactions between men and orderly political competition.[14]

It would be naïve to assume that such devices always work.

Competitions do sometimes escalate into fights: community life can be made intolerable by quarrelling. Astute leaders can manipulate the rites and ceremonies of solidarity to do one another down, by using them as a means of increasing their political credit. Nonetheless, even if every man were a cynic and an unbeliever, man as a collectivity is not: this is why one cannot do without the distinction between normative and pragmatic rules. The normative represents the general interest, a value which is everywhere (in a particular culture) taken to be its own justification, and therefore a religious value. Whether the political competitor accepts any particular normative value or not, he must at least appear to do so.

Finally, to take us into the next section, it should be noticed that many rites and ceremonies which symbolize common acceptance of the rules of political competition have to be stage-managed. There are roles specialized in handling situations in which the normative rules, for one reason or another, have come into question. These are the authorities: men whose job it is to keep the rules of a structure in good order.

AUTHORITIES

It is difficult to find a sufficiently neutral word for the judicial roles which are the subject of this section, for every noun carries some connotations of the power attaching to the role. Judges, arbitrators, referees and umpires all have sanctions at their disposal: mediators, by definition, do not. The role, in fact, covers a wide range of types of action. At one end of this range the task is no more than that of helping the competitors to communicate with one another, of suggesting a possible solution to their difficulty or at least of diminishing the uncertainty about one another's intention.[15] At the other extreme is the judge who announces his decision and is able to enforce it, whether the competitors agree with him or not.

The role may also be filled by a wide variety of persons and even goes beyond the range of human agents to mechanical devices like drawing lots or consulting oracles. The job may be done by a person highly specialized in this role alone: as in the case of a judge. It may be an incidental task attached to some other role, as when a priest is also a mediator. One man may carry out the work: or it may be done by a council. It may even be done in a highly diffuse fashion by public opinion.

These roles—when we need a general word we shall call them 'umpire' roles including in that word even roles which do not command forceful sanctions and where the holder does no more than suggest or help communication—serve to protect the public interest (public, of course, being defined by the structure concerned). It is through them that the public at large seeks to protect itself from violence and disorder and the undue trespass of political activity into other areas of social interaction. The holders of these roles represent the public and they are a means of making articulate and focusing public opinion.

It would, however, be too simple to assume that this is necessarily the gateway for democracy and that in every society one will find in the end that the people control their rulers and the general will reigns supreme. The people, as the word is used when one speaks of democracy, do not always coincide with the public, as the word is used here. Who qualifies to be considered as the public, and to have their interests protected by umpires, is laid down by the personnel rules of the structure concerned. Not everyone is permitted even to watch the competition and have a voice in how it should be played: many more may be excluded and find that their only part in political competition is to pay its costs. In Rajputana the greater part of the peasantry did not constitute the public for the Rajput political structure. There are times when the effective public is a city mob or the students: and devices like property-restricted franchises ensure that the 'public' does not coincide with the 'people'.

One of the tasks of a leader is to be an umpire in his own group. How, then, does one distinguish leadership roles from umpires? Are umpires always also leaders? Empirically it is often the case that they are: but it is both possible and necessary to make an analytic distinction between the two roles.

The distinction lies in the end towards which their activities are directed. A leader's concern is to keep his group strong and to maintain his position as a leader. If he discovers that the structure of rules through which he has been maintaining his group and his own position within it is no longer effective, perhaps because new kinds of political resources have become available, then he has an incentive to modify the structure in order to take advantage of or to keep up with his competitors. For example, the ruler of a small principality in western Orissa did exactly this in the decade following Indian independence. In the days of the British his power was maintained because he received the revenue from extensive estates, because he was formally recognized and supported by the British, because he acted as a magistrate and dispute-settler for his subjects, because he lent them money and because each year he arranged and supervised and paid for the celebration of some spectacular rituals. He kept elephants and horses and a motor-car, was a keen *shikari* (hunter) and in general comported himself in the extravagant and ebullient manner of that anachronistic squirearchy which the British succeeded in creating in some parts of India. When Independence came his office as Raja was formally abolished, although he was allowed a pension and certain privileges. Much of the land he owned was confiscated and his judicial functions were—officially at least—taken over by civil servants. His influence as a moneylender was attacked by the provision of various forms of agricultural credit. Faced with these changes some of the princes took their pensions and went off to live in retirement in Calcutta. But when I met him in 1959, this ruler had become a member of the Orissa Legislative Assembly in the interest of the Ganatantra Parishad, a party formed by the ex-princes and the middle-classes of the hill regions of western Orissa. The prince still lived in his palace and he still put on each year the festivals, but, so he said, with an increasing austerity (he seemed very concerned to play down this side of his life). But he was very anxious that I should be clear about the basis of his success. He saw himself fighting for the people of his constituency (a large number of whom had belonged to his principality) against the Congress government. He provided a detailed account of three agitations which he had inspired and led against the local administrators. These were conducted with that mixture of non-violent protest sitting lightly over a threat of violence and disorder which the Congress itself had perfected in the struggle for Independence. He had been on hunger strike, he had been to jail, he had sat down in the pathway of police and officials. In short he had maintained his leadership of his principality (now part of a Constituency) by an almost total reversal of values and of styles of his political conduct before and after 1947.

An umpire does not do this. In the first place, insofar as he is an umpire, he has no group to maintain. What he must preserve is the structure of rules which regulate political competition. His concern is not a team, but an arena. This does not mean, of course, that the umpire's role is wholly conservative. In practice, most of an umpire's time is spent in seeing that the existing rules are obeyed and that deviant competitors are brought back into line. But the role also includes modifying the existing rules and even making new rules to cope with unanticipated disorders which may break out in the arena. But his goal is always the preservation of that arena and the preservation of those parts of the political structure which are its defining characteristics. An analogy may help to make this clear. The rules of Association football are modified from time to time—offside rules, body-charging, harassing the goalkeeper and so forth. But a defining rule is that only the feet and the head and certain parts of the body may be used to strike the ball: so that when the legendary William Webb Ellis picked up the ball and ran with it, his action created a new kind of game, a new structure of rules. In the same way a political structure contains rules or statements of values which are deemed in the culture concerned to make it what it is: these can be called the definitive rules or definitive values of a political structure.

One can also distinguish the referee from a leader by saying that the role is non-competitive. Firstly the umpire is not—normatively at least—concerned with what goes on in other types of arenas and he is not in any sense in competition with the umpires of those arenas. We shall see later that pragmatically this is not always the case, for in situations of political change, the umpire may find himself striving to keep his structure of rules in general use and to prevent his customers, so to speak, from patronizing another structure. This will be discussed in a later chapter. In the meantime, let it be assumed that the umpire has no external competitor: the football referee does not have to take into account what is being done by referees in boxing rings.

Secondly, the normative rules which lay down the umpire's duties within the arena he is controlling make it quite clear that he must not be a competitor within that arena. He must not be identified with one side or the other. If he does so, then he forfeits his normative authority and both political structures and games tend to develop 'meta-umpire' institutions to deal with situations in which the umpire's impartiality (and, of course, his general fitness for the job as well) has become suspect. Courts of appeal perform this function. So also do election commissions when they judicially hear complaints for bias or incompetence against presiding officers or other officials. There are also sets of rules for ensuring beforehand that the umpire will be neutral. When national teams compete the referee is chosen from a third nation. Jurymen may be rejected if their impartiality is suspected.

Nevertheless, the normative rule insisting upon the umpire's impartiality is frequently broken. An important question is to ask why this occurs and what is its significance.

The umpire's role can be seen as a sequence of tasks. This sequence is initiated when one competitor complains that his opponent has committed a foul. The umpire then has two kinds of task which go on concurrently. One concerns intelligence (in the military sense) and communication: finding out what has happened and deciding whether or not there has been an offence and ascertaining what the parties intend to do. Secondly, a number of practical steps have to be taken: quick action to prevent retaliation and, later, bringing the parties together and either getting them to compromise or making a decision and, if necessary, enforcing it. When this is finished, or perhaps before, some kinds of umpire will look at the rules themselves and ask whether, in the light of what has happened, they should not be modified to prevent such a situation from arising again. The first step is clearly the emergency action to prevent retaliation: the final step is the modification of the rules. Between this beginning and end, the umpire is engaged in gathering information and making use of it for the practical purpose of restoring orderly competition.

When the umpire gathers information he uses it to construct a cognitive map of the situation. This map includes some features which are normative and some which are pragmatic.

The first normative question arises from the complaint that a rule has been broken. To discover whether or not this complaint is justified, the umpire has to satisfy himself that the structure does in fact contain such a rule. This is not always such an easy task as it sounds, particularly when the rules have not been codified. Even when they have been codified—and particularly if they have been codified into a detailed obscurity—it is a pragmatic device for the political adept to invent a plausible-sounding normative rule and use it to bamboozle umpire and opponents alike. It is even easier to work this trick through those normative rules which are so general that they are left uncodified, a useful opening being 'It has long been a tradition in this great institution which we are all here to serve. . . .'

Secondly, the umpire must ask: If there is such a rule, does it apply in the present situation? Rules, as we have said, always contain this element of uncertainty because they are general while situations are particular and can be plausibly connected with a variety of contradictory normative rules. At least in political competition those detected in wrongdoing will usually find some normative cover for what they have done.

Before these two questions can be answered the umpire must find out what in fact happened. Was the act which gave offence in fact committed, or is it a pragmatic move in a game of political denigration?

These three kinds of question are the basis on which the umpire can make a normative assessment of the case. But, if he is to be effective, he must ask other kinds of question as well. He needs, in particular, to make a realistic judgement about whether the altercation in fact concerns the matter raised in the formal complaint, or whether it concerns something else. When the Bisipara Pans brought their dispute with the clean castes to the notice of the authorities for the second time, the judgement delivered was fundamentally irrelevant to the real cause of the dispute and totally inadequate as a means of restoring order. It had to be so for the complaint that the high castes had attacked the Pans with guns was untrue: the Pans had made it because they knew that the scuffle between their man and the Warrior youth was a trivial affair which would never command official attention. The false complaint was in fact a rather inept way of trying to draw official attention to what they considered was continued and illegal discrimination against them on the basis of caste. The official judgement, however, was based on the complaint formally made, and could not be effective in settling the larger issue. The officials who listened to the case saw it—

and from one point of view they were correct—as an attempt by
the Pans to use judicial machinery to harass the clean castes.
In such a situation the umpire has two things to think about:
firstly the misuse of normative rules to harass opponents should
be discouraged; secondly, the misuse may itself have come about
because those particular normative rules are out of touch with
reality, and they should therefore be modified. Sometimes, of
course, as when the basis of the dispute is some deep-felt racial
or communal antagonism, the umpire settling particular disputes does not have the power to remove the cause of the conflict.

Especially when they have few sanctions at their own disposal, umpires must also ask a number of pragmatic questions
about the political resources available to each of the competitors.
If this power is near enough equal, then the possibilities of a
consensual settlement is that much increased. We will look at
the possible variations in this pattern in a moment, but first one
should notice a considerable practical difficulty. The umpire's
job is to see that a violent encounter does not take place. If he
cannot enforce a settlement on both parties and knows that he
must arrange a compromise, then he must not only know how
each of the competitors think they would fare in a fight, but he
must also make his own judgement of who would win and what
would be the cost of victory to the winner, and use this judgement as a means of arguing the disputants into a compromise.
The practical difficulty involved lies in discovering what, so to
speak, collateral each competitor holds to secure his political
credit. Obviously it is in the interest of the competitors to bluff
not only their opponents but also the umpire about their
strength, and the variables involved can be so complex that in
fact the only way to find out may be to allow an encounter.

The amount of attention which the umpire must pay to the
relative strength of each of the competitors depends upon his
own independent political resources. If he has a loyal and
incorruptible and powerful police force to back up his decisions
and to find out for him exactly who did what, he can ignore the
relative strength of the competitors (assuming that neither one
of them is stronger than the police) and make his decision purely
on a normative basis. If he does not have an enforcement agency,
then the effectiveness of his decision depends upon the degree
to which both parties value the rules of the competition and

consider that his decision is in accordance with these rules. The less they value these rules, the more attention must the umpire pay to their relative strength. This can be clarified by looking at what umpires do with the cognitive maps they make of the situation, including, of course, the assessment of their own power relative to that of each of the competitors.

The umpire's first practical task is to prevent hot-blooded revenge and the consequent risk of escalation. When the Pans complained of armed rioting and bloodshed the officials sent out from the District headquarters a single policeman, whom the village awoke to discover next morning sitting in the council house and demanding that someone bring him tea. This—or its equivalent in the local idiom—is all that cultures which have strong umpires need do. They are also likely to make it known that those who retaliate forcefully on their own behalf, and do not give time for the judicial authorities to intervene, will be penalized in the subsequent judicial proceedings unless they can show that they acted only to defend themselves.

Societies which do not have umpires who command forceful sanctions rely upon mystical institutions to stem immediate violence. Among the Pathans the person of a Saint was inviolate and his house was a sanctuary.[16] The Konds, according to one authority who wrote a century ago—I heard nothing of the custom—had the odd belief that the murderer who gained refuge in the house of his victim could not be harmed, the logic being, presumably, that he had delivered himself as a hostage and a pledge that compensation would be paid.[17] The final penalty for disregarding sanctuaries is mystical—punishment by disease falling upon oneself or one's kin—but it is also sometimes true that a man can damage his case and provoke a coalition of men concerned with the public interest against him, if he is seen to violate such mystical norms.

Once the immediate danger is stopped, the umpire who commands his own resources and can enforce a decision gathers information and makes his judgement in the way that I have sketched out above. But the umpire who cannot command sufficient resources to enforce his decision and who does not believe that the competitors will accept, on a moral basis, the rules of fair play, must make an assessment of the relative strength of the competitors.

If he finds (correctly) that the competitor whom he believes to be in the right is also patently the stronger, then there are no difficulties, for he can rely upon the stronger person to provide sanctions for his judgement. Nonetheless, he is likely to communicate with the weaker competitor and try to show him both that he is normatively in the wrong and that pragmatically he has no chance of winning a contest and that, therefore, the least expensive course to be followed is to submit to the judgement and acknowledge the sin: otherwise he will be shown up to be not merely a sinner but also politically bankrupt through being seen to be unable to protect himself.

Now suppose the reverse situation: the stronger competitor is also the man who has broken the rules. If the umpire commands no resources, then he is better out of the situation, for if his decision is ignored with impunity then both he and the rules are tarnished. If he bends the rules and decides in favour of the stronger, then he becomes a partisan and ceases to be an umpire: which is bad for the role of umpire but may not be bad for the political actor concerned. In effect he earns himself a job as a kind of moral consultant and public relations man to the stronger leader.

An interesting situation is that in which the umpire himself has sufficient resources to balance out the disparity between the weaker and the stronger competitors. Then, in the interest of maintaining the rules, he may ally himself with the weaker party in order to make the stronger stay within the rules.[18]

All these procedures have been oversimplified in my description, especially that of the mediating umpire. Such a man cannot merely announce his decision. He has to bring both parties to the frame of mind in which they prefer to collude rather than to fight: where each believes that a small concession will bring a large advantage, because if they fight they might lose. Such an umpire, *par excellence*, is the man who conceals from one hand what the other is doing: he has, ideally, to convince each side that the other is the stronger, and he may drop pragmatic hints that he can use his own power to ensure that this will be so. This is, indeed, a nice contrast to the role which was first set out: with normative rules the umpire's business is to clarify and find the truth; at the pragmatic level of the present discussion his success depends on no-one knowing what the truth is, but each side believing his (contradictory) versions of the other party's strength. Barth reports that one of the Swat Saints said, 'I look like a simple man; I live simply—but oh! the things I do!' [19]

Many men used to frequent the tea room of the Orissa Legislative Assembly trying, to quote one of them, 'to do business without having any capital'. That is, they try to use their skills as negotiators and communication agents to build up a business which will in the end provide them with capital. This can happen also to the umpire whose initial capital is only his skill and whatever mystical sanctions he can command. From being a mediator, if he is successful, he can become an arbitrator and eventually a leader. The man who emerged as ruler of the Swat valley was a Saint. The dynasty which rules Libya began as members of the religious order of Sanusiya, and acted as mediators between the warring Bedouin tribes of Cyrenaica: in the end they became the focus of Arab opposition to Italian rule.[20] De Gaulle's power was reinforced by his successful arbitration of the Algerian question. Sometimes the evolution is truncated as when a 'compromise' candidate is appointed to high office to hold the ring between powerful contenders and in a short time emerges himself as the most powerful of all: Shastri in India was such a man. The umpire turned leader has assumed a competitive role: he may have rivals within his group and he has competitors who lead other groups. In such a position he can no longer afford to make the maintenance of the rules of political interaction through which he rose to power the sole end of his activities. He must now trim his sails to whatever wind will lead him to resources which will keep his group strong and his leadership secure. He is therefore likely to innovate, if necessary, and to be less concerned about the political structure's definitive rules.

CONCLUSION

From time to time we have had to notice the existence of other arenas: the fact that the competitors must regulate their behaviour in one arena according to their needs in a different arena. But the reverse also applies: some resources gained in one arena may be used to win prizes in another arena. The Bisipara Pans were trying to do just this: to make use of their connections with the Congress party and the Administration to give themselves a better standing in the village arena.

This constitutes the use of a new kind of resource. From the point of view of the arena in which the new resources are employed, an element of uncertainty has been introduced and there is a risk of disorder and breakdown. New (and perhaps controlling) prizes are being offered; new forms of confrontation are being used; messages are being misunderstood; normative agreement and pragmatic collusion are both more difficult to achieve; umpires find their decisions unenforceable perhaps because the value basis of their authority has been undermined. But for leaders or would-be leaders who are quicker than others to perceive what is happening, the same set of circumstances are an opportunity.[21]

In the next chapter we examine one type of this situation: that in which a small hitherto relatively self-contained political arena is being progressively encapsulated within a larger arena.

NOTES

1. This pleasantry of phrasing is taken from the verdict of a coroner's jury on a man drowned in a river '. . . met his death by an Act of God, helped out by the scandalous neglect of the way wardens.'
2. See the discussion earlier on innovation. p. 69.
3. See the discussion in *Southwold*, pp. 6–7 on the size of winning coalitions and the relation this bears to their information of the other side's strength.
4. This conflict is more fully described in *Bailey, F. G.* (1), Chapter XI.
5. This was the name coined by Gandhi in his campaign against untouchability. 'Harijan' was a word of great normative potency in Bisipara since it signified that the Big Battalions were on the side of the untouchables. Among the clean castes the word aroused contempt and fear.
6. This instrument was rare in the hills, although common among the more sophisticated plains people of Orissa. The clean castes did not possess one and its use on this occasion is both a symbol of modernity and a way of putting on dog in front of the clean castes.
7. The affair in the Kond village is described in *Bailey, F. G.* (2), Chapter VI and in *Gluckman* (3), Chapter 3.

8. This procedure is described in *Eimerl and De Vore*, p. 109.
9. The ferocity with which this norm is upheld among Arab peasants even to-day is described in *Cohen, A.*, pp. 135–6.
10. See *Bailey, F. G.* (4).
11. See *Bailey, F. G.* (2), p. 51.
12. For example see *Middleton*, Chapter IV.
13. See *Douglas*.
14. The point is eloquently put in *Fortes and Evans-Pritchard*, Introduction, pp. 16–23.
15. Aitken seems to have played such a role in bringing together Lloyd George, Carson and Bonar Law, none of whom, according to Blake, had much liking for one another when the affair began. By some Aitken was represented as the youthful *eminence grise* behind Asquith's downfall. Blake disagrees—see pp. 299–301 of his book—but seems not to be quite sure. Certainly the message-carrier can be a role of great power: cf. the discussion of mediators p. 141 and of middlemen p. 167 and note 18 to Chapter 8.
16. See *Barth* (2), p. 59.
17. The custom is mentioned in *Macpherson*, p. 66.
18. See the incident of the Pathan Saint who took off his turban described on p. 64.
19. *Barth* (2), p. 98.
20. The story of this dynasty is told in *Evans-Pritchard* (2).
21. See Chapter 9, pp. 216–24.

8

Encapsulated Political Structures

The man who votes may also go to church, may raise a family, and certainly makes a living. There are some cultures where politics, religion, kinship and economics are so closely connected with one another, that the people themselves need only one set of terms to describe social interactions in the different fields. For example, to say that a man is an Untouchable in India's traditional rural caste system is to indicate that he owns no land but works for a master as a labourer, that he is politically dependent upon this master, that he observes certain religious customs and possibly holds the corresponding beliefs which account for his humble status,[1] and finally that he can never be related to his master because they belong to different endogamous castes. In other cultures, like our own, there is a much higher degree of specialization, and what we do in politics may have only a marginal connection with our economic or religious life, if only because all these kinds of activity bring us into contact with different sets of people. Of course, not all modern cultures are like this: in the one-party state the dominant party behaves like a python: it feeds not just on political man but on the whole man seeking to mould his religious beliefs, usually into a secular form that serves the party's ends, organizing the way he shall make a living, and even through the provision of welfare activities and through its educational institutions influencing the form that family life will take.[2] Common to all these forms is the fact that political activity nowhere stands on its own: it exists within an environment of other kinds of social interaction and, indeed, of other constraints and resources which are not themselves social.

These propositions can also be put in structural terms. The

set of rules which regulate political competition must find some adjustment with the sets of rules which regulate economic interaction, family life, religious organization, educational opportunities, and so forth. A set of political rules like the caste system which pragmatically prescribes that leaders shall be both rich and of high ritual status, is in difficulties when, as happened with the Bisipara Pans, some of those who had very low political status nevertheless became rich, and at the same time some of the erstwhile dominant caste became poor. One way to understand a political structure is to analyse the process through which the continuing adjustment between it and its environment takes place. In the case just mentioned, either the rich Untouchables must be made poor again or else the rule disqualifying them from positions of power must be changed: perhaps by removing religious purity as a qualification at all, or perhaps by re-defining the Untouchables as having a special kind of hitherto unrecognized purity. If none of these solutions are taken, then uncertainty and the danger of politics trespassing further into other kinds of social interaction grows to the point where all social life is put in jeopardy.

If we stand inside one political structure, then its environment may include, besides economic, religious and other kinds of structure, other political structures. For example, the structure of parliamentary government in the United Kingdom must find adjustment with a variety of other political structures which exist, so to speak, under its umbrella. It must find adjustment with local government structures and they with it. The same is true of other kinds of structure which are called 'parapolitical':[3] those which exist for other purposes but which also have an internal system of political activity; for example, trade unions, employers' organizations, religious groups and so forth. All these structures exist and possess varying degrees of autonomy within the structure of national government. In the same way the French Government had to find adjustment with the trade unions, the bureaucracy, business interests and the peasants and at least in the early years of the Fourth Republic, its party structure was reasonably successful in this task. Secondly, there are other political structures which exist outside the nation, and are independent of it, but with which it must find some adjustment: these are its competitors and potential competitors, the other nation states. In other words, political structures include a set of rules, both normative and pragmatic, under the general heading of 'foreign policy'. For the Fourth Republic the principal strains came from structures which spanned these two categories, namely the colonial empire. With Tunisia and Morocco it was successful: Mendès-France saved something from the embers of Indo-China: it foundered on the rock of Algeria.

The situation can obviously be very complex. Even in such an apparently simple case as that of the Konds of Orissa, the successful Kond 'politician'—that role had hardly yet become specialized in the eyes of the Konds—must be able to manipulate at least four different sets of political rules: the tribal structure of the Konds; the castelike structure of relationships between himself and his Oriya overlords; the rules of the bureaucracy; and, increasingly, the rules of the modern democracy at the State level, at the newly established level of local self-government, and to a very slight extent at the national level. Whatever person we stand beside—Kond tribesman, Oriya chief, bureaucrat, candidate for election in local councils or State assemblies—he seems not merely Janus-faced, but Hydra-headed as well.

Such a situation can only be understood by abstraction: by taking part of it at a time and blanking out the rest, and then seeing whether the propositions arrived at will suit or must be modified when we look at another part. Anthropologists have concentrated upon small-scale face-to-face political communities, and for that reason we will centre our interest in this chapter upon them: upon small-scale relatively undifferentiated tribal or village structures. Almost without exception today these structures exist within larger encapsulating political structures; these were colonial governments but today are virtually all independent nations.[4] These larger structures are, of course, much more specialized and command much greater political resources than the structures which they enclose. It will be convenient if we refer consistently to the smaller enclosed structure as 'Structure A' and the larger encapsulating structure as 'Structure B' (for a mnemonic: 'B' = 'big').

Another simplification has to be made before we can begin. The arrows of causation between a political structure and its environment point both ways. But, as far as is possible, the encapsulated political structure will be treated as the dependent variable and the environment will be the independent variable. State legislatures, political parties and free elections are inevitably to some extent adjusted and modified in their contact with the political structures of Indian villages: but our attention will be directed mainly towards the modifications which take place in village structures. Furthermore, State institutions have to be modified to fit other variables besides the village political structures: for example, they are different in times of peace and war. But we shall take these variables for granted. In other words we are interested in the effects of change at the State level upon village or tribal political structure. We do not enquire into the causes of changes at the State level, even though some of these will be reactions to peasant or trival behaviour.

In this way we isolate two political structures. There are then two logically separate questions to be asked. Firstly, we compare them to find out how similar or dissimilar they are: secondly, one asks how they intereact with one another.

Some formal differences have already been assumed in the conditions set for conducting this experiment: Structure B disposes of greater political resources than Structure A; it is large-scale where Structure A is small-scale; and it tends to be made up of specialized political roles while the roles of Structure A tend to be undifferentiated (like those outlined above for the traditional caste system). But the formal comparison of the structures includes a comparison of values, which underlie some of the other differences, particularly those of role pattern. These values are highly generalized normative rules about what kinds of honour or prestige a political actor should aim for, and equally generalized guides to the kind of conduct thought proper in the competition. Furthermore, behind these prescriptions lie existential propositions—ideas about human nature and the 'natural' condition of human communities and the relation between man and nature.

For example many peasant ideologies differ fundamentally from modern ideologies about the interaction between men in the context of natural resources, and the degree to which man is in control of these resources. Peasants act as if they believed they were playing a zero-sum game: as if the success of any one competitor could be achieved only by some other person's failure. The amount to be shared out is fixed: if one gets more, then another man must get less. This is not an argument that everyone should have equal amounts; rather it turns out to be an argument in favour of the *status quo*. Any change in relative command over material wealth by definition means that the gainer has inflicted harm upon the loser. This is the reason why spectacular success by one man, when many of those around him have failed, leads to charges of witchcraft or of some secular form of dishonest and anti-social behaviour. There is no room for the non-zero-sum situation: that in which everyone can be the winner, in which everyone by co-operation can become richer.[5]

Such ideas have an obvious significance for planning. The statement of a target of increased wealth is both nonsense and is immoral: nonsense because man does not have that degree of control over productive resources; and immoral because it incites some people to make themselves richer when the only means of doing this are anti-social. To state as the aim of one's political endeavour the goal of an increased standard of living for everyone carries with it, for the peasant, the hint of the charlatan.

These ideas also spill over into leadership. Honour or prestige or wealth or ritual purity are goals culturally understood and accepted by the peasant. Dedicated service to the public weal is not, and when used as an appeal seems like hypocrisy. In other words, the transactional element is much nearer the *normative* surface of public life in peasant societies than in the larger encapsulating structures; pragmatically, one suspects, there is little to choose between them.

On the other hand peasant ideologies also have their moral component: they believe that competition for material and political prizes should remain within bounds. We have remarked on the way in which this is symbolized in the periodical rituals of solidarity and the belief that quarrelling and disharmony can damage health and fertility and prosperity. No matter what goes on in reality, the public life of a peasant community is ideally conducted in the idiom of co-operation: fellow-villagers in India are known as 'village-brothers'; public administration is conducted through consensual procedures which emphasize solidarity rather than through the divisive procedure of majority voting.

An influential and highly articulate group of Indian politicians, most of whom have retired from politics and become philosopher-publicists and social workers, have seized upon this normative rule of consensus in village behaviour, and elevated it into being the supreme value of community life. Their argument is that people who live under the rules of Structure *A*, if left to themselves, co-operate with one another and reach decisions by the method of consensus: but values injected from Structure *B* have destroyed this structure by introducing the notion of competition and the procedure of majority-voting. I have discussed the validity of these ideas elsewhere:[6] here they are cited only as an illustration of a difference in the value-systems between encapsulated and encapsulating structures.

Many more examples of striking differences in world-view, in goals thought desirable, in standards of good and bad conduct and judgements of permissible and impermissible tactics in political competition could be adduced. These differences are important because their effect is that the people who work with the rules of Structure *A* and those who work under Structure *B* have difficulty in understanding what they are each doing and why they are doing it. Since they cannot understand they cannot communicate; insofar as they cannot communicate, if they become involved in a contest their mutual confrontations are likely to be crude and misunderstood and to lead to the over-commitment of resources. In short, differences in culture bring about those conditions of uncertainty which inhibit political competition and cause political fighting. Very often this is to some extent a revolutionary situation: the State is trying to bring about a revolution in the villages, by changing fundamentally the rules which regulate political competition between the villagers.

Now let us look at the variables which govern the adaption of Structure *A* to Structure *B*. Firstly, those in command of Structure *B* have a choice to make in the degree to which they concern themselves with what goes on inside Structure *A*. At one extreme is the situation in which the encapsulation is merely nominal, merely, one might say a matter of geography. The leaders of Structure *B* either cannot or choose not to interfere with Structure A. Their decision will depend on some of those considerations which were discussed earlier under the heading of collusion. They might not have the resources to interfere within the encapsulated structure, even if they wished to do so: or they might not consider it worth their while because the pay-off for successful intervention might exceed the cost of the intervention. In the days of the British empire in India there were large areas in the hills that border Assam and China and Burma which were unadministered, or 'administered' by an occasional para-military tour of inspection.[7] In the 1830s there was a cautious debate in the East India Company about the future administration of the Kond hills.[8] Before that time no-one had been into the hills. When an expedition did penetrate the area, in pursuit of a truant tax-defaulting prince from the plains, they discovered that the Konds indulged themselves in the rites of human sacrifice and practised female infanticide. An invasion and subjugation of the hill peoples was reckoned (correctly, as it transpired) to be expensive: mostly because physical communications were very difficult and because the deadly cerebral malaria (not of course then known as malaria) was endemic in the hills. One side argued that no civilized government could tolerate the practice of human sacrifice on its borders: the other side pointed to the difficulties and cost of an invasion, and made it clear that the return in revenue from a mountainous and unproductive area would not pay for the military operations or for the subsequent administration of the area. In the end morality triumphed over prudence, and the East India Company and its successor triumphed over the Konds (after thirty years of intermittent disorder).

The second possible posture for the leaders of Structure B is the predatory one: they do not concern themselves with what goes on inside Structure A so long as the people who live under it pay the revenue. After the harvest is collected troops of soldiers ride out from the capital and, by threat or by siege, collect what they think is their due. Sometimes this took the form of a transaction: the peasants paid up on the understanding that the ruling power would prevent other powers from sending out similar expeditions. This is a form of relationship between Structure B and Structure A which resembles the protection rackets organized by gangsters.[9]

A less disreputable version of this relationship is achieved when the ruling power adopts what is called 'indirect rule'. Here the policy is founded on an agreement to leave intact the broad structure of A, providing this does not do violence to certain fundamental principles ('natural justice') which are embodied in Structure B. For many years this policy directed British imperial rule (even before the phrase 'indirect rule' came into use). In part this policy may be founded on a moral conviction that people are entitled to their own beliefs and should be allowed, as far as possible, to preserve cherished institutions. But it should also be pointed out that, at least in the short run, indirect rule is cheaper than a radical reorganization of the political structure of A. To reorganize means to create conditions of uncertainty, to risk explosions and to incur for certain the expenditure of resources involved in re-training people, even when this is possible.

The final posture is that in which the ruling power has taken the decision that Structure A must be integrated: which, in practice, means radical change, if not abolition. The basis of such a decision is likely to be compounded of many elements: moral repugnance for what goes on in Structure A is certainly one, often phrased in terms of the removal of iniquitous 'feudal' institutions and their replacement by socialist democratic institutions: allied with this goes another kind of moral attitude, that the people of Structure A should devote their energies to a wider polity than their own parish pump. This is in fact a judgement that the costs of incorporating the personnel of Structure A into Structure B will be more than offset by the resources which they put into Structure B. This posture is adopted by virtually all the developing nations: they seek, with varying degrees of determination and success, to put an end to casteism or communalism or tribalism or regionalism and to make a united nation.[10]

The ambitions and intentions of the rulers of Structure B are one thing: their performance can be quite another and will depend on a number of variables. One of these is the resistance which the people of Structure A wish to offer, and this will depend upon the degree to which they esteem their own political institutions and on the extent to which the values of these institutions differ from the values of Structure B. This is a very simple, but also a crucial proposition: for example, other things being equal, an Islamic central government will have less difficulty in integrating an Islamic peasantry than will be the case if either but not both of the parties are Christian. Secondly, the performance will also vary according to the resources of which the people of Structure *A* dispose. These resources may take many forms: a deeply-valued ideology, perhaps in a religious or ethnic form; an inaccessible terrain, as was the case with the Konds; alliance with outsiders; and so forth.

The success of a plan to integrate smaller structures will also depend upon the resources which the leaders of Structure *B* can put into the struggle, and upon their needs in other arenas. Calls to fight on other fronts may work both ways: difficulties with China and Pakistan made it no easier for the Indian government to suppress the Naga rebellions; but they assist other forms of integration by giving appeals to regionalism or caste interests an air of immorality in the hour of national peril.

To summarize. There are situations in which the encapsulation is merely nominal. Structure *A* has complete autonomy: Structure *B* is totally indifferent to what goes on inside Structure *A* or else, even if concerned, it does not have the available resources to do anything about its concern. In such a situation an incongruity between the values exhibited in the rules of the two structures is of no significance, for the people of the two structures do not interact. Once one begins to consider situations in which interaction does take place, then cultural incongruity is important. To simplify the picture we may put together the two Structure *B* variables, determination to interfere and resources to make interference possible: the severity of the situation for the actors in Structure *A* will then depend on two variables. One is the composite interference variable just formulated (determination plus capability): the other is the degree of incongruity between their own values and procedures measured against the values and procedures of Structure *B*.

This, of course, is playing at quantification. We cannot hope to find numerical ways of expressing these variables. But they do provide a method of at least categorizing examples of the encapsulation situation, and even of suggesting conditions under which certain political roles emerge. Certain styles of the middle-man role, to be discussed later in this chapter, are generated by the degree of incongruity between the values of Structure A and Structure B.

So far we have been standing back like spectators beside a sports field. The larger part of this field is taken up by a contest between teams of adepts, highly specialized, expensively equipped, professional, directed by umpires and utilizing an elaborate repertoire of normative and pragmatic rules in their efforts to win a prize. Around the edges of the field, with make-shift equipment, sometimes without a referee, with small prizes, but also with their own established normative and pragmatic rules of behaviour, are many smaller contests. They are not all playing the same kind of game, and they differ, in varying degrees, from the central dominating contest.

As we watch, two kinds of interaction begin to take place between those in the main arena and those in the smaller peripheral arenas. From time to time a player from the larger arena begins to interfere with one of the smaller arenas: he may simply suggest that there are better ways of playing that game; or he may offer a new kind of prize; he may recruit one or two of the smaller players and bring them to play in the main arena, and then send them back; he may demand that the smaller players all make a contribution to the cost of the main arena; he may insist that they stop playing their kind of game and try to replicate exactly what is being played in the main arena.

The effect of this interference on the smaller arenas varies. Some go on playing their own game with great obstinacy. Others make a pretence of accepting the suggestions but find ways of continuing to do just what they had been doing all the time. Sometimes they are helped to do this by imperfections in the new rules. When local government institutions were first widely introduced into rural India in the 1950s, in some areas the revolutionary potential of universal suffrage was dampened down by the practice of voting by a show of hands. Dominant castes, even if numerically inferior were able to dominate elections because they knew who had disobeyed instructions on how to vote and could punish them.[11] In some arenas one team seizes the opportunities being offered from the main arena much more quickly than the other and starts to win regularly: then the other team also begins to change to the new tactics. Bisipara is beginning to go this way.[12] Sometimes the offer of a new kind of prize makes the smaller teams alter their recruitment rules and they line up in quite a different way: sometimes smaller arenas coalesce to make this possible. Caste associations are a phenomenon of this kind.[13] In many cases the smaller arenas are abandoned and all the players either join in the contest in the main arena as is virtually the case in the village of Mohanpur,[14] or, because they are too old to learn or perhaps have been disqualified by the main umpire for sticking obstinately to the rules of their parochial game, they retire to the side and become spectators.

If one watches long enough then out of the many different ways in which the players are changing their tactics or resisting change a few general patterns emerge: patterns of resistance; patterns of change that come about from seized opportunities; and over all a slow drift towards uniformity, as the minor arenas lose their distinctiveness and become the same as, or one with, the main arena.

To distinguish the different ways in which games are played in the smaller arenas and to codify the rules, especially when the players themselves have not codified them, is task enough. It is, indeed, in general what anthropologists have been doing. To identify the circumstances which decide what kind of game is played in each smaller arena is a second task and a more difficult one: but it is also necessary because from this knowledge one might predict which of the lesser arenas will hold out against the main arena and which will give way.

Now let us change the viewpoint. From outside as a spectator one looks for the grand design, the interplay of forces which in their resultant far transcend the doings of the individual men who together make them up, as the body transcends the cells which compose it. Tribalism gives way to feudalism: and it to socialism. From inside, however, one cannot so clearly see the transcendental pattern. The situation is not one for contemplation: a sense of tragedy is a handicap. There are new ways to win prizes: there are new prizes. Feudalism may be giving way to socialism, but in the meantime who is going to help me get a gun licence: the old chief or the party agent? And how much will he want? I am a loyal subject of the chief of my tribe: but my son wears a bush shirt and respects neither the chief nor me. Yet he is my son. So where does my duty lie? These are the tiny transactions, the minute conflicts of loyalties through which the grand design of change is worked out: they constitute the processes through which the forms of Structure *A* and Structure *B* find conflicting expression. We will shortly look at one such situation: the struggle between the clean castes and the Pans in Bisipara.

The people who live in Structure *A* will find the encapsulation situation more or less severe, depending upon the differences in culture between themselves and the outside power, and depending upon the effort which that power puts into creating a 'grass roots revolution'. In the extreme cases not merely the rules of Structure *A* are abolished, but also the people who followed those rules are exterminated. This has been the fate of some tribes in the South American jungles and for a time once looked like being the fate of North American Indians too: there have been outside powers which have tried to create national uniformity by exterminating those who are different rather than by teaching them new ways. Sometimes this may happen not as the result of any deliberate and malign policy formulated by the leaders of Structure *B*, but as the result of their carelessness or incompetence; helped out—to use a phrase which sets more problems than it solves—by a collective loss of the will to live. Bisipara, at the time of what they called the 'Harijan' affair, was far from this extreme: nevertheless, during the temple dispute, and the affair which arose out of the clash between the old man and the boy and for some time afterwards, there was a feeling both among the clean castes and the Untouchables that the situation was out of control. Resources had been committed of such a kind that once committed they could not be withdrawn or even steered, and the result was a feeling of collective apprehension. The more pragmatic outlook mentioned above had not emerged; and it may be that there is a cycle of moral crisis and pragmatic innovation inherent in the encapsulation situation. At any rate, we shall follow this pattern in our exposition: first the moral crisis; later, in the concluding section, the matter-of-fact pragmatic adaptations which those in the smaller arenas can make.

A MORAL CRISIS

The events which made up this crisis have already been described: the temple dispute; the old man and the boy on the
fieldpath; the cutting off of Pan privileges of music-making and
begging; the voluntary withdrawal by the Pans from their
traditional tasks of scavenging; their change of name and their
parade of reformed custom which removed many of the attributes of their low status; and their determined, if clumsy,
attempt to make use of the Administration and the politicians
to raise their status in the village. The root of these disturbances
is also easily perceived; some Pans had become rich and wanted
to be treated as men of wealth and power.

Merely to be rich will not in itself produce political power.
Some positive act of symbolic conversion of wealth into honour
must be made, and it must be generally acknowledged, not least
by those who already possess honour, that the act of conversion
is legitimate. This, we conjectured, is what the Distillers succeeded in doing: through a series of successful confrontations
wealth was converted into political credit.

The more moderate section of the Pan leaders behaved as if
they thought that this avenue to political advancement was
open to them too. The confrontations which they made were
generalized and of such a kind that they were less likely to
provoke the clean castes into direct retaliation. It was as if they
were searching for a bargaining position through which a compromise, acceptable to both sides, could be reached. To give up
or discourage drunkenness, to build their own temple and to
take on other signs of Hindu respectability, even perhaps to
refuse any longer to rid the village of its dead cattle are acts
which put the ball, so to speak, in the other court. To that
extent they are a challenge and a confrontation. On the other
hand the challenge is a 'creeping' one: the confrontation is made
in a form which does not offer to the opponent a clear point at
which he must draw the line. The clean castes were like an army
retreating towards a river over a flat and featureless plain: short
of the river there is no obvious feature at which they can make
up their minds to take a stand. Up to this point neither side has
lost its head, nor feels that the situation has got out of control.
Indeed, the clean castes riposte in an appropriately controlled

fashion by forbidding the use of Pans in music-making and employing other Untouchables, but carefully refraining from interfering with the employment of Pans as daily labourers.

In point of time mild subversive redeployment of political resources came after the indecisive direct confrontation occasioned by the Pan attempt to get into the temple. This was led by a more militant section of the Pans, who differed from Pan moderates in two ways: firstly they employed direct confrontations; secondly they were ready to call into the arena new kinds of political resource.

In the model constructed to explain how the Distillers made their way up the ladder of caste there were also direct confrontations provoking encounters. Indeed, a game without encounters is necessarily a game without winners or losers: moreover, in a 'league-table' sequence such as is involved in caste-climbing, encounters are necessary to mark off the positions (the political credit) of each of the competitors at the beginning of an episode. In the caste-climbing competition a direct confrontation is made when the challenger goes beyond the parading of attributes and demands to interact with his opponent in a way which will validate his claim to the attributes of purity.

Even within this category of direct encounter there is a range of choice between actions which resemble generalized confrontations insofar as the challenged party is left uncertain just where to make a stand and those which unambiguously put him with his back against the river and give no choice but to fight or acknowledge defeat. Interactions, for example, with a Brahmin vary in the degree to which they bestow honorific status on the receiver. One service which the Brahmin gives is to make a horoscope. He gets a fee for this, and he will do the job for anyone of any caste providing they pay the fee: this includes Untouchables. But even in this almost pure transaction there is a symbolic vestige in that the price charged rises for customers from lower castes, perhaps to compensate the Brahmin for the risk of contagion. This apart, the interaction is completely sterile, so to speak: when a Pan employs a Brahmin to make a horoscope this could not be interpreted as a confrontation, let alone a decisive confrontation. From this level there stretches up a graded series of confrontations, each more decisive than the last. To give up drink is a mild challenge; to refuse to cart away dead cattle is more direct, but did not in fact provoke anything more than a mild retaliation; but to claim to go into the temple constituted the directest of confrontations, and could only end in victory or defeat, because the clean castes had no choice but to acquiesce or resist.[15]

The temple confrontation was especially decisive because of its comprehensiveness: all the clean castes were involved, for they all stood to lose if the Pans were successful. This is not like an attempt to subvert a relatively humble member of the caste hierarchy, like the Washerman, and to subvert him alone: it is like driving in the thick end of the wedge. The attempt was bound to fail because the Pans had not accumulated sufficient political credit (in the symbolic form of purity) to bring them within reach of success.

Up to this point the competition is a moral one (a matter of principle), but it is still a competition: it is not yet a fight. Both sides are following the accepted pragmatic rules of caste-climbing. They agree on the definition of what constitute the prizes in this arena: namely honour as symbolized by the deferential services of the village specialists, access to wells and temples and other places of ritual purity, and such symbolic interactions as those involved in commensality. Both sides agree that economic resources can be converted into political credit through the symbols and symbolic interactions just listed. Where they disagree is in the personnel rules: the clean castes implicitly were saying that the political credit (i.e. purity-rating) of the Untouchables was so low that they had no right even to be in the arena as competitors.

It might be argued that this last point of disagreement is a moral one, in that the clean castes did not have a price and were not open to bargaining. One might envisage them saying that no Untouchable, however rich, was entitled to compete for honour; that this was a matter of principle and could not become the subject of a bargain. In other words the gap between Untouchables and clean castes might be one of those definitive rules which are considered by the actors to lie at the heart of the village political structure.

But it is difficult to be sure of this. Firstly, as was pointed out earlier, the Pans as a whole may not have been rich enough to climb up the ladder which the Distillers had used. A few Pans were very rich but only a few; and these were encumbered with a long tail of poor relations whom they would have had to carry with them. Secondly, it may be that the length of time over which I observed the process was too short for Pans to be accepted as clean castes. One might have drawn similar pessimistic conclusions about the chances of the Distillers improving their position in the caste table, had one been in the village at the turn of the century. Moreover there is circumstantial evidence both from this and other parts of India which indicate that barriers of Untouchability have been crossed: for example the Kuli caste of Weavers in Bisipara are reckoned among the clean castes while fifty miles to the north, in the area from which their ancestors came to Bisipara, they are considered Untouchables. Thirdly, even in Bisipara the clean castes do not make a stand on the principles of Untouchability when they have to deal with Untouchables who command very great pragmatic power (through having power in Structure B): the occasional official who is an Untouchable, the touring Ministers of Government, and clerks and policemen are not treated as Untouchables, even when the villagers well know that they are.

Therefore it is possible that given time and sufficient wealth among the Pans, the clean castes might have ceased to condemn Pan candidates for honour and prestige in the village arena purely on the grounds of principle and might have adopted a more pragmatic transactional outlook in the affair. But, as things turned out, the Pans themselves—I think unwittingly— caused a sudden escalation and drove the clean castes into seeing the whole affair as one of principle on which they must take a stand or fall. This escalation was occasioned by the Pans making use of outside (Structure B) resources in an attempt to gain prizes in the village arena.

The normative rules of the village political structure are not designed to regulate contests between castes. Rather they seem to envisage a contest of the *doladoli* type between descent groups or factionally modified descent groups within the dominant caste. The model of Distiller caste-climbing suggests that those normative rules became pragmatically extended to include the conflict between castes involved in caste-climbing. The extension consisted of a tacit admission that men of other caste beside the dominant one were eligible to compete for honour as defined by the ritual usages of village Hinduism. In the first stages of the contest between clean castes and Pans, when the situation was still under control, the issue was whether or not there should be a further pragmatic extension of personnel rules, allowing the Untouchables also to compete for honour. But before this issue had time to work itself towards a solution, the Pans broke another—and quite explicit rule—of the village political structure: that one should not make use of political structures outside the village in order to gain one's end inside the village arena.

The village council used to record its decisions in writing, especially if it was suspected that some of those who had given their agreement during the debate would later retreat. When the decision was to penalize an offender, even he was expected to agree and sometimes made to sign his name or make his mark at the end of the document. Partly this is a manifestation of that deeply rooted tradition, mentioned above, of reaching decisions by the method of consensus: partly it is done in the knowledge that there are often no effective sanctions with which to compel the reluctant, and one at least would have a signature to brandish at them while making accusations of bad faith. But it is also clear that the written document is drawn up with one eye on the controlling judicial institutions which exist outside the village. Villagers, in Bisipara at least, only very occasionally take one another to court: there are sometimes rumours that an aggrieved litigant is planning to sue the village council, but this has not happened in Bisipara. It has happened in other villages in the area, and there are other areas where the government courts provide a regular weapon for villagers intent on harassing one another. Bisipara villagers are acutely aware of the possibility of an appeal to political and judicial power outside the village, and they preface the record of any decision with a statement that the verdict was reached by everyone in common, and accepted by everyone, and that if any person makes an appeal to the government courts, he hereby agrees to pay a fine of Rs. 25 (roughly a month's wages for a labourer) to the village funds. In other words, there is a very strong feeling that to take disputes outside is to initiate that type of non-zero-sum game in which everyone is the loser.

The Pans too see the world outside in this way. Their everyday contacts with the local agents of government contradict the normative tenderness for them and for the tribal peoples which is written into the official policy. On the police crime map in the district headquarters the Bisipara Pans were, at the time when I saw it, represented by a very large black spot. They are a bye-word for rascality, and have been so in the minds of officials ever since the area was administered. Consequently, to under-state the position, Pans do not find their interactions with the official world any less painful than do their clean caste fellow villagers.

One wonders then why, if the Pans too thought that to start this game would make everyone the loser, they nevertheless called for the police and officials and doggedly recalled them, again and again, when they were not satisfied. One explanation might be that they had come to that point, not unknown among contestants, of saying that if they could not win, no-one would win. I doubt this: it is true that like the clean castes the whole affair set them in a panic, but not, I am quite sure, to the extent of contemplating self-destruction. Some of them may have felt at the beginning, and certainly they came later to feel that they had less to lose than the clean castes through govern-ment intervention, although they knew that neither side would find such intervention pleasant. In the event they were right: the long series of judicial setbacks did, as I shall show later, constitute a victory for the Pans.

There were two clear reasons why it made sense for the Pans to call in official support. The Congress government, and to a less extent their British predecessors, had been intent upon improving the political and social standing of the Untouchables. When the Bisipara Pans demanded to enter the temple, they were able to point to a law which made it illegal to keep Hindus out of temples on the grounds of untouchability. There was a continuous propaganda against untouchability and this was becoming increasingly effective. From time to time a social worker came to the village and spoke of the evils of untouch-ability and—with more effect—of the legal penalties for dis-criminating against a man as an untouchable. Clean caste villagers thought of this man as a regular member of the adminis-trative services, referring to him as the 'Harijan Inspector'. They were also convinced that if they were caught discriminating they would suffer a fine of Rs. 500 and six months in jail. They associated Harijan welfare with the Congress government, and, small wonder, voted with the opposition Ganatantra Parishad, almost to a man. All this gave the Pans a clear incentive to make use of outside resources to beat down their own clean castes, although they knew that the local officials, the junior ones at least, would not implement the Government's intentions with much enthusiasm.

The second reason for the Pans calling in help from outside was that in the rules of political competition in that outside world (Structure *B*) caste did not constitute a qualification which a man required before he could seek political prizes. I do not think that they began by saying to themselves: 'If we enter that arena, our Pan status will be no handicap'. They had no intention of withdrawing from Structure *A* and trying their luck in Structure *B* at the time when first they called in the police. All that they could see was a resource in the environment, available to them and not available to the clean castes. But later some of them became drawn into Structure *B*, a point to which I shall return in a moment.

From the point of view of the clean castes, to call in outside aid especially in the form of the police was an entirely illicit move, an indication of Pan depravity and in effect a declaration that this was total war with no limits on the kind of weapons used. It was like that moment during the battle of France in World War II when people in Britain stopped talking about the 'phoney' war, and the facetious language of sport in which operations had hitherto been described fell out of use, and there was a sudden heightening of all the emotions and an unbridled use of the language of hatred and of love. (Even then, it must be added, neither side in Bisipara kept up this feeling long enough to let it interfere with the serious business of getting the fields cultivated.)

What counter-moves were open to the clean castes? There were no practical steps which they could take to cut off Pan access to the new resource. It is true that they could and did state their case and win it several times over before the procession of visiting enquirers. But there was nothing they could do to prevent the general support which Pans received from Congress policies, beyond the ineffective step of voting against the

Congress at the next election. Nor was there an umpire, accept-able both to themselves and the Pans, who might intervene and say that new resources should not be used in village politics. The officials themselves were a kind of umpire, and they did in effect say that they were not going to interfere: but they could hardly declare themselves normatively disqualified from regulat-ing village politics, which is what the clean castes wanted, and, had they been skilfully manipulated, they would have had to enforce Pan access to the village temple. The only other umpire might have been the village council, but this, since it excluded Untouchables, was already committed as a council of war for the clean caste group.

The clean castes were able to counter in two ways. Firstly, they were able to withhold the prize. This amounts to more than the fact that they prevented the Pans from entering the temple. They continued to withhold all the other normative symbols of caste status. No specialists served the Pans; the commensal restrictions were still observed; people were less blatant in avoiding physical contact with Pans, but nonetheless, they continued to avoid it. It is interesting that the Pans themselves co-operated to the extent that none of them forced an actual violation of these rules. Nothing could have been easier than to rush into the temple or the meeting house, to take water from the clean caste well, or deliberately to lay hands upon a clean caste person. The consequences would have been immediate violence; but I do not think the Pans feared this. Rather they held back because the tactic would have been ineffective: the prize is not to get into the temple, or to sit in the meeting house, or to touch a clean caste person but rather to have the right to do all these things acknowledged by the clean castes. To steal an article gives one possession of it, but not ownership. In short, since there is no neutral umpire formally allocating the prize, the clean castes can hold on to the symbols of their own superior-ity until they have to concede defeat or until the attackers give up the attempt: there is no formal way of shortening the contest. This is another sign that we are dealing here more with a fight than with a competition.

The Harijan affair was, of course, both a fight and a competi-tion. There were several restraints, voluntarily observed, especially the tacit agreement not to let the quarrel interfere with making a living. There was also, however, a clear indication not only that this was a conflict about the rules of the game, but also that the clean castes were from time to time being compelled to acknowledge that the rules had changed. Despite, from their point of view, the gross unfairness of using external political resources, they were themselves forced to adopt the same tactics. They could not find a counterforce to put against what they saw as Congress support for the Untouchables: no rival political party would, openly at least, espouse caste discrimination. But the clean castes did prepare an adequate defence against the charges brought before the enquiring officials. Moreover, in 1955, after their vindication in the final enquiry by the Magistrate, they were upset by rumours that the Pans were about to institute civil proceedings and at once set about raising money to find a lawyer who would protect their interests.

They also began to find ways of counting the score in this modified version of the village political structure. I visited the village again in 1959 and my visit happened to coincide with a festival which involved some children's sports. When I had watched this festival in 1953 and 1955, the organizers came from the clean castes: the Pans sat apart and Pan children were allowed to compete after the clean caste children had finished. In 1959 the organizer was a Pan, an ex-policeman and an unsuccessful candidate for a seat in the Orissa Legislative Assembly. A very few young clean caste children took part: the rest were Pan youths. All the audience were Pans with the exception of myself and the village postmaster, on whose veranda we were sitting. I asked him why things were so changed. He said that they (the clean castes) had decided to do without the sports that year, because they didn't want any trouble with the Pans: but the Pans had gone ahead and held the sports, and in their usual place, the street of the Warriors. The postmaster added, bitterly: 'They are the kings now. We are the subjects.'

This incident seemed to indicate that the clean castes were by then virtually bankrupt of political resources, with which they might reassert their control of the village political arena. In effect they had decided to avoid an encounter by not advancing: and were then humiliated by being forced to retreat. Yet the Pans did not press home their attacks. They told me they now had access to the temple. But by 1959 this prize and other similar parochial gains had begun to seem to their more aggressive leaders less important. How did this come about?

The contest was joined in the first place because the Pans accepted the rules of Structure *A* for the definition of political prizes: that is to say, they wanted themselves recognized as a respectable caste no longer tainted with the impurity that had made them untouchable. They could not accept the personnel rules, which would have excluded them from the competition; and they broke one of the 'control' rules by getting aid from outside. But to accept aid is to put oneself under an obligation to the giver. In effect it means to enter another arena and give some of one's resources to a team in that arena. A few Pans actually joined the Congress, one of them becoming a candidate for the Assembly, and many of them voting Congress. The prizes in this arena are defined in quite a different way from the honour-purity symbols of Structure *A*: they consist of being elected to office, and together with this normative prize goes legitimate access to a wide variety of pragmatic prizes—expense accounts, patronage, salaries and so forth.

Those who had caught a sight of these prizes put a lower value on the right to enter the village temple. They also began to feel themselves in a different world from their fellow-villagers who had not, so to speak, seen the promised land. Such an experience changes one's ideas. The Pan who organized the children's sports was not merely cocking a snook at the local self-styled establishment: he was doing what every other man with ambitions to run for office does—hoping to gather a few votes by demonstrating his selflessness and public spirit.

Such a man has put himself outside the structure of village politics. Its prize rules no longer direct his ambitions. Its personnel rules, which bar him from the arena, are no longer relevant because he no longer wants the prize offered in that arena. At first he did want the prize, and for that reason he invoked resources forbidden by the rules of Structure *A*. But now there are both bigger prizes outside the village, and with the new local government institutions being set up, there are also new kinds of prize, for which he as a Pan has a normative right to compete, inside the village.

The final stage in this process will be reached when clean caste men too turn their ambitions outward and find it advantageous to ally themselves with those very Pans who in the village were their enemies.

To summarize. Bisipara's 'Harijan case', as the clean caste villagers call it, is a tea-cup affair. As history, it is nothing: but it has its value as a microcosm in which can be seen some of the political processes which occur in arenas of all sizes from the tea-cup to the ocean. Resources are built up and a decision is taken to commit them to political action. This can be done by a generalized display of symbols which are accepted as indicators of political credit. With varying degrees of subtlety those symbols can be used to challenge competitors. Sometimes these challenges are so delivered that the opponent is thrown off balance and finds it hard to know where and when to make a stand, because none of the encroachments seem enough to justify his committing himself to action. But sooner or later one side is manoeuvred into drawing a line (or itself decides that it will be good tactics to be seen to have reached the point of intransigence) and then an encounter takes place and the relative credit position of each of the competitors is made clear.

'Burning the bridges' (the act of committing oneself to a position from which there can be no retreat) may be a ploy or, if seriously meant, marks the beginning of 'unrealistic' conflict,[16] in the sense that the conflict is now a matter of principle and the contestants have no common ground to use as the basis of a bargain. This may occur as a result of one competitor patently cheating, and driving the other to proclaim that such fundamental values are now at stake that no holds can be barred. In other words, an appeal to principles and morality may be the outcome of panic and uncertainty: the competitor who thinks he has the situation under control will try to keep a bargaining position open. In a situation of encapsulation the use of external resources will be defined as cheating, when the values of the external world contradict those of the encapsulated arena.

The men of Bisipara used external resources in a fumbling uncertain way, and as a result gave themselves much anxiety. Other encapsulated arenas produce roles which serve to regulate the flow of external political resources into the encapsulated arenas. These are the middlemen to be considered in the next section.

MIDDLEMEN

Middlemen, in the situation of encapsulation, are roles which come into existence to bridge a gap in communications between the larger and the smaller structures. The role can take many forms. Sometimes it is consciously created by the larger structure to meet its own deficiencies: the 'ombudsman' is an example. Sometimes it comes into being as a pragmatic addition to a normative role in the larger structure: the District Commissioner in a colonial regime or in any authoritarian bureaucracy may find himself shielding his people from the cold wind of central directives and covertly modifying orders, which if literally applied without regard to local conditions would cause great hardship.[17] The stock in trade of the local politician is the work he does to see that the wishes of his electorate are brought to the notice of the central authorities. Other middlemen spring up from below and carve out roles for themselves, beginning perhaps as mere messengers and ending in some instances as leaders directing and controlling the processes by which Structure *A* is integrated into Structure *B*.

Not all these roles which exist at the point of contact between two structures are to be considered middlemen. The local leader who fights resolutely and single-mindedly for local autonomy is not a middleman: nor is the bureaucrat who intends to and who is able to wipe out the local structure. The essence of the role is to keep a foot in both camps. His interest is to keep going a process of bargaining: either in what he does or in what he says, or both, he must persuade the two sides that this is a situation in which compromise can be made. He must convince them that they are not engaged in pure conflict, but that they have interests in common and that if they keep their eyes upon these interests, both can, to some degree, emerge from the contest as winners. In other words, he has to demonstrate that this is a non-zero-sum game.

The difficulties (and opportunities) of such a role will clearly vary with the gap between the two structures. This gap can be seen at two logically different levels. First the two structures may diverge radically in their cultural base: neither side may understand the other, in extreme cases being reluctant even to see the other side as human beings—a situation in which extermination may be regarded as the best solution by the stronger power and feared by the weaker as the likeliest outcome. Secondly, and independently of the degree of mutual comprehension, there may be a radical divergence of cultural values. Each side knows full well and accurately what the other stands for, and is thereby moved to contempt and hatred. Logically this situation can exist: but, as everyone knows, the effort to understand often leads to empathy and a willingness to see something good at least in the people if not in their political and social structure. This has very often happened with colonial administrators, bringing them to the paradoxical situation of preferring the 'noble savage' to the 'educated nigger', the latter being, incidentally, very often a middleman.

The middleman's difficulties are compounded because very often he is unable to make a normative justification of his activities. The success of a middleman's role, like that of the mediator,[18] as we saw earlier, can depend upon his ability to deceive: to misrepresent the strength and the intentions of both sides to each other. If he is found out, he loses credit. Even if he is not found out, he cannot conceal the fact that his purpose is to work for a compromise and to prove that neither side is as depraved as the other side thinks. He must always, therefore, be regarded with suspicion and contempt by those who have made an ideological commitment to their own cause. If he springs from below, from the lesser structure, then he runs the risk of being branded a renegade: from the other side he may be regarded as a spy, or as a traitor by those who like their savages noble, or—most commonly—as an unprincipled man on the make. In fact, as we shall see, he often is a man on the make.

One should not be deceived by the parade of normative respectability which most middlemen find it necessary to mount. Sometimes this emerges as a vague and generalized statement about doing good for everyone. Sometimes the normative statements accurately reflect quite sincere convictions that mutual understanding will bring mutual accommodation: that Indian village communities can be the basis of the Indian nation: that what is good for General Motors is also good for America. But even such people as Gandhi could not but incur the occasional contemptuous accusations of duplicity—both from the British and from, for example, Dr Ambedkar.[19] Indeed, suspicion of deviousness, if not deceitful activity, is inherent in the middle-man's role, for while it exists to make communications between opponents, its strength depends upon keeping this communication imperfect. Perfect communication will mean that the middleman is out of a job: it may also mean that there is no room for those 'white lies' which formerly deterred the contestants from all-out conflict.

It should be made clear that we are saying that middlemen incur opprobrium: not that they deserve it. Whether they do or not depends upon the way one values Structure A against Structure B. In any case, whatever their intentions, the effect of middlemen's actions may work either for or against integration. Perhaps the only general statement that can be made about what middlemen do is that their activities tend to confuse planned integration or planned resistance to integration and to promote the solution which is got by 'muddling through': bargains and compromises, rather than outright victories for one side or the other.

At first sight it may seem strange that the encapsulation situation is an occasion for mediating at all: by definition Structure B commands vastly greater political resources than Structure A. How, then, can there be room for middlemen? Bargains can be made only when both sides are strong. The answer of course is that Structure B is faced with many Structure As, that it has other arenas in which its resources are required, and that it may be inhibited from imposing its will by force through moral scruples. Another way of looking at this situation is to notice that Bisipara does not enter into a contest with the central government at Delhi; contact is with officials and politicians in the local district headquarters and, for a variety of reasons, only a fraction of the force at the disposal of Structure B can be focused through these persons. It is even possible for villagers to play off the local officials and politicians against their own superiors:[20] in the more orderly intervals of colonial rule to call in the military to keep order was taken as a clear sign of administrative incompetence. One way or another the encapsulation contest is brought to obeying that universal law of political competition: contestants must not be grossly mismatched. Hence there is room for compromises and room for middlemen.

The simplest form of this role is that of the pure messenger. When they are negotiating a marriage, the people of Bisipara use a go-between: in this way they avoid committing themselves in the early stages and neither party risks the humiliation and loss of face and the implied challenge (confrontation) which a rejection might otherwise bring about. Many negotiations, in all walks of life, open with private enquiries about how requests would be received rather than with the public transmission of the requests themselves.

The early reports sent back by the commanders of expeditions into the Kond hills in the first half of the nineteenth century spoke of their contacts being arranged by a tribal official called the 'Digaloo'. The language of the Kond hills was—and still is—Kui, a dialect belonging to the Dravidian language family of South India. On the plains of Orissa people speak Oriya, which belongs to the Sanscritic northern group. The interpreters through whom the East India Company's employees worked spoke Oriya and depended upon finding bilingual contacts among the Konds. There had been Oriya colonies in the hills for several centuries and many of the Konds must have been bilingual: but they had formalized their contacts with Oriya settlers and traders by using an interpreter, whose role was to save the Konds from direct contact with outsiders. This man was the 'Digaloo' and he was invariably an Untouchable, 'Digal' being a common lineage name among Kui-speaking untouchables. Contemporary accounts interpret this custom in the idiom of Hindu concepts of pollution, saying that the Konds were anxious to preserve themselves from contact with outsiders; there are, indeed signs that Konds had a very high opinion of themselves before the British Administration broke them. The custom may also indicate the common idea that messages delivered by very humble persons cannot be construed as challenges (except in special circumstances). At the very least, the use of such an intermediary is a hint that the frequency of interaction is to be kept low.

Middlemen tend to take the form of messengers when the local community (that which afterwards becomes the encapsulated community) has a high degree of autonomy and makes little use of political resources from the world outside. In this situation there is likely to be complete ignorance of the way of

life of the outsiders and a tendency to look upon them either as
not entirely human, or, if men, a different kind of men, so
different that they do not merit consideration as moral beings.
No interaction with them is possible on a moral basis (that is, on
a basis of shared values) and the only possible or desirable contact is through occasional transactions. Hence people like Untouchables, who themselves are at the margins of one's own
moral community, come to be used as messengers: it takes a dog
or a devil to communicate with foreign dogs or foreign devils
and the Konds certainly looked upon their Untouchables in this
light.

For the dog, the situation is not without compensation. The
literature on the Kond hills, almost up to the present day, is full
of outrage and indignation at the way in which Kui Pans cheat
their 'masters', the Konds. The same is true of other tribal areas.
The mistaken high status attributed to the 'Digaloos' was not,
pragmatically speaking, so wide of the mark: in practice they
could not fail to find opportunities for profit, either material or
political, in the Kond refusal to engage themselves directly with
outsiders.

The normative status given to middlemen is indeed an index
of the degree to which the value systems concerned are closed:
that is, are not shared by the two structures. The middleman is
despised in proportion to the disparity of the two cultures. His
pragmatic status is equally an index of the frequency and intensity of interaction between the two cultures, so long as this
interaction remains short of all-out conflict. This can be illustrated by moving from the Kond 'Digaloo' bridging a gap between disparate cultures, and one across which relatively little
interaction took place, to the village broker in Bisipara.

The gap which this broker bridges has already been described.
The peasants must make frequent, if often reluctant, use of
external resources provided by the bureaucracy and they must
observe the rules laid down by that bureaucracy. Their right
to land is validated no longer by belonging to a clan or a caste or
by giving allegiance to a Hindu chieftain but by an entry in the
Record of Rights and by being able to talk successfully to the
clerks in the Revenue department and to the Revenue Inspec-
tors. They must pay taxes; they must observe the law; they
need licences; they can get, sometimes, loans of money to im-

prove cultivation; their children sometimes go to schools; they patronize markets run by the government; they vote; they listen to propaganda; almost every aspect of their lives is touched by the larger society around them. Nevertheless they look upon this outside world with apprehension and they do not accord moral status to its agents: cheating an official is not cheating in the same way as defrauding a fellow villager would be. Equally while only a fool does not watch his step while dealing with fellow-villagers, even with his own brother, yet there are known limits beyond which these people will not go; their ways, even when they are being dishonest, are at least predictable. In other words, interactions with fellow villagers, even transactions, are ultimately controlled by a recognition of common values: an acceptance that the other man is, after all, a man like oneself. But this is not so with outsiders: they are not men like oneself: the degree of shared, and therefore controlling, values is slight. It is a world of danger and uncertainty.

From the other end, that of the agent of government, the picture is not so very different, except that apprehension tends to be replaced by contempt and exasperation at one's own incapacity to get a message across into their thick heads, so to speak. There is the same unwillingness to regard the other party as a man like oneself and I heard one official, to the great embarrassment of his colleagues who were present, say: 'Men I can lead. Animals like those villagers I must drive.' Even the politicians, who most often want only a simple thing like the vote, are very conscious of their own inability to make effective contact with their electorate, although they will more often blame the lack of technical means of communication than the disparity of values embodied in Structures *A* and *B* respectively.

Such a situation, in which interaction must take place through voluntary acts (the peasant must *agree* to give his vote, the clerk *agrees* to issue the licence, and so forth) and in which neither side can communicate sufficiently to be sure that the other side even knows what is required, let alone can be persuaded to do it, is made for the middleman. He is needed by both sides, and both of them know it and pay him, directly or indirectly for his services. In this situation he is not entirely any more the long spoon that the wise man uses to sup with devils: he is the spoon without which a man cannot eat at all. There is

I suppose, a vestige of the face-saving job done by the Digaloo: there are times when the middleman goes to humble places and stoops to do things which his employer in Structure *B* either would not like to do or would not like to be seen doing. But in this situation, in contrast to the Kond Digaloo, the village broker is providing a service that is more a technical than a symbolic necessity. The Kond a century and a half ago would have lost face by negotiating himself with foreigners: but no peasant would feel himself degraded if he could get a gun licence on his own behalf, without going through a broker: he simply does not know how to do it.

Bisipara's broker is still despised—and by those at both ends of his transactions. His fellow-villagers think of him as a liar and a cheat and a hypocrite, a man who has made a fortune (albeit a modest one) out of their predicaments with the administrators, a renegade who pretends to serve his fellow villagers but in fact serves no-one but himself. Officials and politicians see him as a villager with ambitions far above his education and his abilities, an unreliable man, at the behest of the highest bidder and hypocritical in his protestations of concern for the public interest. It may therefore seem odd to argue, as I am about to do, that such a man is well poised to become a leader in the process of encapsulation. Bisipara's broker has tried, and his success has been very modest indeed; but in the next generation there may well be leaders who take off from the position established by him and by some of the Untouchable leaders discussed earlier in this chapter.

The first point to notice is that while the broker is himself vilified, and while the partners linked by his transactions despise one another, the interaction itself is not condemned on moral grounds. It is wrong to appeal to the police against your fellow villagers: but it is not shameful to buy improved seed from the Government farm, to get a gun licence, to buy from a government-run co-operative, to send a letter through the post-office, to make one's children go to school, and so forth. All these actions may be perilous, and the sensible peasant always looks carefully for the snag, but to refuse these interactions on moral grounds would be thought peculiar: like having a conscientious objection to putting up one's umbrella when it rains. In short, while the peasants of Bisipara still have a deeply felt normative sense of their own difference from the officials and other outsiders and of the malevolence of foreigners, and while this feeling still inhibits the growth of that trust which is necessary for a moral relationship, yet they have lived long enough with the outside world, and have been compelled to interact with it on sufficient occasions, for them to begin to ask themselves what is the most effective way of managing this interaction. In other words the 'unrealistic' posture of conflict—that of total moral commitment to a principle, at whatever cost—is giving way to a more pragmatic bargaining posture, which entails some recognition, however grudging, that some values are shared with the other side, and that these values may be used as a basis to make concessions oneself and so bring the other side to make concessions. Another way of looking at this is to say that what is usually done comes to be accepted as the normal thing to do, and in time the normal thing becomes the right thing. Continued pragmatic interactions, other things being equal, begin to achieve normative status.

Even without this development, a middleman is well positioned to build himself a team by transactional means, if, for whatever reason, he has some degree of monopoly of resources which are available from the outside world. We have already touched upon this phenomenon in several situations. Such a man may become the leader of a 'faction' with a heterogeneous following of men whom the traditionalists style 'self-interested' but who may turn out to be the van of some new kind of team which in the end achieves moral standing. Such a man may also be one among several transactional leaders whose interactions constitute a period of experiment and confusion as people learn to make use of new kinds of political resource. One or several of the 'factions' may grow large enough for specialized roles to emerge within it, thus stabilizing the faction with a professional ethic and sometimes equipping it with an ideology and, in either or both ways, providing a core to the group.[21]

This has not happened yet in Bisipara. Their broker stood for the State Assembly, but got no support from his own village. His role remains purely transactional, and even at that level hardly developed enough for him to be able to field a team. The villagers, however, elected him chairman of the new village panchayat, believing that these new bodies were meant to provide spoils for the village, and he was the best equipped to know how to handle the officials who provided the spoils: at the end of a year they had already decided that he had done nothing for the village and would not get their votes again.

There are special conditions in Bisipara which inhibit the evolution of their middleman into a leader. The frequency of interaction between the villagers and the world outside is still low compared to that found in other areas of India and the interaction is itself encumbered by moral ambivalence, as the 'Harijan' dispute demonstrates. Secondly, the village is divided over the parochial issue of caste and does not have its eye sufficiently set upon the changes offered by the world outside to make them value the kind of leader who can effectively tap those resources. Thirdly, it may be that their particular middleman is not very good at his job.

Where conditions are right for the middleman to evolve into a leader (or, as may happen, for a local leader to take on middleman roles by tapping into external political resources) his position changes according to the manners in which the villagers themselves operate in Structure *B*, as independent agents or as a body. At one extreme everything which the villagers know of the world outside, every contact which they have with it, is mediated through their leader. This is the situation of encapsulation proper, and one of the leader's functions is to preserve Structure *A* by controlling its contacts with the world outside. He regulates both the use which the village can make of resources in Structure *B* and the use which Structure *B* leaders can make of the village as a political resource for use in their own arena.[22] This is the situation which obtained in places like Bisipara in the earlier years of British rule, after the disorders. In effect, it is the situation of indirect rule, in which the administrators, so to speak, allow the indigenous chieftains to keep their 'fiefs' so long as there is no disorder and so long as the revenue is paid.

This state of affairs can be changed in two ways. Firstly the monopoly of communication enjoyed by the middleman-leader may break down, because his subjects learn to make their own connections, as has been happening to some extent in Bisipara. Secondly, the controlling power may itself decide that they will no longer tolerate the existence of structures of the *A* type and that the whole country must be 'modernized'. This too is happening in Bisipara. When both these events take place then the situation of encapsulation has given way to integration and the local community has ceased to be an important arena for the people who live there. In such a situation there can still be roles specialized in communication between the elite and the mass of people they govern, but they do not bridge such vast discontinuities as to deserve being called 'middlemen': nor—and this too perhaps should be a defining characteristic of a middleman in situations of encapsulation—are they regulating (whether knowingly or not) the process by which when Structure *A* comes into contact with Structure *B*, common values are brought into the open and what might have been a conflict is kept down to the level of competition.

ENCAPSULATION AND CHANGE

The encapsulation situations described in this chapter happen also to be situations of change. Change is a form of contest, but not everyone agrees that situations of change are also contests. Especially when the contest is between the representatives of a Structure *A* and a Structure *B*, the latter's leaders often try to obscure contradictions by announcing that what they are doing is in everyone's interest (the clichés of democracy are especially useful for this purpose) and that anyone who opposes them is acting against his own interest.[23] The same bias appears in studies done by sociologists hired by management to tell them how to keep the workers happy.[24] Obviously neither the opposition between management and labour or between a reluctant peasantry (Structure *A*) and a modernizing elite (Structure *B*) are situations of pure conflict. Both sides stand to gain by co-operation at least by not allowing their differences to become a war to the death, if not in more positive ways. Yet, it should be stressed, this at the same time looks to the competitors like a zero-sum game for while co-operation may produce bigger profits, the question of how the profits are to be shared still remains. Both sides may be hurt by strikes or lock-outs, but when the time comes to split the spoils, the side which cannot back its demands with a realistic threat to strike (or lock-out as the case may be) is at a disadvantage.

The loud insistence that modernizing measures are for the good of those modernized, even if they suffer temporary discomforts, is the less convincing to peasants because the promised return on the transaction must often be indirect. To pay one's tax is an act of personal and immediate deprivation: the return of a made-up road or efficient policing is much less personal and apparent, especially if the road goes to another man's village and the police are used to provide a ceremonial guard at the Governor's mansion. The fact that next round our village may get a road or that life would be intolerable without the police, seems a distant and academic point, and the tax-payment like a forced loan with little hope of return. Consequently peasants find it much easier to see this as a pure-conflict situation, their own losses being the other side's gain.[25]

The contradiction inherent in this situation is the more obvious when things go wrong; when the whole concern makes a loss, so to speak. When the dam for which the peasants have paid half the cost by giving their labour bursts, or when the improved seed which they have been persuaded to buy from the Government farm fails, the peasants are convinced that they were right to have been suspicious and wrong in co-operating at all.[26] In the same situation the modernizers are tempted to gloss over the technical short-comings of their own plans and to personalize the situation and make it into a contest by looking for scapegoats. They change their order of priorities and decide that before they can improve productivity they must eliminate the headman or wipe out the kulaks: sometimes they may be right in this judgement, for their failures may have been the result of what they think of as sabotage and the other side regards as legitimate resistance to protect its own interests.

It may also happen that the modernizing elite starts right in with these aims, being convinced by its own ideology that nothing can be done until the 'political kingdom' is secured: in other words, until those who support other kinds of rules for controlling political competition have been eliminated, or, if not the men, until the roles have been eliminated.

Sometimes the modernizing elite may wade in regardless of the consequences and the cost. If they do pause first and appraise the situation, there are several kinds of question to be asked. Let us suppose that they suspect that the institution of hereditary headmanship is the obstacle to progress. First they should make sure that it is in fact this institution which is standing in the way of productivity or national unity or whatever is their declared aim. Secondly there are some simple calculations about the size of the task: for example, is there one headman or are there four hundred? Thirdly just what rights and duties are comprised in a headmanship, for without knowing this one may not be able to work out what will be the consequences of removing headmen.[27] Fourthly, and following from the third task, what other roles are functionally linked with the headman's role? By removing each headman will one also upset the lives of several hundred functionaries now employed by him? Fifthly is the role of headman one which his subjects see as a value in itself, a symbol perhaps of their own collective identity or of some fundamental religious value? Or do they have towards that role a transactional attitude, which would allow them to transfer their interactions to some other role which they believed would do the job just as well or perhaps better.

All these are general considerations and could be allowed for in making a plan for the abolition of the headmanship. But, inasmuch as this can only be accomplished by a successful contest with all the headmen concerned, those who are asked to implement such a plan must ask another set of questions about particular headmen and about the resources which they can deploy in the contest. The headman who is imbecile or stupid or impoverished or who has set everyone about the ears—the man whose political credit is low—is more easily shifted than the man who is rich and popular and a personal friend of the Chief Minister. The latter headman too can be dethroned but a different set of moves will have to be used than in the case of the nonentity. In other words headmen will each individually have other roles, and the same assessment of the political potential of these will have to be made as was made for the headmanship role itself.

These contests with individual headmen are not independent of one another. If the man known to be the most formidable of the headmen is made to tumble first, then lesser men will tumble the more easily: if he wins his round, then lesser men will be that much more strengthened. It may seem more politic to take on the smaller adversaries first and follow the pattern of the league table or the caste-climbing game accumulating sufficient political credit to challenge the biggest in the field.

The contests, whether with big or small men, will exhibit most of the features of a competitive arena: subversion, confrontation, collusion, encounter and so forth. But there is one important difference. By definition contests about change belong at that end of the continuum where uncertainty prevails. There is likely to be a wide measure of disagreement about the normative rules. The point at which a contestant finds he has exhausted the latitude he allows himself for bargaining is the more quickly reached, for what is at stake is a normative rule which will be a matter of principle and not a matter to be bargained over at all. The Orissa princes bargained with Patel in 1947 and their capitulation was quite swift: they agreed to their own effective abolition, while retaining titles for themselves and keeping certain minor privileges which they had held as princes and receiving a pension which would prevent too drastic a change in their standard of living. Those to whom I talked ten years later were very quick to point out the normative basis for their action: they capitulated partly for the general good of India, and to try to save their subjects from the consequences of resistance: indeed three of them each opened his account of these events with the proud claim that he had been the first to 'accede to the Indian Union'.[28] Perhaps, given such resources as the Nizam of Hyderabad possessed, they would have been less ready to bargain. Whatever the case, they certainly saw the events of 1947 as quite different from, for example, their own dynastic quarrels, which caused princes to be dethroned from time to time. These dynastic intrigues took place with the British courts poised to intervene as umpires. But in 1947 the princes must have been acutely conscious that the same force which held the ring earlier was now ranged entirely with their opponents: therefore, as is the case in a fight as distinct from a competition, the stronger team made the rules.

There is a second reason why contests which involve change bring uncertainty at least when they first occur. The hints and signals which convey messages about relative strength or about willingness to bargain are more likely to be misread than in such institutionalized arenas as *doladoli*. The Orissa princes had never faced such a situation before: nor, indeed, had the new Government of India. The princes did not know how much force the Indian Government would use, nor, indeed, given the disorders rampant in India at that time, how much it could use. Just before Indian independence came about the princely states of Orissa, southern Bengal and Chattisgarh tried to form an Eastern States Union, in the hope of being a constituent state in the new India, and such a unit, had it been formed, would have been a more formidable opponent than the individual princes, divided among themselves, proved to be.[29] (Some of the princes did join the Congress, and I was told that many more would have liked to join, had not the Orissa Congress suddenly become afraid of alienating its own supporters by admitting erstwhile enemies. The Congress, in other words, probably read offers of capitulation and co-operation as a takeover bid.)[30]

Again, it is in the interest of both sides to stiffen their own supporters by claiming that bargaining is impossible because the opponent is too depraved to keep his word, and by inventing, if necessary, horror stories about the other side's intentions. In *doladoli* no-one could make any headway with a story that the other group planned to burn their opponents' houses and rape their women. It would sound as absurd as a rumour that Labour supporters planned to violate Conservative women or vice-versa. But stories of this kind are not so readily disbelieved in cities where race riots take place. Nor would they have seemed fanciful in India in 1947.

The uncertainty arises because neither team is sure what the the other can do and how it will act. There are reforms in India— like the attempt to abolish the role of the broker and so eliminate corruption, or to eliminate bootleggers in dry areas—which have run into the sand so often that the contest is conducted with a gentlemanly restraint and a wealth of pragmatic bargaining which outshines even *doladoli*. Perhaps the best example of change-contests becoming routinized are the several non-violent protests through which Indians sought to gain Independence. Still in 1959 some agitators considered it only fair—and sensible —to let the police know where and when they proposed to break the law.

But even in these routinized change-contests, because prin-ciples are held to the front, there is a readiness to withdraw recognition of one's opponents' moral status and hit below the belt, pushing back the threshold where bargaining is possible by accusations of 'police provocation' or 'foreign-inspired agitation'. There is, I suppose, a tendency to simplify a contest situation and to pretend—or to believe—that a man who does not share *all* your own principles cannot share *any* principle with you, or perhaps if he does not share your most cherished principles, he cannot be acknowledged to have any principles. How can you, as a believer, enter into a bargain with and so trust a man who announces that God does not exist? The same declaration (that one is not open to compromise) is found when people say: 'The only good X is a dead X,' and mean it.

CONCLUSION

The difficulty that faces encapsulated political structures is the difficulty that faces all political structures: how to maintain themselves by finding adjustment with a changed environment. From the point of view of the people whose political competition is regulated by the structure, their difficulty is how to keep political competition within bounds and to see that it does not wreck other structures of social interaction on which their survival depends.

The chances of a particular political structure and the values upon which it is based surviving can be increased under certain conditions by commitment: by nailing one's moral flag to the mast and proclaiming that the position will be defended to the last man and the last round. But such an act is only effective when the defiance is backed by command of adequate resources and when the opponent can read the message and be deterred by it: defiance will not stop the tide coming in.

If the opponent cannot read the message, or is not impressed, then the chances of keeping a check on the resources spent in political contests are increased by middlemen and by a pragmatic willingness to ditch principles, to deplore moral enthusiasm and see it as fanaticism, and to bargain and seek for compromise. Structures may go to the wall, but people survive.

The sudden introduction of new resources into a political arena may lead to uncertainty and to crisis, and this in turn makes the actors shout defiance and numbs their perceptions of reality with an overdose of principles. But, to echo a phrase, some of the people can be fanatics all of the time, and all of the people can be fanatics some of the time, but all of the people do not behave like fanatics all of the time. If they did there could not be political competition, only fights, which would in the end leave the field empty of players.

NOTES

1. As is well known the myths of classical Hinduism account for a man's status in his present life by his conduct in his previous incarnation. To act well in this life is to be born to a higher status in the next: low status now is a penalty for misbehaviour in the last existence. Misbehaviour is defined as conduct not suited to one's status. Thus, for a low caste man to behave like a Brahmin is to run the risk of yet lower status on the next re-incarnation. Such a myth has obvious relevance to a highly-stratified polity.

   But many of the villagers of Bisipara had never heard the myth: and those who knew it seemed to me to regulate their conduct to it in much the same way as a non-reflective person in Britain consciously behaves himself in order to make it into heaven and avoid hell.
2. An introduction to party structures is given in *Duverger*.
3. I have taken this term from *Easton* (2), p. 52. For my own part, I find it easier to recognize politics as an aspect of interaction at all levels—even the family; what goes on in Ivy Compton Burnet's novels seems to me political. To recognize only one level, or even to focus strongly upon it, is to be ethnocentric and, more importantly, to waste opportunities for comparative insight.
4. A good introductory book to this field of enquiry written from a sociological point of view is that of *Mair*.
5. See *Bailey, F. G.* (7). For the point about witchcraft see *Gluckman* (1), Chapter IV.
6. See *Bailey, F. G.* (6). The most eloquent exponent of these ideas is *Narayan*: see his booklet. A sympathetic opinion on this is given in *Tinker*, p. 194. For a brief but effective criticism see *Morris-Jones* (1).
7. A vivid—and to my knowledge unique—account of one of these expeditions is given in *Fürer-Haimendorf*.
8. Parts of this debate are available in *Selection from the Records*—see references under that title.
9. A seemingly milder form of this is described by *Whyte*, pp. 123–141, in his book about an Italian locality in an American city. The racket was based upon the 'Numbers' a form of illegal

gambling on horse-racing. This required an elaborate organization of collectors and could not easily be kept concealed from the police. Life was made easier for the local policeman, providing he left the 'Numbers' alone, both by small gifts and by helping him out in his police duties. Among other things, he was expected to keep other policemen from butting in.

10. See *Mair*, Chapter 4.
11. Notice that such intimidation could be given a normative cover under the guise of consensus. In some states of India consensus was officially encouraged by giving a *per capita* financial reward for uncontested (i.e. consensual) elections. As *Morris-Jones* (1), says, in such conditions consensus must sometimes have been a fair name for very ugly proceedings.
12. See p. 164.
13. Traditional castes (*jatis*) are relatively small groups of people who intermarry. Many of them are culturally similar to one another: for example, they may practise the same traditional occupation, occupy similar positions in the local caste hierarchy, and even have the same name. But they did not interact with one another and, even where interaction would have been geographically possible, they often were hostile and took care to maintain social distance by denigrating one another.

In some areas of India, from about the 1880s onwards, such groups united and formed themselves into associations with the stated objectives of improving their status both in the religious scale of Hinduism and in the secular world of business, politics and the professions. They became, as it were, pressure groups and it was in their interest to recruit as widely as possible.

Clearly such associations are teams designed for combat in a new arena. The village and the local hierarchy of *jatis* have been abandoned in favour of an arena which is the state or linguistic region.

For a fuller exposition see *Bailey, F. G.* (5).
14. See *Bailey, F. G.* (4), Chapter 2.
15. There have been some examples of this situation already. The message, carried by Bonar Law to Asquith, that the Unionist Ministers would resign if he did not, compelled action. In the same way Lloyd George, once his resignation had been accepted, had to fight or give in: there was no further room for confrontational manoeuvres. The leaders of the Fourth Republic drifted into this situation over Algeria. They, neglecting earlier opportunities of negotiation and other tactics, found themselves with only the option of fighting: it was left to de Gaulle to open up the option of a political settlement.
16. The term is taken from *Coser*, pp. 48ff. Through Coser's book runs a distinction between realistic and non-realistic conflict. The former is conflict rationally directed towards some object, and it is possible that the object might be obtained through

negotiation and agreement and therefore without conflict. The latter is conflict begun to relieve tensions and stresses in one of the contestants: it is therefore rationally 'aimless': it can be diverted only by being turned onto some other victim.

I cannot comment on the idea of 'venting aggression' since this belongs to a field different from that which I am investigating and one in which I am not competent. For me the interest is in the way in which the distinction can be used as a normative gambit. Your opponent can be stigmatized as someone working off his aggressions, and the fact that there is a real bone of contention, an objective and real grievance, may be concealed. Such an argument *ad hominem*, whether it concerns aggressiveness or ambition, is mostly beside the point: Lloyd George's ambitions do not prove or disprove the charge of inefficiency against Asquith.

I cannot, however, resist adding—with the timidity appropriate to an amateur—that to grab for a principle and take a moral stance and refuse compromise or negotiation looks to me like an action which belongs in the same pigeonhole as non-realistic conflict. It is, of course, realistic if the contender is merely using the principle as a normative theme and as a bargaining counter.

17. I owe this to a contribution made to a Wenner-Gren symposium by Max Gluckman in the summer of 1966. See *Gluckman* (4).

18. I am reluctant to use the terms 'middleman' and 'mediator' interchangeably. The latter is primarily a person helping to settle a dispute: the former is a person who assists in communication and this is obviously the more comprehensive term. A middleman, therefore, may also as in the context of the present discussion, act as a mediator. Aitken, therefore, was primarily a middleman, easing communication between Carson, Lloyd George and Bonar Law, but with a tinge of the mediator in that he was hoping to resolve their mutual antipathies. See also note 15 to chapter 7.

19. Dr Ambedkar, a distinguished statesman and himself an Untouchable was an All-India leader of an Untouchable organization, the Scheduled Castes Federation. I heard him in a broadcast, following a number of people who had described Gandhi as a 'saint', say sharply, 'He was no saint: he was a rascal . . .', an epithet which in India does not have the slightly indulgent connotation it has acquired in Britain.

20. There was an example of this in the Kondmals in the first decade of this century. The Sub-Division Officer, a man called Ollenbach, was trying, with the help of some missionaries, to get prohibition introduced. The system of licensed stills was demoralizing the Konds and impoverishing them, while lining the pockets of the Distillers, who monopolized the licences. The latter mounted a vigorous campaign against Ollenbach, impugning him on every count, including his morals: it seems that but for the intervention of missionaries in Calcutta, the Distillers

might have won the day. Ollenbach was a remarkable man who ruled the Kondmals like a prince for twenty years, who spoke Kui, danced the Kui dances, sang their songs and belonged with them as no other European ever did.

The story is briefly told by *Alderson*, who, like Ollenbach, was an SDO in the Kondmals.

21. A detailed analysis of the development of factions within the Congress party of Uttar Pradesh by Bruce Graham suggested this point to me. See *Graham* (3).

22. For the description of such a man in an Indian village see *Beals*, pp. 58–63.

23. This is the situation of unrealistic conflict. See note 16 above.

24. The example of management-labour relations occurs both in *Coser*, p. 24, and in *Mills*, pp. 92ff.

25. See *Bailey, F. G.* (7).

26. Both these disasters occurred in Bisipara. See *Bailey, F. G.* (1), pp. 252–3.

27. I was told (by a politician) that when *zemindari* (the landlord system) was abolished, many peasants were in doubt whether or not they had benefited. Since one official replaced many landlords, at the very least they had further to go to pay their rent. Landlords, too, were a source of ready money for loans and some of them provided relatively informal and inexpensive judicial services for their tenants. See *Bailey, F. G.* (4), pp. 193ff.

28. A little of this story is told in *Bailey, F. G.* (4), pp. 177–81. For a description of the integration of Princely India into the Indian Union, see *Lumby*, Chapter VI.

29. For a description of this 'conspiracy' from the point of view of the Orissa Government, see *Mahtab* (ed.), vol. V, pp. 113–39.

30. See *Bailey, F. G.* (4), p. 211.

9
Change

When, in the 1830s, the servants of the East India Company first learned that the tribes who lived in the Kond hills practised human sacrifice ('meriah') and female infanticide, they were outraged (normatively) at this affront to natural justice, but disinclined (pragmatically) to meet the expense of forcing the Konds to behave in a naturally just fashion. Expeditions sent into the hills were decimated by cerebral malaria and occasionally sniped at by Kond bowmen. But once involved, the Company found it difficult to withdraw and the Meriah Wars, as they came to be called, continued for about twenty years until in the 1850s a regular, if rather patchy, civil administration was established.

Once the Company had launched itself upon a campaign of pacification, another debate arose about how best to bring the Konds to heel. One school of thought, led by a man called Campbell[1]—a soldier in charge of operations in the Meriah Agency—advocated a frontal attack upon Kond society and Kond values. Konds were very elusive and vanished into the jungle as soon as troops appeared. Campbell's method of bringing civilization was to hang the aged and infirm, who could not run fast enough, and to burn the crops and houses. The rival opinion, held by another soldier, Macpherson, whom Campbell replaced, was that such brutal measures were both immoral and impractical and that the area could be pacified more economically by an adroit use of the political structure of the Konds. Kond clans were in a continual state of feud with one another. Macpherson believed that if the Company's servants could act as mediators between clans, they would come to be accepted by the Konds as benefactors, and would become influential enough to put an end to human sacrifice and female infanticide. In the event a policy based more upon brutality than finesse was adopted both before and after the administration was formally established. Until about 1880 the structure of Kond society continued to be dismantled, whenever the administrators had a whim and the opportunity to dismantle it.

In the terminology used in this book Campbell and Macpherson and the Company represent a Structure B, here considered as an independent variable and a 'rival' political structure in the environment of Structure A, the Kond tribal political structure. (We ignore the resident Oriyas.[2]) The courses of action advocated by Campbell and Macpherson stand for two extremes in the possible relationships between Structure B, and Structure A: a totally destructive attack upon everything in sight, as against the manipulation of a single crucial variable in the hope that this change will in turn change other variables, and, so to speak, the structure's own energy may be used to bring about its own reform, or even its own destruction.

It is in this sense that knowledge is power. The man who correctly understands how a particular structure works can prevent it from working or make it work differently with much less effort than a man who does not know these things. If you know how an internal combustion engine works, a spoonful of sugar, or a cup of water, or a potato can be used to immobilize a motorcar. Indian agitators whom I knew planned exactly where and when to employ their limited resources to encompass maximum disruption.[3] The man who understands the working of any organization or institution can find out which roles are crucial to the maintenance of those structures, and among these roles which are the most vulnerable. The point is very obvious and would not be worth making, were there not evidence from all around that actions are often taken without previous analysis and out of ignorance. This is true of community development projects, of attempts to 'modernize' political and social systems, even of new universities or of the construction of new courses within universities.[4]

This story of the extension of British imperial rule into the Kond Hills will be used, together with other examples, to formulate questions which can be asked about political change, and to discuss some of the difficulties which arise out of those questions. The situation is one in which principles come into conflict: in which the contestants cannot agree about the rules of the game and do not so much compete for agreed prizes, as fight about what will be the rules of political competition in the future. This more distant perspective shows, in the example just given, three different sets of rules for ordering political competition in the Kond hills. The Konds have their own system of feuding between clans, which are teams recruited through descent and territorial affiliation. Macpherson's plan would have been to provide umpires who would regulate this competition, thus creating a kind of indirect rule adapted to a society without strong chieftains. Campbell advocated direct and forceful rule.

These were the three types of 'game' suggested for politics in the Kond Hills in the first half of the nineteenth century. But, at a second level of enquiry, each game has a particular advocate, and one can envisage the whole process as a contest between the different advocates. Thus, while changes in the end may often be the result of forces beyond the control or the intentions of any particular man, it is still possible to identify an area in which men are aware of what is happening and are able to gain partial control over events by intelligent anticipation and by manipulation. Furthermore the concepts used for the study of competition (in which notionally at least there is no disagreement about the rules of the game being played) can be used: subversion, confrontation, encounter, collusion, and so forth.

The analysis of this book is based upon a simple classification of political contests. At one extreme are those contests which are completely under control insofar as the possibility of escalation is remote: social resources are used to keep the competition going, but there is no danger of this use becoming excessive and so preventing the carrying out of other necessary social tasks. *Doladoli*, at least as it appeared in the 1950s in Bisipara, comes near to this kind of political contest. Such politics are in effect a kind of game, and this represents one end of a continuum. Other kinds of contest are plotted further along the line of the continuum according as the chances of escalation increases. This happens when new kinds of resources are brought into use, for one reason because uncertainty about how best to use them causes them to be used prodigally, and invites prodigal counteraction, and so on until the point of explosion is reached. In Bisipara the Pan dispute represents this end of the continuum: so too, for the French Fourth Republic, did the Algerian affair.

Another criterion for placing a particular contest along this line which stretches between stability and explosion, is to estimate the ratio of normative to pragmatic rules used in regulating the contest. Pragmatic rules govern the use of resources which have not yet been formally and publicly accepted as proper to be used in that arena. As their use becomes more widespread, more blatant and obtrusive, so the point of crisis approaches, when either they must be normatively legitimized or suppressed. Each course of action is likely to have its partisans and so a fight ensues. Hence the ratio of normative to pragmatic rules can be taken as an indicator of potential instability. The ratio is not, of course, the *cause* of this instability: it is a sign only. The cause is a maladjustment between the normative structure and its environment.

This chapter is about that end of the continuum at which the dangers of escalation are greatest. It should be emphasized, however, that these contests are still on the same continuum which includes the perfectly ordered and controlled political 'game'. We are not going beyond the end of the continuum and asking: What happens when total breakdown occurs, when there is an explosion, when there are absolutely no holds barred? Rather we ask about how, even at this extremity, the contest is kept within bounds and how one set of rules for regulating political competition can give way to another set of rules, without entailing total breakdown. It would, of course, be foolish to pretend that one can fix upon a definition of 'total breakdown' good for all situations: nor is it necessary to find such a definition. If, even in the most bitterly fought civil war, men are able still to get food and other necessities for themselves and their families, and to reproduce themselves, then to that extent the war has been kept in bounds: one may then ask what these bounds are and how they are maintained. In other words, so long as life continues, no matter how nasty, brutish and short that life is, there must be rules regulating political contests. This does not, of course, necessarily mean that the contestants observe rules of fair play (although even in the most savage wars there may be some normative restraint): but it does mean that they share to some degree at least a common language of confrontation and an ability to predict what the other man *can* do with the political resources at his disposal, even if they cannot foretell exactly what he *will* do. It is, perhaps, a matter of constraint rather than restraint.

Out of this minimal degree of shared perceptions comes the possibility of compromise and bargaining, from which may emerge a new kind of political structure.

ENVIRONMENT AND LIMITED CHANGE

The seeds of change lie in the environment of a political structure. New resources may become available for use in political competition and the rules may not give sufficient guidance for their use. It may also happen that resources for the use of which there are adequate rules are no longer available and so drive people to extemporize and cast about them for substitutes. The political structure of the Konds could operate, as was described earlier, only if the ratio of people to land was suitable. There were normative rules of adoption and of fictive clan brotherhood which allowed for local discrepancies in this balance of land to people to be adjusted.[5] But, as was noticed, even with these adjustment mechanisms, the Kond political structure could not have survived an overall increase of population, assuming, of course, no changes in the techniques of producing food from the land available. The structure depended upon adequate adjustment to a demographic variable in its environment.

When the British invaded the Kond Hills and eventually brought the inhabitants to heel they altered the environments of the different political structures, which existed there, in several ways. Their arrival made possible new kinds of Kond local community, for land came to be bought and sold, and title to occupation could be validated by the British administrators and did not any longer require the underpinning of Kond usages of clan brotherhood and Kond mystical beliefs about the Earth. Increased interaction with outsiders must have given the Kond Pans ('Digaloos') a less humble position than before, although no evidence has survived from the early days to make us sure of this. It is more certain that the Oriya chieftains of settlements like Bisipara, just because they spoke Oriya and understood the ways of the new administrators better than did the Konds, gained a new degree of power over the Konds and became able to treat as subjects men whom formerly they would have considered allies.[6] Later the colonial ideology of 'fair play' which meant that the innocent, if savage, tribals must be protected from the wily Hindus reversed this process, although not very effectively.

Other changes were less directly political. By unwittingly giving the Distillers a monopoly of the drink trade, the Administration made available new resources for village politics and brought about the pragmatic adjustment to the village political structure which allowed the Distillers to convert some of their wealth to honour and prestige. Again, when the area was pacified trade increased and eventually even some of the Pans benefited: with this new-found wealth and with wealth got from jobs reserved for them as under-privileged persons the Pans were able to mount their challenge to the rules which had formerly regulated political competition in the village. This process was helped out by yet another change in the environment: Gandhi's campaign against untouchability.

It is clear from this that the term 'environment' is defined very widely: it may mean a new law, a new ideology, an increase or decrease in population, a plague, a new technique of cultivation, a tender-hearted or a rigid administrator, or many other things, singly or in combination with one another. In effect, the environment is defined as everything which is not part of that particular political structure. Therefore the possibilities of disturbing influences are immense and the chances of a stable political structure existing would seem remote.

In fact, of course, a political structure is not at the mercy of every change in the environment. Some environmental changes prove irrelevant to the political structure: others are, so to speak, anticipated by the structure, which itself contains rules excluding personnel of certain categories or certain resources from the political arena. Moreover, as we noted earlier, every political structure has sets of rules for dealing with recurrent crises; rules for succession; the reading of the Riot Act; the declaration of martial law; coalition governments in war-time; and so forth.

Even in the case of encapsulated political structures the crises are not so frequent as would seem likely from a survey of formal contradictions between Structure A and Structure B. For example, in the Pan dispute there is an obvious contradiction between the personnel rules of Structures A and B: in the former a Pan is disqualified from seeking political honours; in the latter, caste is not considered a qualification for entering the political arena. The prizes, too, are differently defined: Structure A concerns access to temples and various other indicators of ritual purity; Structure B is concerned with the choice of people to fill specialized power roles—chairmen of councils, members of assemblies and the various positions of command in the administrative services. For all these roles caste purity is explicitly *not* a criterion of choice and penalties are prescribed for those who make use of caste prejudices in elections.[7]

These contradictory rules were points at issue in the dispute outlined in the preceding chapter. But when one makes a further examination of the two sets of rules, there are other formal contradictions which in fact had not become an issue in Bisipara, although it is possible that they may do so in the future. The status given to women is a good example. So far as the villagers are concerned, the civic status of women, even perhaps their social status, is marginal. In common with many peasant and primitive people the world over, women belong in the home and are not considered fit to play an active part in public life: sometimes they are considered positively irresponsible and there are many symbolic observances behind which one can detect the theme that women are a source of danger to society, a temptation to evil and anti-social behaviour.[8] Women are excluded from the competition for honour in the village political structure: they should not hold land; they have no seat on the village council; and a woman's honour is not her own responsibility, but that of the man who is her guardian. But in the normative rules of Structure B sex is not used as a qualification for political activity. Women may vote and they may seek office no less than men. Yet, in the event, this formal contradiction over the status of women between Structures A and B did not become an issue in Bisipara. The formal contradiction between the two structures was not translated into an empirical contradiction.

It is then necessary to explain why some formal contradictions emerge in action and others do not: or, to put the point more generally, why some environmental changes call for a reaction from the political structure and others do not. At both levels one finds that there are pragmatic rules which serve to insulate the political structure, or, if they do not insulate, they prescribe the appropriate adjustment. It was a pragmatic rule of the latter kind which allowed, we conjectured, the Distillers to convert their wealth into political status. Also in this category are the rules in this country which allow interest groups of all kinds to keep their end up in Parliament and in the bureaucracy, although they have no formal representation in either institution.[9] As for peasant women in India, although normatively included in the arena governed by the rules of Structure *B*, they are pragmatically excluded by the rule that those who wish to enter the competition must have the resources to do so. The great majority of peasant women do not have such resources, and even as voters they often turn out to be dependents of their husbands.[10] Until they acquire such resources—management of property, control of dependents and above all education—the formal contradiction of their roles in Structures *A* and *B* cannot emerge in action.

The general point which emerges from this discussion is that while political structures are connected with an environment and must continually find adjustment with that environment, there is nevertheless a discontinuity inasmuch as *not* every change in the environment feeds back onto the structure. One might, of course, recognize this fact by defining the environment more narrowly, as consisting only of those variables which do in fact impinge upon a political structure. But the wider definition is preferable because it draws our attention to the possibility of new variables coming to affect the structure, and it makes it easier for us to notice formal contradictions which are not empirically realized, as in the case of the political status of women in Bisipara.

REPETITIVE CHANGE

Political structures survive because they need not be affected by every change in their environment. They may also be maintained because they are able to cope with disturbances in the environment without changing their own form. This is done by means of rules designed to redress the balance and to restore equilibrium. This phenomenon has been noticed again and again in the course of the book, especially in the discussion of the role of umpires and of other institutionalized devices for the control of deviants. We return to it again, for the last time, to prepare the ground for a discussion of what is meant by other kinds of political change.

A disturbance from the environment becomes manifested in behaviour when someone either cannot or will not fulfil the obligations expected of him in a particular role. The mechanisms of social control, by which deviants are brought into line, are discussed in other places in this book. In this section we will look rather at those situations in which roles cannot be performed for reasons other than the incumbent's indiscipline. One occasion on which this occurs is when the incumbent of the role dies.

Every social structure has to be equipped with rules to deal with personnel changes. People are born and they die, and they grow out of some roles and into others. Therefore every society has rules about which groups the newly-born will be enrolled into, about who will succeed to particular statuses when the incumbent dies or moves out, and about who will take over the property (and the attached obligations) of a dead man. These are, respectively, the rules of descent, succession and inheritance. The passage of people through these roles is called variously social circulation, dynamics or repetitive change. These rules can be regarded as devices to ensure that an environmental disturbance (e.g. the removal of personnel through death) does not break down the social structure. When an umpire dies, a swift, agreed and unambiguous method of naming his successor is required to prevent the game turning into a free-for-all. Kingdoms which do not have such explicit rules for nominating the heir pay the penalty in succession wars.[11]

But this is too simply put. As written, the description takes in only two kinds of situation: kingly rule, then succession (whether by war or not), then kingly rule, then succession and so on; more generally put, normality is broken by crisis, which brings in redressive institutions which restore normality and so on. But if one examines the process more carefully, the clear distinction between normality and crisis is not so easily made. One normative rule for domestic life in many parts of rural India is the patrilineal joint family, which should consist of a man and his wife, his grown sons and their wives and children, his unmarried sons and daughters, and perhaps various family retainers. This is the equilibrium position, so to speak. When the old man dies, the eldest son will step into his place and there are various rituals in the funeral ceremony which symbolize this rule of succession. The father's death constitutes the disturbance, which is controlled by rules of succession and inheritance so as to bring back the equilibrium of joint-family living.

But if one looks at actual families, the norm is seldom realized. Actual families seem to be 'incomplete' by the normative standards of jointness, or sometimes 'overcomplete'. They may contain widowed or divorced daughters of the family: one or both of the old parents may be missing; there may be only man and wife and minor children; or a widow with children, and so forth. In other words, the simple monolithic version of what constitutes the equilibrium position has vanished and in its place appear a variety of forms which eventually sort themselves out as stages in a cyclical process through which joint families break up into nuclear families, some of which will pass through various stages until they are themselves joint families.[12] In short, the idea of a static position of equilibrium is replaced by the idea of a cyclical process, which from the point of view of an individual family is just like the passage of an individual man from birth to death.

This cycle constitutes repetitive change. But while in one sense everything is changing, in another sense everything is the same. A man moves through the seven stages of life, and from his point of view, life is ever-changing. But, seen from outside, there are always the same seven stages through which men travel. An analogous pattern appears in a league table: teams may go up and down but there are always the twenty-two positions from the top to the bottom. It is this larger framework which constitutes the equilibrium: in our terminology this is the structure which is being maintained in the face of environmental disturbances: and, in the usual sense of the word change (the the introduction of something novel), developmental cycles and repetitive change in general are models which tell us how structures do *not* change in spite of changes in their environment.

Another kind of cyclical change is suggested by Leach in his book *Political Systems of Highland Burma*.[13] He describes an oscillation between two 'models' (sc. 'political structures'). One model is the feudal Shan state, with specialized political roles, concentration of power, elaborately marked rank differences, and so forth. The other is the Kachin model of, roughly speaking, an egalitarian society achieving what order it can through the balance of force between opposed groups; not unlike the Kond tribal society. The reality of political behaviour, however, lies between these extremes. A leader builds and schemes towards creating for himself a feudal kingdom: but in the process of doing this, the nearer he gets to the mark the more difficult the process becomes—like climbing a greasy pole. Eventually the princedom breaks apart and the political structure moves back towards leaderless egalitarian opposed groups. Then the process begins again. A similar pattern of events has been described earlier in the discussion of transactional groups and the necessary limitations upon their size.

Leach has certainly described two structures which are rivals to one another. He is not, like his anthropological predecessors, concerned with the maintenance of a single internally consistent structure in the face of environmental disturbance. But, although these are rival political structures, they are not envisaged in the same way that we have set up Structure *A* and Structure *B*. These suggest change. But Leach has outlined an equilibrium system, an endless cycle of opposites like the light and dark phases of the moon. Nothing appears to be cumulative in the political systems of Highland Burma.

Like the earlier example of the bureaucratic cycle of pragmatic slackness stopped by a reassertion of the rules of normative impersonality, these examples show structures maintaining a pattern, albeit a complicated pattern of process, in spite of changes in the environment. In the next section we begin to look at the possibility of the environment, so to speak, winning in a small way and causing the structure to adapt itself.

ADAPTIVE CHANGE

A political structure is in a process of constant adjustment with its environment, and to a change in the environment it has four ways of responding. The first is that no response may be called for, since the structure is, so to speak, insulated from that part of its environment. The second response, which we have just discussed, is to bring into play redressive rules which restore

equilibrium and these rules allow the structure to persist unchanged in spite of disturbances in its environment. The third
outcome, now to be considered, is that the environmental disturbance may modify the rules which make up the political
structure. In a later section we discuss radical change.

When surveying actual events, it is seldom possible to be sure
which kind of change is under way. While one may reasonably
expect that highly routinized repetitive changes, like those
which follow on a death or retirement of the holder of an office
in a stable society, will be that kind of change and nothing more,
it is only after the event that one is able to distinguish adaptive
from radical change.

The theoretical distinctions are easier to make. Repetitive
change is quite without a cumulative element: that is to say,
so far as the rules and roles are concerned there is a complete
return to the *status quo*. In radical change there is no such
return, because the normative rules which give shape to the
system have been abandoned in favour of a different set of
normative rules. Adaptive change comes in between these two
extremes. Those normative rules which are felt by the actors
to be definitive of the system are preserved: but the pragmatic
rules by which these normative rules found adjustment with
their environment are changed, because the environment has
changed. The structure does not move back to the *status quo*:
it has found a new level of pragmatic adjustment with its environment, without, however, altering its definitive values. The
progress of the Distillers up Bisipara's caste hierarchy is an
example of adaptive change.

For a more complicated example of adaptive change we will
take the structure of French politics between the end of World
War II and the elections of 1951. During this period (and, indeed,
on until 1962 when the UNR won an absolute majority) governments were always formed as coalitions, because no one party
commanded an absolute majority of seats in the National
Assembly. A parliamentary majority was always an alliance,
and usually between groups which differed sharply from one
another on certain normative themes. These themes were used
to bid for votes in elections, so that parliamentary alliances had
to be managed with some degree of adroitness. Our concern in
this section is to examine, very briefly, a change in the alliance

structure between the periods 1945–47 (the period of *tripartisme*) and 1947–51 when a structure known as the third force alliance was employed. We will also look at factors in the environment which brought about this change.

The elections for the First Constituent Assembly were held in October 1945 and more than two thirds of the seats were divided between the Communists (PFC), the Socialists (SFIO) and the Christian Democratic group, the Mouvement républicain populaire (MRP). De Gaulle, who had been President of the Provisional government which returned to France in the wake of the advancing allied armies in late 1944, had included representatives of the parties in his ministry; but had not recognized its responsibility to the Consultative Assembly. After the general elections of October 1945 (for the First Constituent Assembly) he formed a new coalition ministry but this time based specifically on the three largest parties and responsible to the Assembly. This became known as the first government of *tripartisme*, the alliance of the 'three large parties'. De Gaulle resigned in January 1946. A second tripartite ministry was then formed by a Socialist, Gouin. In May that year, the alliance was shaken because the MRP, for reasons to be given shortly, opposed the First Constitution Bill and the government fell.

The second Constituent Assembly was composed much like the first, except that the MRP considerably increased their strength. In June Bidault (MRP) formed the third tripartite ministry, and in October, under this ministry the Second Constitutional Bill was approved, despite criticism from de Gaulle.

In the elections which followed (November 1946) there were some Communist gains. The pattern of party representation was still suited to a tripartite ministry, but the MRP was unwilling to serve. There was a stop-gap Socialist ministry between mid-December 1946 and mid-January 1947 when Ramadier (Socialist) succeeded in forming a ministry. This contained representatives of the three parties of the left and left centre (PFC, SFIO, MRP), but also included men from the right centre and the right (Radicals and Conservatives). In early May of that year the Communists voted against this ministry, and a week later Ramadier formed another ministry, this time excluding the Communists. In November that year Ramadier's government fell, following labour unrest and strikes and parliamentary attacks from the RPF, a rally (styling itself not a party but behaving like one) formed by de Gaulle in 1947 and, as noted earlier, a rallying point for those disenchanted with the parliamentary regime. At the end of November 1947 Schuman (MRP) formed a government of the right centre, and this government marks the beginning of the third force alliance structure which characterized subsequent ministries with one or two exceptions, up to the 1951 elections.

These events bear witness to a shift from the left or left centre towards the right centre and the right, a trend which continued in a rather irregular fashion up to 1958, when it culminated in the institution of the Fifth Republic and the election of de Gaulle as president. The two processes which stand out in the period 1945–49 are the increasing restiveness of the MRP when harnessed in a left centre alliance, and the exclusion of the Communists from the ministries in 1947 and afterwards. Let us now try to account for these two changes in terms of the structure of French politics at this period.

Tripartisme was an attempt to restore and stabilize republican norms. Most of the politicians had lived through the troubled second half of the thirties and had also seen or experienced the authoritarian regime of Vichy, the antithesis of republican norms. There were, as we have noted, exceptions and these were the people who rallied to de Gaulle and his RPF. But the rest, it seems, wanted genuinely republican institutions and were prepared to exercise restraint in order to have them.

This restraint took the form of generalized alliances in parliament and in the ministries, which in effect were agreements not to play upon normative themes which would make life impossible for another party in the alliance and so drive it to extremes. It is exactly that kind of collusive situation which was described earlier: restraining one's opposition short of the point which might drive an opponent to upset the applecart. Thus both the PFC and the MRP avoid, with the help of SFIO as mediators, the point of no return on such issues as state aid for religious schools and economic reforms.

Restraint on such issues could not have been easy, for each party was answerable to a clientele in the electorate, and its performance was judged by the electors in the light of their particular normative themes on these issues. For example, the

PFC politicians in the ministries had to watch the effect of their performance in economic matters upon the trade unions and the workers of the big cities who elected them. Moreover, restraint was doubly necessary since there were rivals for these normative themes: both Socialists and Communists were linked with trade unions and workpeople. The MRP had to keep an eye on parties further right and, after 1947, on the rating of de Gaulle's RPF, for the right-wing themes of all these groups overlapped with one another.

Nevertheless, for the period of *tripartisme* the structure seems to have held. In effect the parties acted as 'gatekeepers'[14] for demands from the environment: the left-wing parties controlling demands from the labour force and the MRP from business, the professions and various right-wing interests. The demands would be filtered and restrained, all in the interests of keeping the republic intact. Government was a kind of marketplace of interests and ideologies, with the parties acting as brokers, each party having a stable relationship with its sector of the environment, and the parties together forming a stable alliance. This restraint was helped by a partial diversification of interests *within* each of the parties. The MRP in particular ministered to a wide range of clients: some trade unionists; some professional people; some parts of big business; and some regional interests, for example Alsace Lorraine.

But it did not last. Let us begin by looking at the environmental pressures on the MRP. The MRP constituted the right flank of the tripartite alliances and drew some of its support from those who questioned the idea of republican institutions and favoured a presidential regime. De Gaulle's withdrawal and, after his period of contemplation, re-entry into politics in June 1946 with a speech advocating a presidential regime and his subsequent (April 1947) formation of the RPF were immediate threats to the hold of the MRP over part of their clientele and they caused the party to move further to the right. Such straws in the wind made them vote against the First Constitution: and made them reluctant to join another left centre tripartite ministry in December 1946. They had troubles too on the colonial front: when the war broke out in Indo-China they found themselves using procolonial normative themes. In short, changes in the environment—de Gaulle's activities and colonial crises—

broke the stable relationship which the MRP had had with a part of their clientele, forced them to intensify their use of environmental resources against their partners in the alliance, and so threatened its stability.

Structurally the same thing happened with the PFC. Inflation and pressures for higher wages led to strikes in April and May 1947, which put pressure on the unions, which in turn pushed the PFC into a more militant role within the alliance: and so, quite soon, out of the alliance altogether. Later that year they were helping to maintain strikes against the Ramadier government and had reactivated their links with Moscow through the Comintern.

The structure which followed (third force alliance) was in some ways similar to *tripartisme*. The definitive norm of maintaining republican institutions still held good: indeed, if anything this was strengthened insofar as the Radicals and some others further to the right were admitted into the ministries; after 1952 even the RPF was, so to speak, domesticated, its members accepting office and de Gaulle abandoning it. It is true that the PFC was now on the outside and generally in a normative role of total opposition, but Communists were still represented on Assembly committees and their relationships with the Socialists were not unfriendly in the period under review.

The difference between the two structures lay in the stability of relationships and the gatekeeping arrangements which made for stability. In the third force alliance both on the left and on the right parties were outbidding one another for the allegiance of sections of the electors. Within the parliament and within even ministries there were no comprehensive alliances: only limited contracts for particular purposes—to bring down a ministry, to get a particular measure through, or a man in or a man out and so forth. There were schisms between groups of ministers; between the ministers and the parliament; sometimes within the group of temporary allies who formed the parliamentary majority. In short, pressures from the environment and the consequent injection of new resources (new or intensified normative themes) into the structure of parties and parliament, put a strain on the institutions of the Fourth Republic; but the pressures were contained short of the point of breakdown. They did, however, bring about important adaptive changes in the pragmatic rules which regulated the behaviour of the politicians.

This was not radical change. The Fourth Republic survived until 1958. But the adaptive changes were cumulative. At no stage was there a return to the relative stability of the first years of *tripartisme*.[15]

Now let us look at radical change.

IDENTIFYING RADICAL CHANGE

Some changes may be dramatic, very obvious, and at least at first sight, very complete. The Russian Revolution, the attaining of independence by India and the many other countries formerly under colonial rule in the two decades following World War II, or the collapse of the Austro-Hungarian Empire are events which no-one could fail to recognize as major discontinuities in the history of those countries. On a smaller scale the abolition of the landlord system (zemindari) in India or the passing of laws which forbade the custom of untouchability can also be seen as radical changes in the Indian social system. But when one looks closer the apparent discontinuities are not always so sharp as they appear from a distance. The landlord system was abolished in India but in at least some areas landlords have continued to be powerful: Untouchability has been legally abolished, but in places it continues to be an important issue, as some of the examples given in this book demonstrate. When one looks back from a more distant future the abolition of Untouchability may appear not as a single sharp, dramatic discontinuity but as a number of small steps (including some backwards) over a long period of time, no single step serving to mark the moment when Untouchability was in fact abolished.

Other changes, no less radical than those mentioned, may take place so gradually and so painlessly for the people experiencing them, that they may not realize until they look back long after the event, that a change has taken place. *The Last Hurrah*,[16] a novel about a city politician in the American east, tells how the slow integration of immigrant groups into the mass of the population and the simultaneous development of methods of communicating with electors in the mass, put machine politics—and the machine politician who is the hero of the book—out of business: but he did not perceive that he was out of business until he lost an election which he expected to win by methods which had always brought him success in the past. In England, over the last three to four decades wider opportunities for education and the power and responsibility given to men with technical qualifications and training seems to be bringing about a similar silent revolution in the composition of our 'power elite'. Here again, to be able to put one's finger on a particular event or to select a particular time and say that this was when and where the change occurred is difficult.

One of the reasons why it is difficult to perceive radical changes from the close perspective used in this book is that the actors themselves are often unwilling to face the fact of change. Men whom historians can later see to have been reformers and innovators are written off as deviants and troublemakers. Gandhi appeared in this light to many British administrators, as no doubt did Jesus Christ to most of the Jews and Romans. To have admitted that such men might be the heralds of a new social or political or religious structure is also to allow that there is something amiss with the existing social structure.

The same reluctance to admit that what is already established as the rule of behaviour may not be good enough also appears after the event. Even when changes are agreed upon, then especially in bureaucracies and legal systems, great pains may be taken to show that there is in fact a precedent for such a measure, that the new measure is not new at all but merely a slight addition to, or a truer interpretation of an existing norma- tive principle. From the point of view of general stability and good order this pretence is quite sensible for its effect is to mini- mize the uncertainty which the use of proclaimed new kinds of resource might induce.

Men are particularly disposed to throw a smoke-screen over the fact of change when this change is the outcome of a bargain between contestants supporting rival structures. The victorious leader of a revolutionary army may throw his hat in the air and proclaim that the old order is now swept away, and then both publicize the fact and make it literally true by lining up the leaders of the old order in the main square and shooting them. But other leaders, who perhaps fear that such demonstrations may create uncertainty and provoke further violence, may allow the old leaders to save their faces by pretending that the old order has not been abolished, but merely modified. It appears that the military leaders in Indonesia, anxious to avoid further bloodshed, went through a period of trying to use President Sukarno to give themselves and their regime normative justification in this way.

These difficulties in ascertaining just what is happening arise because situations of change are also situations of contest: to put the matter at its simplest, one side favours change and the other favours the *status quo*. It has been made clear in earlier chapters that in a contest, although the two opponents must be able to communicate with one another, it is sometimes to their advantage to communicate false information: they bluff about their own strength; they collude to present a misleading picture of reality, when they both decide that a bargain would be to their advantage; and so forth. Inasmuch as change comes about through bargaining and compromise, then the account which both contestants publicly present of what they have done and why they have done it, is likely to be less than the truth.

Moreover, the deception may be in the other direction: the contestants may pretend that change has taken place when in fact the change is only nominal.[17] Sometimes this can be a move in the game, on the principle that if one makes a statement often enough, people will come to believe it, and eventually will make it come true. At the time when the Pans were at the height of their dispute with the clean castes in Bisipara, I used to receive letters which were franked with the words, in English, 'Untouchability has been abolished'. To have put the matter more accurately and said that Untouchability was in the course of being abolished or even more accurately by saying that the Government was attempting to abolish Untouchability, would have robbed the phrase of its force as propaganda and would have lessened its chances of becoming a self-fulfilling prophecy.

On other occasions the fact of no-change may be concealed by one of the contestants in order to protect himself. When the Pans first attempted to gain access to the Bisipara temple, the clean caste leaders did not say that Untouchables should not be allowed into sacred places. They claimed that for their own part they had accepted the new legal position and would never try to keep Untouchables out of temples: but this temple was not theirs alone. It belonged to all the clean castes of the Kondmals and, on good democratic principles,[18] the police should organize a referendum of all these people before they allowed the doors of the temple to be opened to Pans. A more general example of allowing the old order to carry on behind a new normative façade is provided by the community development projects in much of rural India. One of the aims of this movement was to raise the standard of living of the under-privileged: to give land to the landless and power to those formerly excluded from the management of village affairs. But in fact it was often the rich peasant who got the pickings, and the dominant castes continued to rule the village, although in form caste was no longer a qualification for public office and public responsibility.[19] To protect themselves the dominant castes pretend that they are operating political competition under the new rules—to some extent, of course, they are: but pragmatically they have succeeded in maintaining the caste criterion for personnel recruitment which operated in the old system and which is expressly forbidden in the new system.[20] In short, there have been some changes: but it is in the interest of one of the contestants to pretend that the change has been more pervasive than in fact is the case. It also happens that sometimes the other contestants may tacitly collude in this deception, perhaps because they despair of being able to do anything about it. In other words some administrators and politicians may turn a blind eye to the fact that community development projects have sometimes benefited the privileged peasants rather than the under-privileged.

Is it necessary to try to penetrate this smoke-screen in order to decide whether change has or has not taken place? In the case just discussed it seems to me pointless to try to decide whether this is or is not change. The important task is to be able to sort the situation out sufficiently to be able to say what has changed and what has not, and this in fact is not very difficult. The prizes have changed, inasmuch as the contestants seek for public office and control of patronage and development monies, and they justify their activities more in the idiom of public service than, as in days gone by, in the idiom of honour and purity. Moreover these new resources have projected many of the competitors out of the village arena into the wider world of local and state government, and this certainly constitutes a change in the structure of village politics by diminishing its significance. What has not changed is a pragmatic rule, common to both Structure A and Structure B, that a contestant must be able, so to speak, to buy his way into the arena before he can compete for control of further resources and bigger prizes: it is still the case, to quote Lord Beaverbrook that 'the first five thousand is the hardest'.

A similar reckoning of what has and what has not changed could be made about the abolition of untouchability as it appears in Bisipara, and this has been done in the preceding chapter. The effect of trying to reach a decision in the form of yes /no, would be to line up with one or the other of the contestants, for it is in their interest rather than that of the analyst to simplify and so distort a complex and incomplete series of events. For example, it only makes sense to insist that rural local government reform has brought about no change in the political structure of Indian villages, if it is your intention to provoke a more resolute attack on the over-privileged or to cast doubt upon the sincerity of Congress politicians or to serve some other political purpose: it is not sensible to look for a yes /no decision if your interest is in understanding what is going on.

While it is sensible to take this attitude towards total situations and to refuse to label them, in their totality, as change or no-change, this still leaves the difficulty of deciding when a particular rule, which forms part of a political structure, has changed. Can this be formulated as a yes /no question?

Once again the position of the Bisipara Pans provides a good example. The personnel rules of the village political structure (seen as Structure A) quite clearly exclude Pans from village government. This is normatively in the hands of the village council: the council meets in a sacred building, which would no longer be sacred if Pans were to enter and so pollute it. When their attendance is required, for example as witnesses or defendents or occasionally plaintiffs before the council meeting as a judicial body, they are made to stand outside the building in the street and speak in a loud voice, and only when spoken to. But nowadays it is not always expedient to exclude Pans from village affairs, because some of them have an expertize which no-one of clean caste can command. Given the state of hostility between the clean castes and the Pans this expertize is, of course, only available when the Pans themselves see they have something to gain. For example, in 1959 the people of Bisipara were trying to convince the education department that Bisipara's school should be raised from the category of 'Upper Primary' to the more prestigious level of 'Middle English'. One of the several moves which the villagers made in this campaign, which they saw as being waged against the district education officials, was a deputation sent to intercept the Chief Minister's car which was scheduled to pass a cross-roads a mile from the village. This deputation was made up of important men of the village and it included three Pans, one an agent for the Congress Party, one a wealthy schoolmaster and the third a retired policeman. Two of these men had been candidates for seats in the Legislative Assembly. These three were the *de facto* leaders of the deputation, and they took a main part in other moves in the attempt to raise the village school's standing.

There were other occasions too, in the government of the village, when leading Pans were invited to collaborate in matters of mutual interest. These occasions appear as pragmatic exceptions to the rule that Pans have no say in village government. Now suppose that the occasions when the villagers have to manipulate the official world continue to increase: it will become, other things being equal, more and more necessary to involve Pans in village affairs, until a point is reached at which both sides feel that there is something unusual about an occasion on which Pans are not consulted. The clean caste villagers at first say to themselves that it would be expedient to involve the Pans in this particular affair: at the end of the series they are saying rather that the normal and the proper thing to do is to consult X, Y and Z and they are not taking into account the fact that X, Y and Z are Pans. When this stage is reached, the normative rule which excludes Pans from village government has gone, being replaced by a rule which picks upon experience and training as a criterion for selecting village leaders. A pragmatic rider to this rule would be that caste status did not count: but it is very unlikely that this negative ruling would be formally announced, for such an announcement would be a challenge and a confrontation. Rather the new rule would slide into place without any formal and open abolition of the old rule.[21] When a bargain is struck in order to co-operate for some common end, those who make the bargain do not begin their co-operation by emphasizing the enmity that lay between them.

Once again we see the pretence involved in successful bargaining throwing a smoke-screen over the course of change. Nevertheless it seems to me that there is a point in the process of change which deserves to be marked as the critical point. This is the point where someone says that the time has come to make the best use of talents available in the interests of the village and to follow the advice of those best qualified to know how to get the village school upgraded, *and this statement receives general acceptance*. This is not, let it be noted, the point at which the best qualified men are actually used for the job: the threshold of change occurs when it is explicitly said that this is the right thing to do.

Action and the normative approval of action are not directly linked with one another. The pragmatic exceptions may be formally recognized as such, the clean castes saying 'We will make use of X, Y and Z, although they are Pans, for these particular purposes. But this does not prejudice their continued status as Pans and their general exclusion from village government.' It is theoretically possible to maintain this position indefinitely, but in practice men tend to bring their ideas of what ought to be done into line with what actually is being done, or to make their behaviour accord with their ideas. When pragmatic exceptions build up against the normative rule to a sufficient extent, then something gets done: either men put an end to the pragmatic exceptions, or they change the normative rule.

We have come back to the notion of a periodical 'tidying-up' or 'reckoning-up' in human affairs. A period of debate is ended and the situation 'officially' clarified by a decision; which is itself the starting point for a new period of debate. The indeterminacies and deliberate obfuscations of a period of subversions and confrontations are ended by an encounter, and the scores are counted, so to speak, and the contestants positioned for a new round of subversions and confrontations. In many cultures a man's passage through life is punctuated by rites which indicate that he is now 'officially' ready to take on the responsibilities of a new role—to take part in warfare, to get married, to join the council and so forth; this too is a process of 'tidying-up'. Civil servants, as we have noticed, lose their pure impersonality and begin to treat those clients whom they know better than those whom they do not, until someone decides that things have slid far enough, and the rules are re-asserted and they are poised once again in a universalistic posture, ready for a new slide into particularistic relationships.

This periodical 'tidying-up' is the moment when change either does or does not take place. Consider again the bureaucratic cycle of sin and penance, as Wilbert Moore[22] calls it. A period of increasing corruption and favouritism is terminated by sharp punishments and the vehement re-assertion of the rule of bureaucratic honesty and impartiality. But it is conceivable that the reformers might come to the conclusion that some of their rules are unworkable and it is therefore necessary to bend these rules to accommodate some of the practices hitherto officially condemned. If the civil servants have been conducting under-hand transactions in order to secure places for their children in favoured educational institutions, it might be thought tidier to reserve places officially in these institutions for the children of civil servants. In the same way it is conceivable that in Bisipara, when someone draws public attention to the fact the X, Y and Z are being continually consulted on village government, the clean castes might decide *either* to exclude X, Y and Z in the future *or* to use the principle that village affairs should be in the hands of those with the longest experience of manipulating the outside world. In either case a decision is reached which enables us to decide in theory whether or not that particular role has been changed.

In practice there are almost as many difficulties in saying yes or no to a question as to whether a particular rule has changed, as there are to the more general question about change in a total situation. There are the same pressures not to draw attention to changes, and to cloud them in highly general statements of the public interest: or, alternatively, to profess acceptance of new rules of behaviour while not in practice being guided by them. Also, if we disregard these difficulties, we still face the practical statistical difficulty of deciding how many people must agree to a new normative rule before we consider it to have been accepted.

Nevertheless there is a difference between recognizing the moment of change in one particular rule and distinguishing between total situations as change or no-change. Total situations are the concern of us, the investigators: we are interested in understanding as much of the complexity of the situation as we can, for we are not being pressed to take action. But a rule of behaviour is very much closer to action, and the actors themselves are constantly trying to make these rules clear and unambiguous guides to action. The periodical 'tidying-up' constitutes a test case and its purpose is to remove the uncertainty engendered by pragmatic behaviour and the use of new resources in political competition.

In the last resort we, as investigators, must take the word of the contestants about whether or not a rule has changed. After all, the rules of a political structure are what the contestants agree are the rules. There is no difficulty at all in observing that two centuries ago the then rulers of metropolitan India were not in control of the Kond hills and that to-day they are. But this tells us nothing directly about the structure of politics in Bisipara: it tells us only about the environment of that structure. When the villagers begin to make use of the local administration as a resource in their own village political arena, then the village political structure has changed to the extent of developing pragmatic rules for the use of external administrative resources. We have suggested that the use of such new resources creates conditions of uncertainty and that there will occur periodical attempts to tidy the situation, either by forbidding continued pragmatic use of external resources or by making their use legitimate and altering the normative rules. These statements of normative rule are made in the context of an arena and are therefore often claims and counterclaims rather than agreed statements. But claims and counterclaims are confrontations which may eventually terminate in an encounter the effect of which is to provide an agreed statement of win or loss or drawn game: that is, an agreed statement of whether the rule in question should be kept, discarded or modified.

This approach also has the advantage of avoiding the practical difficulties involved in recognizing change by counting the heads of those who accept a new rule. Head-counting itself introduces the difficulty of knowing firstly which heads to count and how to weight them, and secondly whether or not to believe peoples' responses to the question, for they may afterwards do what they said they would not do. A new rule is not proved, accepted or rejected by peoples' statements of intention, but by where they line up when an encounter takes place, and by the agreed outcome of that encounter. Head-counting in Bisipara on the question of whether or not Pans were entitled to a share in village government would have produced a four to one majority against the Pans, since there are approximately four people of clean case to every Pan in Bisipara. But the last encounter which I described (the festival run by the Pan expoliceman) and the inclusion of Pans in the deputation to accost the Chief Minister in fact indicate that the normative rule of Pan exclusion from the public affairs of the village is being superseded by the rule that village affairs should be in the hands of those best equipped to represent village interests in the world outside.

We have been discussing the difficulties involved in recognizing change. It is not always important for the analyst to be able to say whether a total situation is or is not one of change: nor need he arrive at his own decision about the change or constancy of a particular normative rule within a structure. A normative rule has changed when the people who live under that rule agree that it has changed, and they signal agreement about such changes to one another through encounters. These encounters are not statements of intention like 'Untouchability has been abolished', or 'We agree that Pans may go into temples' which are either confrontations or bluffs: the encounter is rather a show-down which demonstrates which side (or in this case which rule) has prevailed. Finally the encounters are preceded by a period of pragmatic evasions of the normative rule in question which come to be seen as confrontations; this period ends in an encounter which results either in change or in the reassertion of the existing structure.

MANIPULATED CHANGE: THE KOND HILLS

The British first invaded the Kond Hills because they felt it their duty to put an end to two Kond customs: the rite of human sacrifice and the practice of female infanticide. To do this they were drawn into two more general tasks: they had to gain control of the hill areas and they soon began to think of themselves as bringing civilization to the Konds. They set up jails and courthouses, sent infant girls to orphanages outside the hills and treated these children as wards of the Government, rescued children who were destined to be the victims of sacrifice, gave their wards in marriage to Konds and so established a kind of kinship link with some Konds, built roads and later schools, and from the very earliest days established markets and encouraged trade.

This suggests the very obvious fact that a particular rule of behaviour (in this example, human sacrifice) does not stand on its own, but is connected with other kinds of behaviour. Moreover the connection is of a kind which suggests that the reformer should think in terms of a linear programme. If he wishes to change a particular rule then there are antecedent steps to be taken, in a particular order, to make the change possible: and when the change has been effected, then it will be followed by a further sequence of consequential changes.

Furthermore any such situation will offer the possibility not of one but of several programmes, some more costly than others, some taking a longer time, and each, perhaps, with different consequential changes. The time and resources available to the reformer will narrow the range of programmes open to him, and may, of course, make it impossible for him to carry through the changes at all. The following skeleton of possibilities can be used to explore different pathways which may be open to those wishing to change an encapsulated political structure:

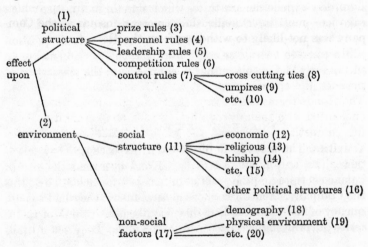

This diagram is a skeleton. From each terminal point we could spread out a fan of lines showing more detailed components, listed in earlier chapters.

Campbell's policy for eradicating human sacrifice in the Kond hills begins with an attack upon (18) and (12)—hanging Konds and burning crops. Those who employ such strategies seldom feel it necessary to explain the logic of their conduct, except to say that this is the quickest way to show who is boss: that is, the quickest way of achieving an authoritarian version of (9), the role of umpire and rule-maker. More generally stated, the logic behind such a policy is that a destruction of personnel and economic resources will prevent roles being carried out in Structure *A*. In the resulting vacuum the rules of Structure *B* can be brought into operation. Moreover, the surviving Konds can bargain their way to a compromise by giving up (13) the rite of human sacrifice.

In fact such a programme, which began with an attempt to terrorize the Konds, proved expensive because it did not take into account the extreme difficulties of the terrain and the endemic cerebral malaria (19). It is also likely that no-one allowed sufficiently for the Kond belief that their own material prosperity (12) depended upon regular performance of the ritual, nor upon a possible link between sponsoring the sacrifice and gaining influence (5): consequently they underestimated the resistance which Konds would offer. Thirdly the bargain implicit in the Company's policies—peace at the price of giving up human sacrifice—must have seemed unattractive, insofar as the Company was not likely to withdraw from the Hills.

Macpherson's strategy was based upon a closer examination of (1) to (10). Control rules (7) are insufficiently developed to produce the standards of order which the Konds would like. The Konds themselves, Macpherson thought, have become disenchanted with their own political structure because it is allowing competition to spread too far into other kinds of social activities. The main form of control is a variety of balance of power (10) and it allows too frequent encounters in which the balance is tested out. If umpire roles (9) could be introduced by the Company, then these would diminish the intensity and frequency of inter-clan conflict; this in turn would lessen the importance of clan solidarity, and of the cult of the Earth, and hence of such objectionable ritual features as human sacrifice. Macpherson himself did not write down the last steps in this argument and I have supplied them. He contented himself with saying that Konds wanted mediators to put an end to feuding, that they would like and respect the officials who became mediators, and the latter would thus have enough influence to persuade them to hand over their stock of potential victims and to sacrifice buffaloes or monkeys instead. One could work out what might have been the pathway through the diagram of such a policy, had it been adopted.

It is also possible to use the diagram to carry out *post mortem* examinations, so to speak, on changes that have taken place or are taking place. In the case of the Bisipara Pans Structure *A* is undermined in several ways. Changes in economic roles (12)— the fact that Pans are able to make a living without being dependent upon Warriors—upsets the dependency role which is put upon Pans in Structure *A*. At the same time a Structure *B* umpire role (9) has been introduced, and this prevents the Warriors from forcibly putting the Pans back into their Structure *A* places. Furthermore Structure *A* has been under continuous attack through the inspiration of Gandhi and his attack upon certain of its religious roles (13) in the campaign to abolish Untouchability.

Gandhi's campaign was conducted throughout India and it was not everywhere as successful as it appears to have been in Bisipara. There are many villages where Untouchables are both treated as untouchable (as they are in Bisipara) and are of no significance in village politics. There are other accounts of places where the Untouchables have reached the point of trying to assert themselves, but have then been decisively worsted, frequently in spite of the support of the local Congress party.[23] It has also been recently reported that in areas of Maharashtra and Madhya Pradesh there have been mass conversions to Buddhism, an attempt to find a normative escape from Hinduism and the status of being an Untouchable.[24]

This suggests that certain preliminary changes must take place before propaganda or even changes in the law can become effective. The Bisipara Pans have had the political successes which other Untouchables have not because they first became prosperous and so were able to free themselves from economic dependency on their former masters, the Warriors; and because the proclamation of their improved status was backed up by the threat of force, made even more immediate to the clean castes by the way in which the Pans seemed to be able to make contact with and manipulate politicians and officials. In other words, from the point of view of Structure B, if the aim is to manipulate (13) (the rules of ritual interation) then it is necessary to prepare the ground by changing (12) (the rules of economic interaction) and (16) (invoking forceful sanctions): the result will be, whether intended or not, a modification of the whole of (1), which is Structure A.

It is also clear that there are discontinuities within this diagram. Religious roles in the case of the Untouchables can only be changed if there is first a change in economic roles: but kinship roles (14) remain irrelevant in this particular case. It is of course conceivable that they could become relevant: one of the most direct ways of ending Untouchability would be to get rid of the rule of endogamy, for sufficient mixed marriages would make everyone an Untouchable, which is as good as abolishing Untouchability. In fact, of course, no reformer has the resources to make a start by overcoming such deep-rooted prejudices and forcing mixed marriages. There are other pathways towards the ending of Untouchability, suggested as theoretical possibilities by the diagram but unlikely to be possible in practice. The specialization and differentiation involved in a caste system clearly could not be maintained if everyone's living standard was drastically reduced to the point at which every hour and every ounce of energy went into getting enough food and raising children. Again, if the whole population were removed and set to work in a totally different environment, Untouchability might vanish. The caste system practised by Indians who were taken overseas as indentured labourers to work on plantations is very much less elaborate than in India.[25] Thus there are two limitations on the construction of pathways through the diagram: in the first, the path is blocked by an absence of connection between a role which can be altered and the role which it is desired to alter: in the second, although there is the required connection between the variables, the process cannot be initiated for lack of adequate resources (e.g. the mixed marriage solution) or is itself considered undesirable (e.g. bringing everyone down to the point of starvation or adopting a Sodom and Gomorrah plan by eliminating Untouchables, or the clean castes, or both).

Other things being equal, manipulating changes in Structure *A* from a position in Structure *B* will depend for its success upon two variables: the first is the amount of resources which Structure *B* is willing or able to put into the task: the second is the choice of an efficient pathway or combination of pathways through the map of Structure *A* and its environment. The efficiency of this pathway is also calculated in two ways: one is the degree to which actual connections are discerned and used. For example—and very simply—elections are not won by addressing even the most convincing propaganda to those who do not have the vote: or—less simply—while it may be true that the tenant does not trouble himself to improve the land for the landlord's benefit, it may not be true that to introduce local self-government will intensify local efforts to raise production levels, as was assumed by some Indian planners.[26] The second factor in calculating the efficiency of a pathway is in ascertaining the degree to which particular roles are vulnerable, that is, how much their alteration will be resisted. At this point we have come back from manipulation and administration to politics. Ascertaining the degree to which particular roles are vulnerable in fact means identifying and sizing up those who will resist that particular role change: and to change that role is to enter into a contest with the upholders of that role.

DE GAULLE, FRANCE AND ALGERIA[27]

Political change seems always to be a contest. Although the cause of structural change is a maladjustment between that structure and its environment, the change is worked out through the actions of men and through their failure to act. Perhaps one can imagine situations of total enlightenment in which wholly rational leaders, in response to environmental pressures of a non-human kind, dissolve the structure which has given them power and substitute another structure for it. But in life it seems that the environmental pressures making for change include usually other would-be leaders, whose ambitions and ideals are frustrated by the present structure. Therefore a contest arises: therefore we are able, to some extent, to understand change by using the categories of competition and contest. All change, in other words, contains an element of manipulation: at least this is true of adaptive and radical change and probably very often too of repetitive change.

We will test out these propositions by looking at some aspects of the struggle which terminated the French Fourth Republic and eventually gave de Gaulle presidential power in the Fifth Republic. Manipulated change in the Kond Hills is an example of limited utility, for while the rival strategies are clear enough, we lack information about the details of what happened on the ground. This is also true, but to a lesser extent, of the story of de Gaulle's manoeuvres. But one does get a broadly comprehensive picture of his strategy, sufficient at least to see how far such concepts as subversion, confrontation etc., such roles as that of the arbitrator, the idea of a more and less efficient pathway through a programme of change, and so forth, are of use.

De Gaulle substituted presidential rule for parliamentary rule. In the latter structure the major stabilizing role is taken by the parties: it is their job to channel the demands from the environment and decisions are reached, personnel chosen, policies selected and so on through orderly competition between the parties in parliament. For this structure to work successfully, as we have seen, there must be stable and predictable relationships between the parties and the appropriate sectors of the environment, and there has to be a generalized restraint upon the use of resources for competition, particularly inflammatory normative themes. The justification for a change to a presidential regime is that the party structure, so far from regulating competition and making it orderly, exacerbates it. Heightened competition makes it impossible for the structure to react appropriately to pressures from the environment and so control them, because it makes decision-taking impossible. The president, on the other hand, is able to take rational decisions quickly and in the general interest of the nation and to act as an arbitrator in political competition. He is helped by administrative agencies, who are responsible to him and who are in a stable relationship with interest groups in the environment. A parliament, if there is one, is primarily an advisory and consultative body. The general public participate in politics not through parties in competition with one another, but through a single party or rally,

which emphasizes unity and consensus, and through interest
associations and professional bodies which develop contacts with
the various governmental agencies.

De Gaulle's *apologia*, therefore, would be based upon an
analysis of the structure of politics in the Fourth Republic. In
this structure control rules were insufficiently developed to produce standards of order which the French nation would like. A
significant number of Frenchmen had become disenchanted
with this political structure, because it was allowing competition
to stray too far into other structures and was producing *immobilisme*: that is, necessary things were not done because all
the energy went into 'sterile games'. The main form of control
was a variety of the balance of power and it allowed too frequent encounters in which this balance was tested out.[28] The
parliamentary marketplace was an insufficient umpire: the clash
of conflicting interests called for a presidential umpire.

De Gaulle, as we have seen earlier, was not alone in these
thoughts. One of the hazards in the environment of the Fourth
Republic was *bonapartisme*, that not inconsiderable body of
Frenchmen who believed that France's greatness depended upon
strong leadership and centralized government and whose experiences and humiliations under the Third Republic had made them
welcome the authoritarian Vichy regime. At first de Gaulle, so
strongly associated with the Resistance and the demolition of
the Vichy regime, must have been suspect: but he soon emerged
as the champion of those who saw authoritarian rule as the
answer to France's difficulties. After only three months he had
resigned, in 1946, as President of the first Provisional Government and in May that year he came back into politics with a
speech advocating a presidential regime. In 1947 he had formed
his 'rally' (RPF). This had electoral successes and was powerful
in parliament, but, as noted above, the Fourth Republic succeeded in domesticating it. Members accepted office and their
name was changed to Social Republicans. By May 1953 de
Gaulle had already abandoned them. The parliamentarians of
the Fourth Republic, had, so to speak, won this round, although
there persisted still a *'mouvement Gaulliste'*, broader and more
diffuse than the RPF itself. De Gaulle's opportunity did not
come again until five years later, when the Algerian war produced an environmental pressure which was strong enough to

demonstrate beyond doubt the regime's political bankruptcy.[29]

The Algerian insurrection began on November 1st 1954. The French Government, under Mendès-France, decided that it must be suppressed, but an analysis of social and economic discontent in Algeria led the government to believe that reforms might take popular support away from the rebels. Soustelle was sent out as Governor-General, in the hope that he could resist pressures from the French *colons* (settlers), who wanted Algeria to remain an integral part of France, and win the confidence of the Arabs. Evidently the three possibilities of military victory, of undermining the support for the rebels by social and economic reform, and of a political settlement, were being kept open.

From that point onwards there is an almost continuous hardening of attitudes: a series of developments on the French side led to confrontations the nature of which diminished the chance of a compromise settlement and made victory or defeat in war seem the only possible outcome. Soustelle threw in his lot with the *colons* and became a firm advocate of *Algérie Française*. A government which took office after the elections of 1956 (January) was expected to work for a negotiated peace with the Algerian rebels (FLN), and appointed a soldier with a liberal reputation in place of Soustelle. But when in February the Prime Minister Mollet visited Algiers, he gave way to pressure from the *colons* and appointed instead Robert Lacoste, who was not interested in negotiations. Secret talks were in fact begun with the FLN, but these were broken off when the FLN leader, Ben Bella, was kidnapped in October 1956. In 1957 his lawyer was arrested by the order of the Ministry of the Interior. The chance of a negotiated political settlement—or a settlement by any means other than military victory—seemed to have been lost.

But by 1957 the army was no longer sure that victory could be won, so long as the war was confined to Algerian territory and attacks on rebel bases in Tunisia were forbidden. The army wanted the right to bomb these bases and to pursue rebels into Tunisia and Morocco, and they put pressure on home governments to modify the crucial policy decision that the war should be kept within Algeria. This would bring down the displeasure of the international world on France and the government did not have a mandate either in the parliament or in the country to escalate the war. The army, however, took the decision for it and bombed Sakhiet in Tunisia.

The army and the *colons* were in fact in control of policy in Algeria and the bombing of Sakhiet only made clear to the world a process which had been going on since Mollet permitted the appointment of Lacoste, bowing to settler pressure to do so. From March 1956, under a special powers decree, Lacoste and the Army were the effective decision-takers for French actions in Algeria.

These men in Algeria were not, of course, able to act quite independently or to sever their links with metropolitan France. Their actions were directed rather to ensuring that ministries in France should support their hard-line policy: that is, should abandon the policy of a negotiated settlement and strive for a military victory, whatever the cost in men, money, international displeasure and so forth. But in effect the protagonists had become the various Paris governments on the one side and the army and the *colons* on the other. The latter succeeded to the extent that they did through subversions and confrontations. They subverted the civilian authorities in Algeria; the army commanders; even the Ministry of Defence and the Parisian police. The appointment of Lacoste, the kidnapping of Ben Bella and the arrest of his lawyer, the refusal to put in hand social and economic reforms in Algeria and the bombing of Sakhiet were confrontations. These confrontations were directed not only against the FLN, to make it impossible for them to allow a negotiated settlement: they were also challenges to the authority of the Paris governments.

The process is analogous to that which we discussed in the context of leadership. Subordinate leaders had achieved a command over resources which enabled them to challenge the authority of their former superiors: what had been a group, hierarchically organized, had become an arena. It is also an example of the reversal of a process which we touched upon in the context of encapsulation: those in the lesser arena, forbidden to compete in the way that they want to, invade the larger arena and try to impose their style upon it. From being in a position of subordination and dependence, like the Pans of Bisipara, the Algerian colonels were now challenging their former masters and trying to force them to modify their policies, as the Warriors of Bisipara were being driven by the Pans towards a change which they did not want. Perhaps these comparisons are at a level of structural abstraction which border on the algebraic: but, whether so or not, the situation between the Paris Government and the authorities in Algiers had become, as Bisipara sometimes seemed, an arena in which the contest was almost out of control. There seemed to be no way of lowering the tension. Paris could not control the men in Algiers: they, for all the noise and disorders and uprisings, were in no position to take over the government of metropolitan France, risking a civil war in the process. This was stalemate: and a situation ripe for an arbitrator: ripe for de Gaulle. He was invested as Prime Minister on June 1st 1958.

What were his qualifications and his resources? We have already looked at the situation which called for an arbitrator. Now let us ask why de Gaulle was a suitable man.

For more than ten years de Gaulle had been the symbol of a regime that would put decisions and order, the re-establishment of the State, as its first consideration. The increasing disarray of the Fourth Republic, the accelerating disrepute of the governments, especially in the period after Mollet's capitulation to the *colons* and the blatant disorders of the spring of 1958, all greatly enhanced the values for which de Gaulle stood. He symbolized the need to preserve France and the social order. Secondly he had at his disposal an efficient network of agents and sympathizers who kept him informed of what was going on not only in France but also in Algiers. Thirdly, he had personal links not only with the army but also with the higher ranks of the civil service and with politicians including those who were not his own declared supporters. Consequently, when the time came to act, he was able to mobilize quickly an efficient *core* of supporters both in the civil and the military echelons; men who served him because they thought it their duty and not as contractual followers.

When he did act, he followed an appropriate pathway through the map of political options open to him. Let us look at some of his actions.

He became Prime Minister on June 1st 1958. On June 2nd, the National Assembly passed a bill for constitutional reform. De Gaulle chose his own way of doing this and the new constitution was drawn up by committees rather than a Constituent Assembly. In form the new regime was presidential but the departures from the parliamentary pattern were not obtrusive and the actual presidential working of the new constitution emerged in action rather than in the codification. In practice he treated parliament as a consultative body and kept a relationship directly with the people: also his cabinet was responsible to him rather than to the parliament. But this followed from the way he interpreted the constitution rather than from the way it was written. It should be noticed that he took the trouble to go through the forms of establishing a new constitution, and having it ratified by a referendum. He was using traditional republican norms to legitimize his new regime: the message of these actions was that the change contemplated was an adaptation of republican institutions to changed circumstances, not their abolition. The old values remained intact and re-inforced: only the means had changed.

Elections were held in November 1958 and a new rally (UNR), although hastily put into the field, won two-thirds of the Assembly seats. This was a Gaulliste party, although de Gaulle himself refused to acknowledge it as such. A government then remained in office, with Debré as Prime Minister, from January 1959 until April 1962. De Gaulle himself had been elected president in December 1958.

De Gaulle succeeded in attaining the presidency, because he alone seemed likely to resolve the problem of Algeria. To people in France he, alone among the politicians, seemed the man with sufficient resources to make the army and the *colons* accept arbitration and so end the Algerian war. Those in Algiers had the opposite impression: this was the only politician sufficiently strong and sufficiently concerned with the honour of France to hold Algeria within the nation and win the war. In short, he was in an ideal position for an arbitrator: both sides expected to gain from his arbitration.

This was clearly a situation which called for those qualities found in the successful Pathan saints: blinkering each hand from what the other is doing. Looking back it seems that de Gaulle had opted for a negotiated settlement, one which would go against the army and the *colons*. But this could not be announced until the army and the *colons* had been brought back under metropolitan control. Consequently he was careful not to say things which might make the army and the *colons* feel that their values were at risk. Algerians, he said on his first visit there, were Frenchmen. Similar messages went to the army and in August 1958, on a visit to Algiers, he spoke of 'the necessary evolution of Algeria within the French framework'. The phrase is not without its ambiguities in retrospect, but at the time the meaning must have seemed clear: that Algeria would remain part of France.

But these speeches were also used to subvert the followers of the Algiers group. In a speech in October in Algeria he outlined a five-year development plan, most of it concerning economic and social improvements for the Arab population. This speech, too, seemed to carry the implication of France's continued interest in holding Algeria and it won the support of the greater part of *colons* and soldiers in Algeria, only the extremists dissenting.

Behind the cover of the speeches, more direct methods were being employed. General Salan, already in power in Algiers, had been officially appointed Delegate General on June 9th (and given a medal). Officers were transferred and replaced, promoted and posted elsewhere until in October de Gaulle was able to order Salan to ensure that the forthcoming elections would be free to all, and to order all military personnel to withdraw from political organizations in Algeria: which they did. In November Salan was appointed Inspector-General of the Army and later (in December) transferred to Paris, being replaced by a civilian, Delouvrier. By the end of the year, the process of subversion had gone a long way: the army in Algeria was separated from the *colons* and could be used to keep them in order; a significant part of both groups supported de Gaulle's regime; recalcitrant officers had been moved out of Algeria. Moreover the option of social and economic reform had been restored, and de Gaulle had already offered to open negotiations with the FLN.

Eventually it became clear that de Gaulle was working towards a negotiated settlement. This again set off violent confrontations from the extremists: the week of the barricades in January 1960; the Generals' plot in April 1961; and OAS terrorism in 1962. But by then de Gaulle was ready and these confrontations ended in encounters in which de Gaulle was clearly seen to be the victor. Negotiations with the Algerian Nationalists had been

opened officially in June 1960 and these ended successfully in
March 1962, with the Evian agreement, bringing the war in
Algeria to a close.

The story of the rise of de Gaulle and the emergence of the
Fifth Republic adapts itself well to the framework of concepts
used in this book. Notice that although these concepts are developed first for the examination of competitive situations in
which there is a broad agreement about the norms which will
restrain and direct the contest, they have been useful also in
analysing a revolutionary situation. In both cases we look for a
structure and its environment, which will, in the second case,
contain a rival political structure; in both cases we need to
distinguish normative from pragmatic rules, and we have to
look particularly at the latter if we are investigating a revolutionary situation; in both cases we have to ask questions about
leaders, distinguishing core from followers, and categorizing the
different kinds of resources open to them; in both cases we see
subversion, confrontations and encounters, and in both there
can be episodes and sequences as a contestant climbs to the
point where he can make the final decisive confrontation which
brings about change; finally, even in revolutionary situations it
is necessary to look at control rules, both to see where they have
failed and also because the effective revolutionary is likely to
be the man who obeys the 'laws' (in the scientific sense) of
competitive behaviour.

Change is a contest: but it is that kind of contest which can
easily become a fight, in which more and more social resources
are consumed to the point where the outcome can only be a loss
for both sides. Men destroy themselves not always because they
have to in order to defend a principle, but sometimes merely
because they have not learned how to communicate through
confrontations and how to keep their encounters socially
inexpensive.

NOTES

1. When General Campbell retired he wrote two books about his
   exploits in the Kond Hills and elsewhere (*Campbell* (1) and (2)).
   In these he cast some aspersions on the conduct of Captain
   Macpherson, long-since dead. Macpherson's brother thereupon
   compiled a book from articles written by his brother and from

his letters, and included, as an appendix, a gentlemanly but vitriolic exchange of letters with Campbell (*Macpherson*). From the perspective of to-day Macpherson seems much the more perceptive and sympathetic of the two. One wonders whether the Konds, some of whom played off one soldier against the other, would have been pleased to know that the Campbell clan and the Macpherson clan were traditional enemies.

Besides these two books the principal published source which I have used is *Selections from the Records* No. V. There is also an account in *Alderson*, and this is my authority for the concluding two sentences of this paragraph. Alderson, presumably, had access to local records and informants not available when I was in the area.

2. The resident Oriyas were, I think, the ones who principally made mischief between Campbell and Macpherson. One Sam Bissye (*sc.* Syamo Bisoi) is a hero in Campbell's account and a villain for Macpherson.

3. I talked with a young man who had played a leading part in the agitations in Orissa which followed the States Re-organization Commission of 1956. He had a very clear picture of how to build up disorders, including even ways of judging when the time was ripe to provoke violence from the authorities (i.e. police 'firings').

4. The weakness lies in those innovators who act as if fervour and a crusading spirit is enough. In fact, even if there is the fervour to begin with, men swiftly lose their goodwill if enthusiasm is not backed by adequate logistic planning. This was, from what I saw of it in Orissa, the principal weakness of Vinoba Bhave's land reform movements.

5. See p. 13 and *Bailey, F. G.* (2), part I.

6. See *Bailey, F. G.* (2), Chapter VII.

7. There is, however, official discrimination *in favour* of tribal people and Untouchables in the competition for scholarships and positions in government service. There are also seats in Legislative Assemblies reserved for candidates from these two categories.

8. Descriptions and discussions of this phenomenon are to be found in *Burridge, Antoun* and *Yalman*.

9. See *Finer*.

10. See *Bailey, F. G.* (4), pp. 37 and 40. This discussion, of course, applies to *peasant* women. The Indian middle class has produced some formidable female politicians.

11. See *Southwold* and *Goody* (2).

12. See *Goody* (1), and *Bailey, F. G.* (3).

13. See *Leach*.

14. I take this term from *Easton* (1), pp. 87–96.

15. For both facts and ideas in this and the later section on de Gaulle, I acknowledge my debt to conversations with and notes prepared by Bruce Graham. See also *Graham* (2), and *Werth*.

16. The author of this novel is Edwin O'Connor, 1959.
17. See pp. 222 of this chapter.
18. Notice also that such a referendum would also accord with the principle of consensus, through which villagers believed decisions ought to be reached.
19. For an example see *Epstein's* discussion of Wangala. For an exemplary display of how to test propositions about the sharing of new resources see *Mayer* (3).
20. See note 11 to Chapter 8 and p. 153.
21. To act discreetly in this way would be in accordance with the general normative rule of village society that nothing should be done to provoke quarrels. The consensus rule is a part of this general pressure towards not stepping needlessly on other men's toes. Even in societies which codify their constitutions, care is usually taken not to advertise too brutally the break with the past. See the remarks on de Gaulle's tactics on p. 222.
22. See *Moore*, p. 58.
23. *Cohn* (1) reports that the Camar untouchables of Senapur, in spite of Congress support which extended to maintaining them for a long period outside their village, were unable successfully to prosecute a case in the law courts against the dominant caste of Thakur landlords.
24. See *Zelliot*.
25. There is now a considerable number of books about overseas Indians, both those who went as indentured labourers and others. For Fiji, see *Mayer* (2): for Mauritius, see *Benedict*: one should also look at *Desai's* book about Indians in Britain.
26. For a discussion of Panchayat Raj (local self-government) see *Morris-Jones* (2), pp. 145–7 and 188–90.
27. See note 15.
28. The phrasing in this paragraph follows almost exactly that on p. 213, which discusses Macpherson's strategy for bringing order to the Kond Hills.
29. This section should not be taken to mean that the Fourth Republic accomplished nothing. We have highlighted its short-comings, which led to its downfall, rather than its achievements. As we have noticed, it tamed the RPF. Somewhat painfully, it settled the war in Indo-China. Tunisia and Morocco were given independence. Its economic policies eventually brought prosperity from the mid-1950s onwards.

References

ALDERSON, H. W. *The Khonds* unpublished mss., *n.d.*

ANTOUN, Richard. 'On the modesty of women in Moslem Villages' unpublished mss., n.d.

BAILEY, F. G.

(1) *Caste and the Economic Frontier* Manchester: University Press, 1957.

(2) *Tribe, Caste and Nation* Manchester: University Press, 1960.

(3) 'The Joint Family in India: a Framework for Discussion' *Economic Weekly* Vol. 12, No. 8, 1960.

(4) *Politics and Social Change* Berkeley: California University Press, 1963.

(5) 'Closed Social Stratification in India' *Archives Européenes de Sociologie* IV, 1963.

(6) 'Decisions by Consensus in Councils and Committees' *Political Systems and the Distribution of Power* A.S.A. Monographs 2, London: Tavistock Publications, 1965.

(7) 'The Peasant View of the Bad Life' *Advancement of Science* Vol. 23, No. 114, 1966.

BAILEY, S. K. *Congress makes a Law* New York: Columbia University Press, 1950.

BARTH, Fredrik.

(1) 'Segmentary opposition and the Theory of Games: a Study of Pathan Organization' *Journal of the Royal Anthropological Institute* Vol. 89, Pt. 1, 1959.

(2) *Political Leadership among Swat Pathans* London: Athlone Press, 1959.

(3) *Models of Social Organization* London: Royal Anthropological Institute: Occasional Paper No. 23, 1966.

BEALS, Alan R. *Gopalpur: a South Indian Village* New York: Holt, Rinehart & Winston, 1962.

BEAVERBROOK, Lord. *Politicians and the War 1914–1916* London: Collins, 1960.

BENEDICT, Burton. *Indians in a Plural Society* London: H.M.S.O., 1961.

BLAKE, Robert. *The Unknown Prime Minister* London: Eyre & Spottiswood, 1955.

BOUGLÉ, C. *Essais sur le régime des castes* Paris: Alcan, 1908.

BOULDING, Kenneth, E. *Conflict and Defence: a general theory* New York: Harper & Row, 1962.

BURRIDGE, K. O. L. *Tangu Traditions* (forthcoming).

CAMPBELL, J.
(1) *Narrative of Operations in the Hill Tracts of Orissa for the Suppression of Human Sacrifice and Infanticide* London: Hurst & Blackett, 1861.
(2) *Personal Narrative of Thirteen Years' Service among the Wild Tribes of Khondistan for the Suppression of Human Sacrifice* London: Hurst & Blackett, 1864.

CHAMBERLAIN, Sir Austen. *Down the Years* London: Cassell, 1935.

COHEN, Abner. *Arab Border-Villages in Israel* Manchester: University Press, 1965.

COHN, Bernard S.
(1) 'The Changing Status of a Depressed Caste' in Marriott (ed.) *Village India* Chicago: University Press, 1955.
(2) 'Some notes on Law and Change in North India' *Economic Development and Cultural Change* Vol. VIII, No. I, 1959.

COLSON, Elizabeth. *The Plateau Tonga of Northern Rhodesia* Manchester: University Press, 1962.

CORNFORD, F. M. *Microcosmographia Academica* Cambridge: Bowes & Bowes, 1953.

COSER, Lewis A. *The Functions of Social Conflict* London: Routledge & Kegan Paul, 1956.

DESAI, Rashmi. *Indian Immigrants in Britain* London: Oxford University Press, 1963.

DOUGLAS, Mary. 'The Lele of Kasai' *African Worlds* (ed. Daryll Forde), London: Oxford University Press, 1954.

DUMONT, Louis. *Homo Hierarchicus* Paris: Gallimard, 1966.

DUTRA, S. *Political System of the Rajputs* M.A. Thesis. London University, 1958.

DUVERGER, Maurice. *Political Parties* London: Methuen, 1959.

EASTON, David.
(1) *A systems analysis of political life* New York: Wiley, 1965.
(2) *A framework for Political Analysis* Englewood Cliffs: N. J. Prentice-Hall, 1965

EIMERL, Sarel and DEVORE, Irven. *The Primates* New York: Time Inc., 1965.

EPSTEIN, T. Scarlett. *Economic Development and Social Change in South India* Manchester: University Press, 1962.

EVANS-PRITCHARD, E. E.
(1) *The Nuer* London: Oxford University Press, 1940.
(2) *The Sanusi of Cyrenaica* London: Oxford University Press, 1949.

FAIRLIE, Henry. 'The Lives of Politicians' *Encounter* Vol. XXVIII, No. 8, 1967.

FEILING, K. *A History of England* London: Macmillan, 1950.

FINER, S. E. *Anonymous Empire* London: Pall Mall, 1958.

FIRTH, Raymond.
(1) *Elements of Social Organization* London: Watts, 1961.
(2) *Essays in Social Organization and values* London: Athlone Press, 1964.

FORSTER, E. M. *Where Angels Fear to Tread* London: Edward Arnold, 1947.

FORTES, Meyer.
(1) *The Dynamics of Clanship among the Tallensi* London: Oxford University Press, 1945.
(2) *The Web of Kinship among the Tallensi* London: Oxford University Press, 1949.

FORTES, M. and EVANS-PRITCHARD, E. E. *African Political Systems* London: Oxford University Press, 1940.

FRANKENBERG, R. *Village on the Border* London: Cohen & West, 1957.

FREUD, S. and BULLITT, W. C. 'Woodrow Wilson' (I) and (II) *Encounter* Vol. XXVIII, Nos. 1 and 2, 1967.

FRIEDRICH, Paul. 'A Mexican Cacicazgo' *Ethnology* Vol. 4, No. 2, 1965

FÜRER-HAIMENDORF, C. von. *The Naked Nagas* London: Methuen, 1939.

GALLIN, Bernard. 'Political Factionalism in Rural Taiwan and its Impact on Village Social Organization' Mimeographed for Wenner-Gren symposium, No. 32, 1966.

GEORGE, David Lloyd. *War Memoirs* London: Nicholson,1933–6.

GLUCKMAN, Max.

    (1) *Custom and Conflict in Africa* Oxford: Blackwell, 1955.

    (2) (ed.). *Essays on the Ritual of Social Relations* Manchester: University Press, 1962.

    (3) (ed.). *Closed Systems and Open Minds* Edinburgh: Oliver and Boyd, 1964.

    (4) 'Inter-Calary Roles: Professional and Party Ethics in Tribal Areas in South and Central Africa' Mimeographed for Wenner-Gren symposium, No. 32, 1966.

GOODY, Jack.

    (1) (ed.). *The Developmental Cycle in Domestic Groups* Cambridge: University Press, 1962.

    (2) (ed.). *Succession to High Office* Cambridge: University Press, 1966.

GRAHAM, B. D.

    (1) 'Theories of the French Party System under the Third Republic' *Political Studies* Vol. XII, No. 1, 1964.

    (2) *The French Socialists and Tripartisme 1944–1947* London: Weidenfeld & Nicolson, 1965.

    (3) 'The Succession of Factional Systems in the Uttar Pradesh Congress Party, 1937–1965' Mimeographed for Wenner-Gren symposium, No. 32, 1966.

HITCHCOCK, J. T. 'Dominant Caste Politics in a North Indian Village' Mimeographed: Center for South Asian Studies, University of California, 1959.

KARVE, Irawati. *Hindu Society—an Interpretation* Poona: Deccan College, 1961.

KAUTILYA. *Arthasastra* see Shamasastry, R.

LEACH, E. R. *Political Systems of Highland Burma* London: Bell, 1954.

LUMBY, E. W. R. *The Transfer of Power in India* London: Allen & Unwin, 1954.

MACHIAVELLI, Nicolo. *The Prince* (Everyman Edition) London: Dent, 1944.

MACKENZIE, W. J. M. *Politics and Social Science* Harmondsworth: Penguin, 1967.

MACPHERSON, William (ed.). *Memorials of service in India* London: John Murray, 1865.

MAHTAB, Harekrushna (ed.). *History of the Freedom Movement in Orissa* Cuttack: Manmohan Press, 1959.

MAIR, Lucy. *New Nations* London: Weidenfeld & Nicolson, 1963.

MARRIOTT, McKim (ed.). *Village India* Chicago: University Press, 1955.

MAYER, A. C.
(1) *Caste and Kinship in Central India* London: Routledge & Kegan Paul, 1960.
(2) *Peasants in the Pacific* London: Routledge & Kegan Paul, 1961.
(3) 'Some Political Implications of Community Development in India' *Archives Européennes de Sociologie* Vol. IV, No. 1, 1963.

MIDDLETON, J. *Lugbara Religion* London: Oxford University Press, 1960.

MIDDLETON, J. and TAIT, D. *Tribes without Rulers* London: Routledge & Kegan Paul, 1958.

MILLS, C. Wright. *The Sociological Imagination* New York: Oxford University Press, 1959.

MOORE, Wilbert E. *Social Change* Englewood Cliffs N.J.: Prentice-Hall, 1963.

MORRIS-JONES, W. H.
(1) 'The Unhappy Utopia—J.P. in Wonderland' *Economic Weekly*, Vol. 12, 1960.
(2) *The Government and Politics of India* London: Hutchinson, 1964.

NARAYAN, J. P. *A Plea for Reconstruction of Indian Polity* Wardha, n.d. (c. 1960).

NEWTON, Lord. *Lord Lansdowne: a biography* London: Macmillan, 1929.

NICHOLAS, Ralph.
(1) (with Tarashish Mukhopadhyay) 'Politics and Law in Two West Bengal Villages' *Bulletin of the Anthropological Survey of India* Vol. XI, No. 1, 1962.
(2) 'Village Factions and Political Parties in Rural West Bengal' *Journal of Commonwealth Political Studies* Vol. II, No. 1, 1963.

(3) 'Factions: a comparative analysis' *Political Systems and the Distribution of Power* A.SA. Monographs 2, London: Tavistock Publications, 1965.

NICOLSON, Sir Harold. *Diaries and Letters, 1930–1939* London: Collins, 1966.

O'CONNOR, Edwin. *The Last Hurrah* Pan: London, 1959.

O'RIORDAN, William L. *Plunkitt of Tammany Hall* New York: Dutton, 1963.

PLUNKITT. see O'Riordan, William L.

RAPOPORT, Anatol. *Fights, Games and Debates* Ann Arbor: Michigan University Press, 1960.

REEVES, Peter D. 'The Politics of Order' *Journal of Asian Studies* Vol. XXV, No. 2, 1966.

SCHAFFER, B. B. and CORBETT, D. C. (eds.). *Decisions* Melbourne: F. W. Cheshire Pty Ltd., 1966.

SCHELLING, Thomas C. *The Strategy of Conflict* New York: Oxford University Press, 1963.

Selections from the Records of the Government of India No. V, Calcutta: Bengal Military Orphan Press, 1854.

SHAMASASTRY, R. *Kautilya's Artasastra* Mysore: Sri Raghuveer Printing Press, 1951.

SMITH, Donald E. (ed.). *South Asian Politics and Religion* Princeton: University Press, 1966.

SOUTHWOLD, Martin. 'A Games Model in African Tribal Politics' Mimeographed, 1966.

SPENDER, J. A. and ASQUITH, Cyril. *Life of Herbert Henry, Lord Oxford and Asquith* London: Hutchinson, 1932.

SRINIVAS, M. N.

(1) (ed.). *India's Villages* London: Asia Publishing House, 1960.

(2) *Caste in Modern India* Bombay: Asia Publishing House, 1962.

(3) *Social Change in Modern India* Berkeley: University of California Press, 1966.

TINKER, Hugh. *India and Pakistan: a Political Analysis* New York: Praeger, 1962.

TOD, James. *Annals and Antiquities of Rajasthan* London: Routledge, 1914.

TURNER, V. W. *Schism and Continuity* Manchester: University Press, 1957.

VON NEUMAN, John and MORGENSTERN, Oskar. *Theory of Games and Economic Behaviour* New York: Wiley, 1964.

WERTH, Alexander. *De Gaulle* Harmondsworth: Penguin Books, 1967.

WHYTE, William F. *Street Corner Society* Chicago: University Press, 1955.

WILLIAMS, Philip M. *Crisis and Compromise* London: Longmans, 1964.

YALMAN, Nur. 'On the Purity of Women in the Castes of Ceylon and Malabar' *Journal of the Royal Anthropological Institute* Vol. 93, Part 1, 1963.

ZELLIOT, Eleanor. 'Buddhism and Politics in Maharashtra' in Smith, Donald, E. (ed.), 1966.

Index